Conversations with Artists

in

San Miguel de Allende

M. B. Paul

Photographs by Mariah Sirius

Copyright © 2014 M. B. Paul
All rights reserved.
ISBN: 149474645X
ISBN-13: 978-1494746452

Cover photograph taken by Lander Rodriguez.
Concept and artistic direction for the cover photograph
by Toller Cranston who himself is posing as the alchemist.
My thanks also to Laurie Richards, the computer wizard.

ARTISTS

Ed Osman	2
Peter Leventhal	14
Mai Onno	32
Erv Kaczmarek	40
Keith Miller	62
Marion Perlet	72
Toller Cranston	88
Mary Rapp	108
Tim Hazell	124
Leonard Brooks	142
Tom and Donna Dickson	152
Christina Sol	172
Santiago Corral Gutierrez	180
Pedro Friedeberg	198
Stephen Eaker and Bea Aaronson	212
Edgar Soberon	226
Mary Breneman	244

PROLOGUE

When I began this project some years ago, I had no expectations. It was an idea, a whim really, to produce an inventory of the artists living in San Miguel de Allende where I had been living off and on since 2001. It surprised me that no one had attempted such a thing before and because I was recently retired and needed something to do, I thought why not. I did very little more about it until a few months later when purely by chance, I met an artist in India who was also traveling alone and miraculously, happened to live in San Miguel. She encouraged me to forge ahead with my scheme and even gave me the name of a contact who eventually paved the way for me to meet some of the most notable artists in the city. One artist recommended me to the next and soon I was well beyond making a list. I was learning what being an artist means and what being an artist in San Miguel has meant to many of the artists who have lived here for fifty years or more. But most of all, I was learning about art itself, what it is and why it is such a force in the human narrative.

The conversations I had with these fascinating people are recorded here and I share them with you as a testament to a way of life that has all but disappeared except in the most remote parts of the world. Mexico in the forties, fifties, and sixties was a unique place. It is still remarkably different from the United States or Canada and I am so grateful for that. It's unfamiliarity is what draws people like me here, but I don't kid myself. The comforts I enjoy in San Miguel today are far more middle class than was possible when many of the old timers, young people then, arrived to study art at the Instituto or to eagerly paint what they saw around them.

Not all the artists I interviewed are senior citizens but all are aging and three of them have died since I first spoke with them. I miss their presence much as one feels the loss of a candle's light when the night wind suddenly rises. Those individuals took with them a living account of the past. I was extremely fortunate to have met them and to have had the opportunity to talk with all the maestros whose experiences and reflections are set down in these pages. I interviewed twenty-two artists but selected seventeen for the final manuscript because I felt each of the conversations present in this collection had its own point of view, its own theme that revealed particular aspects of life in San Miguel. I tried very hard to find the heart of the men and women I interviewed and I think I got better at doing that as I went along. If I did succeed in capturing their voices, it was because I fell in love with every one and I hope that my affection and respect was evident in my questions and in my attention to their responses.

I am grateful to all who were a part of this endeavor, and especially to lovely Mariah Sirius who agreed to take the photographs for the best reason and in the same spirit as I believe guides every happy adventure, to go where life leads us. I hope those of you who read this book will come to know a little more about art, about artists, and about San Miguel de Allende, a place that has always been and continues to be, extraordinary.

Ed Osman

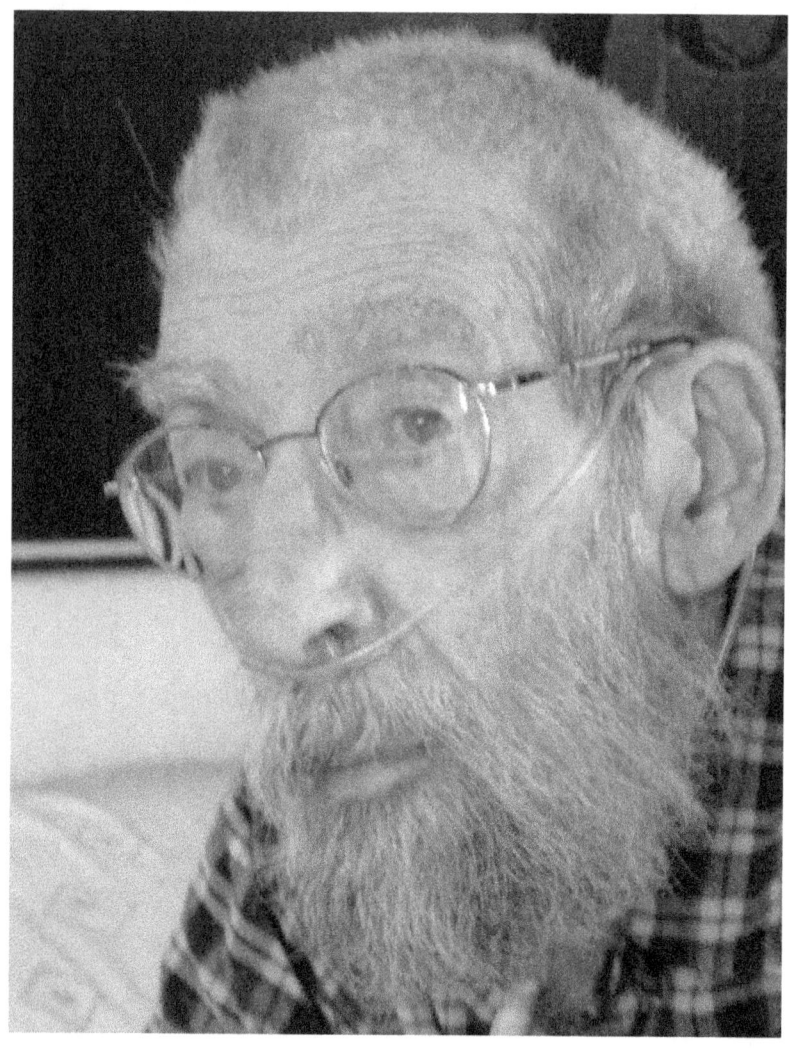

It's another beautiful day in San Miguel and I decide to attend an informal gathering of people in support of a small community of monks in Tibet. As I nibble my cheese and cracker in the condominium courtyard, I happen to mention to one of my hosts that I am writing about artists in San Miguel. She reacts immediately, "You have to talk to Ed." I wait while she goes to a nearby door and after disappearing briefly into the darkened space within, she returns and tells me that Ed hasn't been well but he has agreed to speak with me. I have no idea what to expect and am a little apprehensive about this impromptu meeting with a man I have never heard of, but I summon my faith in the universe, knock lightly, and enter, only to be temporarily blinded by the sudden change in light.

As my eyes adjust, I begin to see what looks like a very old man seated on the edge of a single bed in a small room that serves as kitchen, bedroom, sitting room, and painting studio. Through a low door next to the kitchen I can make out a tiny bathroom. There is a shelf containing half a dozen books, a few papers on a small table, and an unfinished painting on the easel at the end of the room where I entered. Ed himself has white hair which hangs to his shoulders. He has a long thin white beard, is extremely thin, and even though he is sitting down, I can see he is a tall man. The sound of a small motor running draws my attention to the clear plastic respirator tube clipped into his nose. In order to be heard above the respirator, I must speak into a microphone attached to his hearing aid. He appears ancient and frail. But appearances can be deceiving because Ed's memories are fresh and his damaged body when he talks about painting, impels him forward and he exudes all the enthusiasm of a kid.

Edward Osman was born in Newark, New Jersey on January 1, 1927. "As a student, I did ok but one thing, all through my early years I could draw and I loved art." In 1945 he left high school to join the merchant marines where he worked aboard cargo ships as the second cook and baker and enjoyed the opportunity to see something of the world. While their ship was in the Philippines, peace was declared with Japan and the cargo ship was quickly converted to a troop ship carrying 900 soldiers back to California. The war with Germany continued and because Ed was still eligible for the draft, he decided to enlist in the army. "In those days if you enlisted you only had to serve for eighteen months. If you were drafted you were in for three years." As Ed described it, "I did the one thing you should never do in the army. I volunteered. In basic training, when one of the commanding officers asked if anyone could cook, I put up my hand and three months later I had been promoted all the way up to mess sergeant." The war ended a short time later so Ed knocked around, baking and working in restaurants until eventually he decided that he didn't want to remain a cook all his life. Fortunately, having signed up for the army just before the war was over, he was eligible for G.I. benefits and on the G.I. Bill, enrolled in The Newark School of Fine and Industrial Arts. When he told his parents at the dinner table one night that he was going to attend art school, his father who had emigrated from Turkey when he was sixteen and had become a successful tool and dye maker, made his opinion about Ed's decision to go to art school clear. "My father stood up and the table got up with him. I had to move out of the house then and things weren't the same between us after that."

Not one to be deterred, Ed graduated four years later and took a job with an advertising agency in their art department where, he tells me, he learned the business from top to bottom. Art school and the time he spent in his job had taught him to see the world with an artist's eye. "Look around you. Everything you see at one time or another has to go through the head of an artist." After some years at the agency and doing freelance work, Ed bought himself a Volkswagen and decided to take a couple of months vacation. A former professor had often talked about his experiences in Mexico so Ed packed up and started to drive south.

Seated on a wooden chair opposite this unlikely man, I hear the flowing discourse of Jack Kerouac and am captivated by Ed's description of his first encounter with Mexico. His words summon the energy of the beat generation that I am too young to have known but have loved through its literature. "I'm driving down. They had no highways then. They were all farm roads. So I'm driving down and it's my second day and I'm driving south and it's getting late. I got a map from the Esso gas company. I break out this map and I think, 'Where am I?' I don't think I can make Mexico City so I have to stop somewhere along the way, maybe in Queretaro. I'm driving and I see a sign, 'San Miguel de Allende'. I look on the map and it says on the map, 'artist's colony'. It had a reputation even then. So I drive in. I came in off the Mirador. That's the top of the hill where you can look across the valley and see the whole city. The sun is going down and the sky is beautiful. 'Oooh', I say, 'this is something!' I drive down into the town and find a place to stay that night and the next morning, Mexico opens up for me. I hear this singing real early in the morning like Gregorian chants and I wonder what it is. I'm out of bed and it's just starting to get light. The night before I hadn't seen the church so I walk across the Jardín and I go into that church and there's women in there and they're wailing and singing and I think, 'Wow, wow, wow, wow, this is really something. Already I'm almost hooked, you know and I thought, what I'm going to do is spend a few days here." Ed laughs. "A few days. Yeah, fifty years."

During that first year in San Miguel, in 1962, Ed met his wife Guadalupe at a party and later when Guadalupe moved up to Mexico City to work, Ed followed. I am eager for details, but his description of their romance is brief. "I painted her portrait and eventually we got married." Life in Mexico City was good. Ed was selling pictures at a local park, the Jardín del Artes, where artists could set up their easels on Sundays and Ed and a friend opened a gallery in Zona Rosa, a popular tourist area nearby. Things went well until Mexico's currency was devalued and art sales slowed. At about the same time, Guadalupe gave birth to twins prematurely. Ed speaks of this event with a sadness that is clearly undiminished by time. "They died from fluid in their lungs. It was something simple that today could have been cured but in those days, well I became a little disillusioned. I took Guadalupe back to San Miguel to stay with her family and I headed for the States with Bill, an old art school friend of mine, and a car load of paintings."

While living in Mexico City, the two had made a connection with the Thompson family. Joe Thompson and his partner were the originators of the first convenience store in North America in 1927, the now famous 7-11. "In 1963 we went to Dallas where Peggy Thompson had just finished building a large house with forty rooms. She agreed to host a gala inauguration of the new house along with an art show. She gave us one month to get enough work ready. Well Bill and I had a hundred dollars between us and no place to stay so we looked around and we meet a guy who was just closing up his apartment to go to Europe for six months. He says, 'I tell you what. Let me see what you have.' So we take him outside and open up the trunk of the car and he says, 'I'll give you my apartment for one month for that painting.' He takes one of the paintings and so now we had a place to live. The only problem was food. We solved that problem more or less by going to the supermarkets and eating in the aisles when no one was looking. Anyway, we're working day and night. I had a number of paintings but I wanted more. Working, working, working. One morning I come downstairs and on my easel is a cheque. Bill said a big Texan had come in and said he just loved boots and had bought my picture of a pair of boots. On the night of the opening we had our paintings up all through the house. There was a buffet, drinks. It was a complete sell out. On Monday morning Peggy collected from all her friends and wrote out two cheques, one for me and one for Bill. She called up her bank to say two young men were coming down and she wanted the bank to honour the cheques. Bill had a bundle and I had a bundle so we drove up to Jersey where Bill is from. He stayed there and I hopped in my Volkswagen and came back here."

When Ed returned to San Miguel, he got a job at the Instituto, the art school in the city that had been promoted by the American government as a place where ex-servicemen could come to study art. It was an experience he remembers with affection and some bitterness. He was a popular instructor and often had classes of thirty to forty students. Every four months the faculty had an art sale and his work always sold out. "It was a good deal but I had a falling out with the Instituto. They said I was creating a disturbance. I told them they weren't treating us fairly. That was in 1971, the first time I split. After that I taught my own students. If I hadn't been married to my wife with all her family and friends in San Miguel, the Instituto could have created a problem and had me deported. This way they couldn't touch me because if they did something to me they were doing something to my wife and she was Mexican. Years later a friend of mine was in charge there and he asked me to come back so I taught at the Instituto for three more years.

"In those days there was a bar in San Miguel where all the Americans congregated. It was called the Cucaracha. We used to call it the Kook. On any given night I could sit in there and talk to Jason Robards or Robert Ryan. Anthony Quinn was renting the apartment across the street. One night Ann Baxter and I sat at my place and ate chestnuts and popcorn and talked."

"We had another good deal in Acapulco. There's an organization of Americans there called The Foreign Friends. Every year in February, they had a big art sale. I don't know what they're doing now but in those days they had a deal with the artists that the artist got 60% and they took 40% for charity. You wouldn't believe the kind of people that were there. Merle Oberon was selling my paintings. Douglas Fairbanks Junior was selling my paintings. They had this big enormous ballroom all criss-crossed with pegboards and the paintings were hung front and back. It was always a big success. I did that two years. Bill and I would take our families and go down. We had the use of all the facilities in the hotel, the swimming pool, the restaurant. In those days you could get a whole red snapper for eleven pesos. Those were good years. They were all good years."

I ask Ed to tell me what it is about San Miguel that has kept him here. His answer tells me more about the San Miguel that was, than the city of today but as I am learning, there is a quality of timelessness here which is difficult to rationalize. "When you're living in San Miguel you're living in two different times in history. You're living in the past and you're living in the present. You can go out to the country and find people wearing the robozo. You don't see that anymore in town. When I first came here, they had what they called a promenade. On a Sunday the young boys and the young girls would promenade around the jardín with their chaperones and exchange glances with one another. What I fell in love with in Mexico, more than anything was the naturalism. Huntervasser said there are no straight lines in art. Well, there are no straight lines in Mexico. There's give and take. Things happen spontaneously. These are all elements that you rely upon when you're painting. It's your intuition. Now the way I work, I work in reverse. It's not what you put on the canvas, it's what comes out of the canvas. I'm interested in how colours influence one another. You see that black area there?" Ed points to a painting resting on a ledge not far away. "You see that red area there? You see how the black affects the red?" He gestures toward the unfinished canvas on the easel. "In this other painting, the first figure is going to be black. Then I'm going to put the red in and that is going to be the key to the whole painting. It's a language. Paint is a language. The colour of paint is a language."

"Here in San Miguel the light is a lot stronger. That's why the European painters always went to the south of France. Some ventured across into Morocco. They were like I am here. Germany and France was overdeveloped and they needed that natural intake so they went down to a primitive country. Mexico is primitive. You take a look at what's happened here. You come into a country and you take away the customs, you take away the religion, you take away the language. The Mexican is a lost person. How are they going to find themselves? They don't know whether to become Spanish. They don't know whether to go back to being an indigenous, so-called Indian. Here they have the influence of the United States and all the gadgets and the money. I read in this week's paper that Starbucks is coming to Mexico. It's over."

"Mexico had a tremendous influence on me. I remember when I was up in the States when I was working for the advertising agency, I might have one or two days when I would throw a canvas up on the easel. Nothing would come of it. What am I going to paint? When I came here to Mexico, this is the story I tell people, when I start to paint, the paintbrush leaves my hand and paints by itself. The creative energy coming out, I don't know whether it comes from above or whether it comes from out of the ground but everything I touched, turned into something that surprised me. Where it was coming from, I thank you, I thank it, I thank whatever. It's pure magic. It's coming out of me or it's something that already exists and it's coming through me. I'm still intrigued by it, with the mystery."

Ed has saved a couple of photographs of himself as a young man in the army and he takes them from the bedside table and hands them over to me. He is dark and handsome and later an acquaintance in town tells me he was quite the ladies man. I confess he has captured my heart. Ed hasn't walked for three years, not since he took a bad fall in town. He was recovering when he fell again at home. He thinks it is partly a mental thing now but he hasn't walked since that last fall. He lives in a suburb of San Miguel on the edge of the dry Mexican hills. Opposite his bed on a ledge in his room, sits a painting of a woman and he asks me to move it aside to reveal another painting of a young man playing a violin. It is a portrait of Ed's son by his second marriage and it is so beautiful I feel sudden tears in my eyes. Ed speaks softly, "It's pure love." He adds that he hasn't seen his son for some time, he's not certain how long, and he asks that I cover the painting again before I leave.

A few months later in July, I visited Ed again and was heartened to see that he looked quite well. His hair was cut, his beard was trimmed short, and the curtains in his small room had been opened to let in some light. The noisy respirator had been replaced by a newer, quieter model and Ed was sitting up on the side of his bed looking thin but substantial and pleased to have a visitor. I had brought a chocolate cake because I know how Ed once loved to bake. He asked his housekeeper to cut us both a piece but he took only a couple of bites before putting his plate aside. I said that I was glad that he had his Klimt calendar clipped to the headboard of his bed and he said he loved that calendar. I wasn't entirely sure he remembered I had given it to him for Christmas but I was happy to know it gave him pleasure. We talked about a picture on the nearby easel he said he was working on. It had a dark background with three female figures that he explained were representations of the past, the present, and the future. The painting of his son that had been hidden during my first visit, was in full sight and I wondered if there had been a reconciliation. Our conversation was not long. I promised to return in October and kissed him lightly on the forehead before saying good-bye.

It is nearing the end of October and the end of my brief stay in San Miguel. My intention to visit Ed before I leave is on my mind and so at around ten in the morning I call his number. I'm a bit worried when he doesn't answer the phone but I put my apprehensions aside in order to concentrate on an interview with Mary Rapp scheduled for later in the day. At her studio, Mary and I talk for a couple of hours and during our conversation we touch on her connection to the Beats. I mention my fondness for Ed and my intention to see him before I return to Canada and she tells me he died, only a week ago.

All day today, the sky is not as blue, the light is not as bright, and the landscape is flat. I move through it without remembering why it is until the question rises in my consciousness again, and the answer comes. Ed has gone.

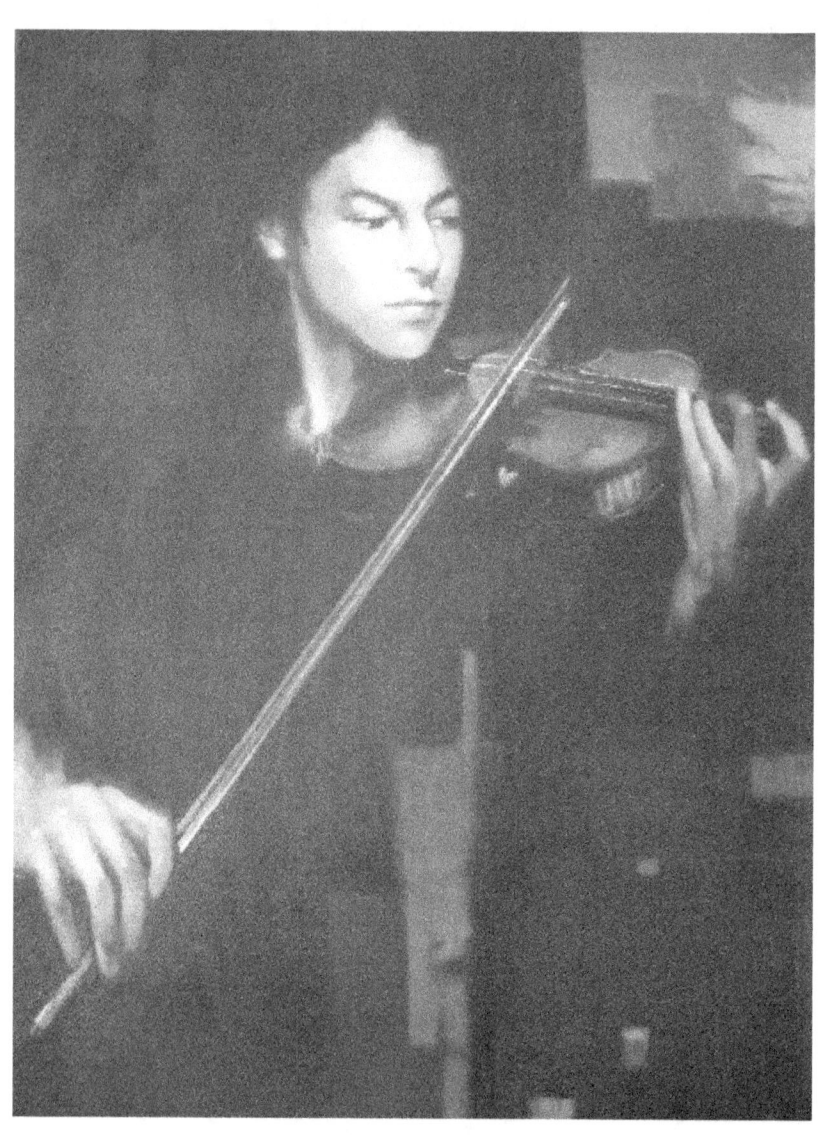

Peter Leventhal

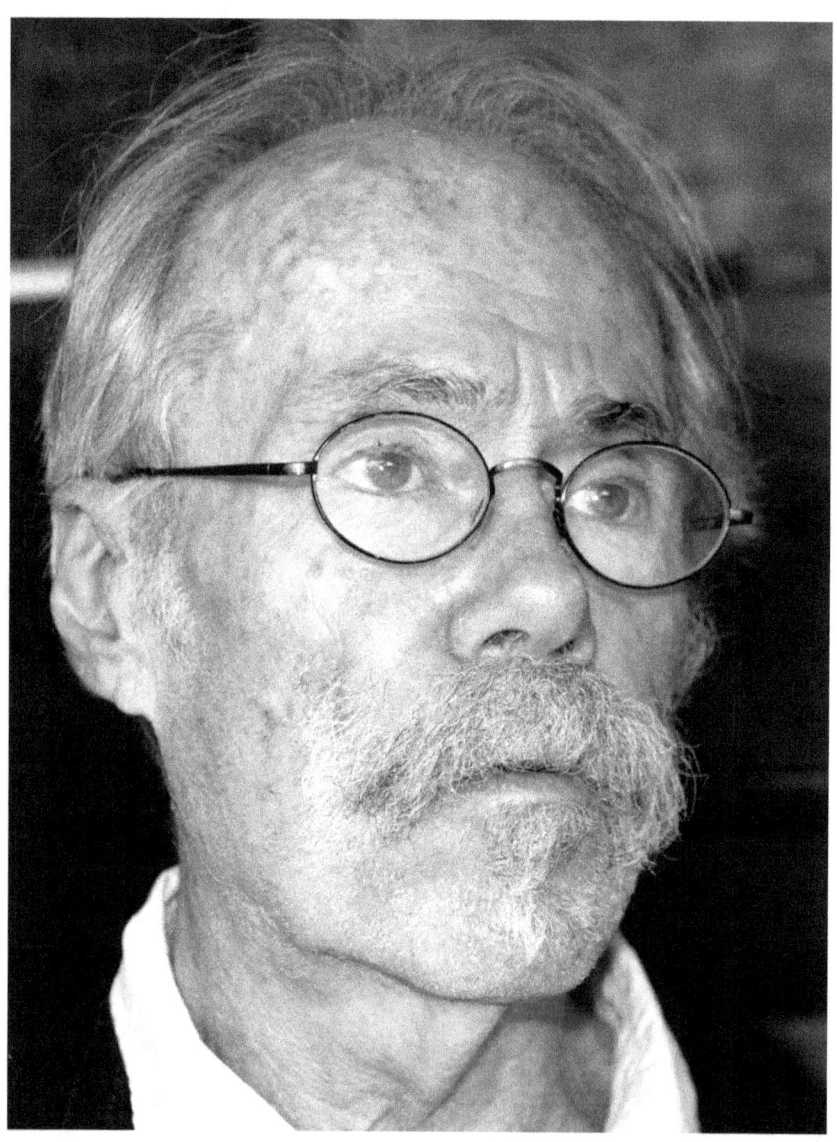

I've seen a number of his paintings, large canvases that hit you in the face with strength of purpose and things going on, so when I first see Peter Leventhal from a distance, he seems leaner than expected, scaled down by his quiet presence and an inconspicuous ego, but nevertheless a man one would notice in San Miguel or in New York. Today he is wearing a white shirt and a black vest that hangs loosely on a frame that one suspects was once more substantial. His white hair and long white mustache give him the appearance of a gentleman rancher who finds himself in unfamiliar territory, not entirely sure what his proper context might be. I extend my hand and notice Peter's hand is shaking as he reaches for mine, but his grasp is firm and his eyes are clear and direct. I like him immediately.

Born in New York City in 1939 on March 14, the same birth day as Albert Einstein, ("He got all the brains and I got all the looks."), Peter Leventhal was raised in an Italian neighbourhood by parents who had emigrated from Russia and Poland. "I had a very strong connection to Europe through them and with parts of European culture that were perhaps less known in the west and I think somewhere there is still a connection. I had a very interesting and good childhood in spite of the fact that my formative years were spent during the war. My father was away in the service and still I had a fairly tranquil childhood. I have a couple of younger sisters and my family was what used to be characterized as lower middle class in terms of income. Later on my father began to do economically better but he had the same bent gene that I have which he passed on to me. Neither of us has been good with finances. He had been trained in Europe and when he came to the United States he went to work in a textile design studio. After the war he started his own studio and it was his profession that led me into art. He had various design studios for much of my life and I had a very strong link to that world. I like to say I was very privileged. First of all I grew up in a city in which there was a tremendous amount of art to see if you chose.

I grew up in a house in which paints and brushes, paper and pencils, the arts were just a part of my existence. There was music in the house all the time. At an early age I was taken to the opera. We had books, so I can say it was a lovely home, very modest but stimulating and instructive for me. On top of that, I happened to be going into my majority in a New York that was to my mind, in one of the great periods in its history. My parents had been part of a huge immigration from Europe of people who were extremely critical, by that I mean very discerning about the arts and had an appreciation, gave it a value that was extraordinary. The intellectual and artistic temper of New York was beginning to germinate in a very exciting way. My father took me to exhibits and we would have discussions, well, I would listen to his monologues, sometimes a harangue but he had very definite opinions about things. For example, he used to tell me that great painting ended with Fragonard in the 18th century. And yet I remember so vividly, he took me to an exhibit of Amadeo Modigliani and he spoke rapturously about the painting. So there was a paradox about what I would hear him say at the kitchen table and what he would say when we went to an exhibit. I remember on my tenth birthday we went to the Metropolitan Museum and the Dutch government had sent a huge show of Van Gogh as a thank you for the war effort. I always knew I wanted to draw and paint, that it was my place, but that show made me formulate the idea that it was possible to do it as a lifelong career."

What do you remember about that exhibit?

"I can tell you right away. The exhibit was chronological so the early paintings were dark and kind of dreary but there was an excitement to them. I realized later that I was looking at work that was representational but not realistic. It had a tremendous power, a transformative power. When you were looking at those paintings, you were somewhere outside of yourself. It was the invention in the painting. As I moved into the next room the paintings started to lighten up. I didn't understand it then but there was the influence of Japanese painting in the work. And then I stopped in front of a painting of a drawbridge from a series of pictures he did of drawbridges. Something kept pulling me into the picture and then I realized that underneath the bridge where the water passed through was a patch of blue that was stunning to me. This was of course not formulated at that time but I can talk about it now after reflection. What I remember most is the excitement."

"After we went through the show we sat down to have a cup of tea and my father asked me if I had any questions. I said I wanted to know how to make a blue like the blue in that picture and my father who was very quick but often very caustic, said, 'In order to make that blue, you have to learn how to make all the other colours around it because that is what makes that blue.' It was perhaps not the response that a ten-year-old boy wanted to hear but it was true. That was like an epiphany. That was the moment I said, 'I want to do this.' Afterwards I drew all the time. I spent much of my class time in school making drawings. This is not an uncommon story with young people, especially young boys who become artists."

"The next thing I remember was we went to the museum again a year or so later. By this time I was close to twelve, and there was a small show in the museum of Rubens and some of the people that he influenced. I guess I was growing into that phase of my life but it was the first time I ever had a sensual response to women, to the shapes, the form and the light and the textures. It staggered me. The drawbridge was the stimulus but I wasn't going to spend my life painting drawbridges. Those two events didn't simply make an impact. Somehow they just went through me like lightening. My father had known a number of artists, some of them successful, most of them not and he explained to me that he would rather I had a trade with which I could make a living because the life of an artist was very difficult. But it didn't register with me. I had already made up my mind."

"We lived in a very interesting part of New York in Greenwich Village and some distance away there was an Italian coffee house called the Peacock, an intriguing place and my father and I went there for the first time after a concert at Carnegie Hall. They had huge canvases on the wall. The paintings were copies but they were first class copies. I remember there was one by the Italian Baroque painter Giordano and there was a bust of Cosimo de Medici, beautifully done. Later the owners moved the coffee shop down closer to where we lived so I would go down there often to have a cocoa or whatever. I just loved to look at those pictures. My father also liked to take me to the boxing matches and on our way home one night we stopped at a cafeteria instead of the Peacock, which I thought was unusual. We were sitting there having a cup of tea and my father pointed out a man sitting with a group of people at another table. 'You see that guy sitting there. They say he is the future of American art. His name is Jackson Pollock.' Then he went around the table and pointed out the other people. I don't know how he knew them but he told me if he ever caught me making work like that, he'd wring my neck. My father was completely dismissive of contemporary trends in American art and yet it wasn't a blanket dismissal because he took me several times to see the work of Paul Klee. He was a great admirer of Klee."

"If it sounds like my father was a dominating figure in my life, there is no doubt about it. He was a complicated man. He did very interesting work and he did it very well. His profession was and still remains for me a very honourable one. Because of him, I started out using a lot of textile design in my work. Through textile design, and my father's profession, I came to discover Raul Dufy who for a long time, was a very important influence. He has a reputation for painting light lovely paintings but if you look carefully there's a profundity to them. He was probably the greatest textile designer who ever lived which was one of the reasons that my father showed him to me. My father also had great reverence for a company called Liberty of London which is still in production."

"They set a standard for beauty that is respected everywhere."

"I'm glad you mention beauty. I have always had an interest in reading philosophy and in reading critical essays. As I said, partly coming out of my familial background, either I knew their work or I knew the philosophies of eastern European writers. I've always read philosophy, particularly German philosophers. I read Schiller as a young man and Schiller says something like this, 'What first comes to us as beautiful, ultimately comes to us as the truth.' People say beauty is subjective but I believe the test of beauty is over time and whether it continues to have a veracity or continues to have a voice that speaks of something that may not be definable but is certainly something that one feels. An opinion is of the mind. It is facile and easy and I don't believe we are in the world simply in our mind. That has always remained a maxim. What first comes to us as beautiful, ultimately comes to us as the truth."

"When I was painting as a young man, I didn't see my father very much for various reasons. I didn't like him to come to my studio because he was very critical. When he did come, he said, 'Your technique is good but the people you paint are so ugly.' It always hurt. It always hurt like a punch in the stomach. That having been said, it is important for me to know that there are various things in the work as a process that are essential. I am not afraid of elegance which is an aspect of American painting that in my time was disdained. Sensitivity was rejected, even facility. One of the things I always loved to hear about Dufy was that he drew beautifully. He drew quickly, very spontaneously. He started out drawing with his right hand which was his dominant hand but after a few years he started to draw with his left hand so he could be more fully conscious of the process. He said that drawing with his right hand was so effortless, it took him too far away from himself. He wanted to be right there and connected to what he was doing. Now I can't draw at all with my right hand, and I had to begin to train myself to draw with my left and I was surprised at the progress I was making. It was going pretty well until my left hand began to shake."

Peter has Parkinson's disease, a progressive disease of the nervous system, and is finding that his ability to draw is gradually disappearing.

"I think there is a confusion in the modern world that makes beauty suspect. There is a profundity to beauty, an insight in beauty that is omnipresent in things that have it. It is not about fashion. It is not about taste. It goes deeper than that. I feel that I can see it, even in work I don't like. I recognize there is an investment of beauty in the approach that is intriguing to me. There is no doubt that there are beautiful arrangements of colour and there are ugly arrangements of colour. I guess what I am trying to say is there is an affection and taste for ugliness that has grown up in the contemporary world that makes me feel that unless there is a standard, it just leads to an anarchic mess and I don't want to be part of that. It's possible my father was right that I paint a lot of ugly people but maybe it was his shortcoming, wanting them to look a certain way. He was in love with 18th century painting and maybe that clouded his view because beauty is complex. It contains a whole world of aspects.

"I happen to have a great love for the history of things. Since I learned to use the internet I have probably seen 100,000 images of paintings, much of it just gorgeous work. I have come across painting from Hungary and Spain for example, that is staggering, painters that I have never heard of and I'm talking about painters of the last couple of hundred years and what characterizes all the work that I see is a certain sense of beauty. It is beautifully done, beautifully painted. Its first value is not, oh look how different I am, look how unique I am. It accepts that it is part of a much larger program. Which reminds me, I had a friend who was much older than I, twenty-five years older, a wonderful abstract painter in New York whose work is in many galleries now and when I asked him how his work was going, he'd say, "I won't know what my work is until the day after I die. Your work is what you do over time." He also said to me once that time is the greatest luxury there is. To be able to take the time necessary to do things is the greatest gift. Today I feel we don't live in the best of times. Something has taken over and dismissed what for me is very valuable territory. Along with what the French called "nostalgia for the mud", there is an anti historical attitude. Many don't want to know what happened longer than five minutes ago."

"The Buddha said beauty is something we should actively seek. Is there something that is common to all of us that makes it possible for us to recognize beauty?"

"I go back to that statement of Schiller. I'm not interested in getting into a philosophical discussion about it. I prefer to be with people or to be with work that seems to be exploring for the truth. Whether we ever get there or not is immaterial to me."

"Perhaps that is what legitimizes the work that has endured through the ages. It deals with that fundamental idea of seeking truth. The art that is only interested in itself and only interested in the moment, is outside of those bounds."

"I think that is the case. Truth is transcendent. We all live as human beings on various levels. Sometimes the level is gross, sometimes it is sublime. While I don't think anybody has a lock on what is the truth, I think that the impulse, the impetus to search for it is what separates what I would call beautiful from not beautiful. You mention the Buddha. That's what the Buddha says. It's the search. It is not for everybody to have the realization. We're listening to Vivaldi now and its beautiful no matter who you are and when I look at material that was designed early in the 20th century, whether it was by Dufy, although I'm thinking of Dufy, it's very beautiful and over time it has held its position. It can be dismissed for a while because attitudes of the moment feel it's redundant or passé but it holds its ground. And again that's the test. The test comes with time. If you are involved with the search, you have the privilege to say this is really beautiful. If you are not involved in the search, how do you make a discernment about what is beautiful or not beautiful?"

"So that's what I feel about beauty. I'm always looking for it. How can I express this? It can be in a fragment of what you are doing. There is a felicity, an engagement, a stimulation that comes from it that is both outside of itself and inside the observer. I recently saw a video of a neurobiologist who was talking about the neurons in the brain. They have an extraordinary ability to empathize so it appears on a neurobiological basis that the empathic response in human beings is built in. And yet we know that human beings are capable of doing horrible things to one another. There is a contradiction there but I'm not going to dismiss something because there is a contradiction. I am going to try to discover why there is a contradiction and to find the truth in what seems the better part of it. I used to look at classical Greek art often. Eventually as I looked at it, I discerned two aspects. One of the aspects that got tired for me was the image, what one might call the subject. But the process and the touch in the work never got tired for me. It remains always as a source of solace. It is like listening to the music of Mozart. It is 18th century, it is nothing to do with the contemporary world but it always brings a certain comfort to the soul. For me, that is the work of the artist."

"Rilke the poet said a lot of things I was not particularly interested in but he did say, 'Art repairs the torn fabric of the soul.' The condition in which we live as human beings means that we are going to have hurt, pain, stress, as well as joy and pleasure. The work that can repair the torn fabric isn't necessarily that of joy and pleasure but it can be. I am a great believer in pleasure as an essential aspect of beauty, but it is not the only aspect of beauty. I will take it back to my early years and make it personal. When I started out painting, I did not have an interest in abstraction although having said that, I think some of it is very impactful but I only wanted to paint representational paintings, and moreover, narrative paintings, paintings that told stories. There was no place to show the work in New York when I was young. I was so shell shocked from being rejected that I once went to a gallery to show them my work and the guy was really interested. He looked at my slides and looked at them. When he finally handed them back to me he said, 'I haven't seen painting like this in four hundred years.' I took it as a criticism and I turned and left and went back to the studio. To this day, I think I made a mistake. I should have stayed and talked to him but the rejection had come so often. Now there has been a return to representational painting but when I look online and see what the galleries are showing, they have chosen an aspect of representation that is worn out and boring and doesn't sustain itself, that is to say, academic realism."

"I have always wanted to paint people and things. In my lifetime, things seem to have changed a lot and in other ways they seem not to have changed much at all. It was very difficult for me in New York. It was very frustrating. I knew what I was supposed to do and I couldn't do it, particularly the socializing. It just seemed crude. It wasn't until I decided to move from New York to north Florida and started to work and show there that I had some success. They were much more receptive to my work and it gave my work a boost that comes from having a little success. When I think about Van Gogh, he spent only ten years painting. He did all those paintings in just ten years. No matter what strength he had, in the end he had to be devastated by the neglect."

You went to Florida. How did you eventually arrive in San Miguel?

The first time I came to San Miguel was in 1990 under sort of strange circumstances, I didn't particularly want to come and didn't particularly like it and thought I would never come back again. But after that I had occasion to be in Mexico City and I came up to San Miguel and it was a little more agreeable and I wound up being shown a piece of property that I bought. I was in a relationship and we agreed that it was a good place to buy a house. Of course the place was very small and seemed very far away. It could take five or six hours to get here from Mexico City by bus. Because it was more isolated and small, I didn't feel I could make a living here so I was commuting between New York and here. When I found myself going to Florida, I stopped coming here for three or four years. My work didn't fit the standards or the interest in New York and Florida proved a very good move economically but it was very stressful in terms of culture. In spite of the fact that there were any number of wonderful, engaging people there, I never felt comfortable in Florida. I decided to come back to San Miguel in 2000 or 2001 and I found a very changed place. It was booming or starting to boom. It was wealthier and people were building houses and there was a call for my work so I decided to stay. I have a lot of problems being in San Miguel in some ways because in spite of what people politely say about its being a gringo town, it is not. It is very much a Mexican town. I have had trouble learning the language. I have get-by Spanish. I read a lot better than I speak but it is sometimes difficult for me to work in an environment in which I am not understanding as much as I would like to understand. That having been said, people have been very kind, I'm talking of Mexican people. I love using them in my work but the high desert environment is not inspiring to me and so in a sense, the move and the duration of my stay has been by default. I sometimes think it is time to move on but given the state of the world, where to move becomes a problem. Not only that, I am not a young man anymore and I have picked up and moved three or four times in the last twenty years and I don't know whether I have the strength to do that again. I have a great longing to live in a Mediterranean area. It has always seemed to be the most compatible for me artistically and culturally but I haven't been to Europe, except on short visits, for a long time and given the homogenization of culture, I'm liable to go there and find that what I am looking for has disappeared anyway.

"I remember when I was a child hearing the older people around me talking about the loss of their culture and now I am the one talking like that. I just finished reading a book about a Sephartic Jewish family who had put down roots in Greece and by the 20th century everything had changed. The book is written by a French philosopher who says this is what happens to cultures, they just disappear. They may linger in a sweet bun of your grandmother's but that is about all that is left. It is sad. The younger generation sees only what is. Talleyrand said, 'Only those who lived before the revolution know how sweet life can be.' and I understand that now. The First World War was a suicide attempt on the part of western civilization. They shot themselves in the head but they didn't die so they tried again and I think you can date the beginning of the Second World War as the final stage in the collapse of the civilization. I'm sure there are people who find that agreeable, God knows western imperialism has been horrible for millions of people, but I think that the history of Europe in the 20th and 21st centuries speaks of what happens when you lose hold of the past."

"A couple of decades ago it would have surprised me to hear myself saying this because I was always more radical in my view about the need for change but there was a kind of conservatism that was conservative only in relation to the ethos of the new world, especially the United States. When I met contemporary Italian painters for instance, they talked about the burden they were working under, being next to the greatest art that had ever been produced. But they didn't particularly want to go anywhere. That's what I mean about the conservatives. There was an acknowledgement and an empathy for what had been produced and the perpetuation of that tradition. For me, there were significant aspects of that culture and it's not that I romance the history, it has been as dreadful as anywhere, but there was a cognizance about the traditions that incorporated language, aesthetic attitudes, mythological and psychological attitudes. If you ask me to demonstrate that in the particular, it would be very difficult but I don't think I'm wrong when I say that something has changed radically in the world in the last twenty years. There is a global culture now and I don't find it attractive, it's not one I can feel comfortable with."

Is there anything you admire in the artwork of the last half century?

"The internet has made images from all over available and the talent is very humbling. It would be impossible to have any overweening self-worth looking at all the talent that exists in the world. I found the first ten or twenty years of modernism heroic. I have never been an abstract painter and I had a certain animus about it because it drove figurative painting right out of the market and you were considered a non-entity if you were a figurative painter. And so I have had an animosity towards it but I look at it now and for the first time I am able to allow myself to say it is beautiful, but it is interesting only up to a point. What happens after you get past the initial esthetic experience? How does it engage you? How does it stay with you? Recently I have been looking at some of the great paintings, paintings I know very well but I am looking at them again and the success of those paintings is staggering. What they do to your psyche or your soul is amplified in a way that is just thrilling and deeply enriching and I can't say there is much contemporary work that engages me that way."

When you are doing your own painting, do you think about that?

"Yes, oh yes. A friend of mine once said that when you go into your studio you bring everybody in with you, your parents, your grandparents, your wife, your children, and about a hundred thousand critics. You have to send them all out. One by one you send them out until you are all by yourself in your studio and then you have to send yourself out and that is when you can begin your painting. I found that a very risible and profound way of looking at it except I have never been able to do it. A thousand images stay with me, the collective work of the culture. I can't get that out of mind. I'm always contending with it. That's the power of the experience that I have with painting. I was fortunate or unfortunate enough to have seen so much great work face to face. It probably was exotic of me, let's say, to think that I could even begin to compete with it but it was a way of pushing myself, of aspiring to something, probably beyond my reach but it was the beginning."

You have lived in San Miguel for many years now. Would you say there is a distinct Mexican culture that endures here and has influenced your work?

"I have learned that I know very little about the Mexican culture. What you see is not necessarily what is deeply there. I don't have admission into that. I have a superficial admission because I paint Mexican people and I can look into their eyes and think that I see something but whether it is there or not, I don't know. What I do like about San Miguel is that it has been behind the times. That is true of Mexico generally but I think that is changing and to me, it is less engaging. A few years ago I got an idea to do something that correlated with the bicentennial and the centennial of the revolution and initially the project was going to be about the history of the Mexican Communist Party as it related to the arts in Mexico in the early part of the 20th century. At that time, most of the great Mexican painters were politically involved in the Communist Party. When I started to do the research, I found much of the material was so horrendous that I got discouraged. I became depressed and decided I didn't want to do it. I don't know why I love reading history because it makes me very disconsolate. It makes me feel that the collective behaviour of human beings is pretty appalling. Then I came across the work of Antonietta Rivas Mercado and I started again. Of course everything had to be visually presented. I did a number of paintings and as I got closer to the bicentennial I found that I couldn't get the backing I needed and I understood that. It was a Mexican event and there were a thousand Mexican painters on line, why would I be chosen? I did fifteen or sixteen canvases but I couldn't get it organized into a show and maybe it was too ambitious a project. I could have simplified it but it was an interesting endeavor and I made some very nice paintings. It gave me a chance to work on more dynamically composed images, historical images and now I am thinking of applying that in an allegorical sense."

There is a painting behind us on the brick wall of the open-air café where Peter and I are seated. It is one of Peter's paintings, a large work depicting two men with some children in the foreground. One of the men looks like Diego Rivera.

"It is Diego Rivera but the man who sat for it is actually a man who has a gallery here. The other man is Orozco but I used a printmaking teacher at Bellas Artes as a model. The kids are little kids from the around the neighbourhood. These are fun to do, like the project I was working on for the Centennial. What I did was I found people here in San Miguel who looked like the historical personages. This picture is a little more illustrative than I ordinarily do. When I say my paintings are narrative I mean they tell a story but the story is often obscured. You know something is going on there but what I'm trying to do is get the psychological implications of the story into the painting, not necessarily literal action. In this case, there was a story going around about Rivera and Orozco, whether it was true or not I'll never know, but they were working on their murals at the same time in the Bellas Artes in Mexico City. Much to everyone's surprise Orozco finished first. Diego was having trouble on his mural. They were both members of the Party but they didn't like one another and Orozco, very few people know that he had no left hand, wrapped his brushes up after cleaning them carefully, walked around the balcony because they were working on opposite sides of the balcony, and whistled over to Rivera and offered his own brushes to Rivera saying, 'Maybe if you use these you can find a way to finish your work.' This was about as literal as I got. There is a story happening but I'm not interested in delineating the story as in a novel. Every viewer sees something of his own in the painting."

May I ask one more question? You were saying earlier that your Parkinson's disease has been worsening and you aren't interested in hearing about new treatments. Why is that and how has your illness effected your painting?

"Here is one way. I completely can't use my right hand for anything. It is so bad that it adds to the misery. If I try to pick up a cup it just flies all over the place. I was able to draw and paint with my left hand for a while and I liked the aspect of the line and the brushwork but now my left hand has started to shake. I don't know how much longer I can draw or paint but it doesn't seem to affect me when I sculpt so I have that to look forward to. But the symptoms of the disease are stronger and I don't have the energy I had even a few years ago. I am seventy-four years old now and I'm not so valuable that I think it is important to spend hundreds of thousands of dollars exploring ways to prolong my life. I have always believed that we each have a certain number of years to live and seventy-four is a good number of years. I lost my 36 year-old daughter a couple of years ago. I have had double that time and if I haven't done what I needed to do by now, I am probably too late."

The young waitress comes to take our empty coffee cups and I ask for the bill. "La cuenta por favor." Peter tells me he must return to his work in his studio, a space he shares with his wife, just a few steps away from where we are sitting. For me, it is a wistful parting as I relinquish our time together, knowing that it won't be repeated. Our confidences exist in a separate realm, a place where we are intimately connected but one that is bound by its own schedule and purpose.

Sometime later I find myself reflecting on the significance of one individual's existence. Since the age of ten, Peter Leventhal has dedicated his life to his painting, and more, to painting what he interpreted as truth. Has he achieved something of lasting consequence? Ultimately, what contribution do any of us make to the larger world? As Peter correctly points out, the real test is time. For the present, maybe all we can say with any certainty is that pursuing the beauty in a patch of blue isn't a bad way to spend one's life. Quite possibly, the search for beauty is the noblest quest any of us can undertake.

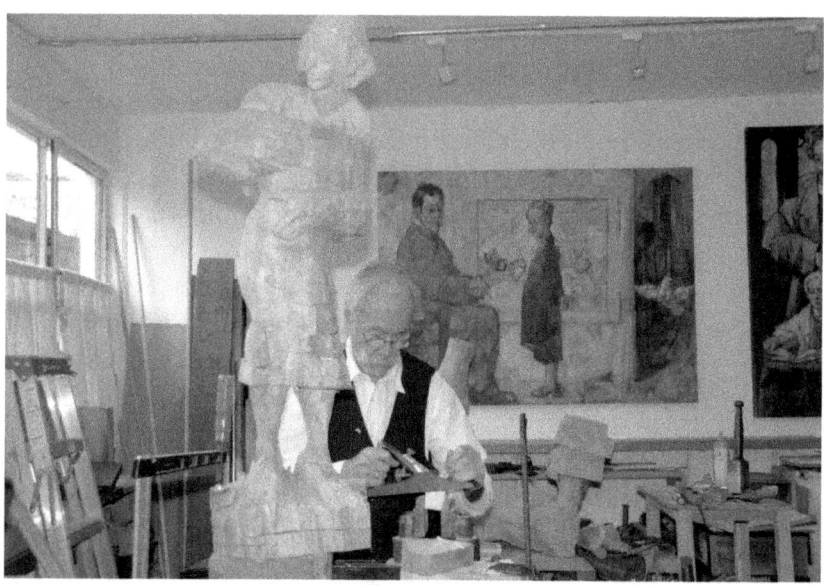

Mai Onno

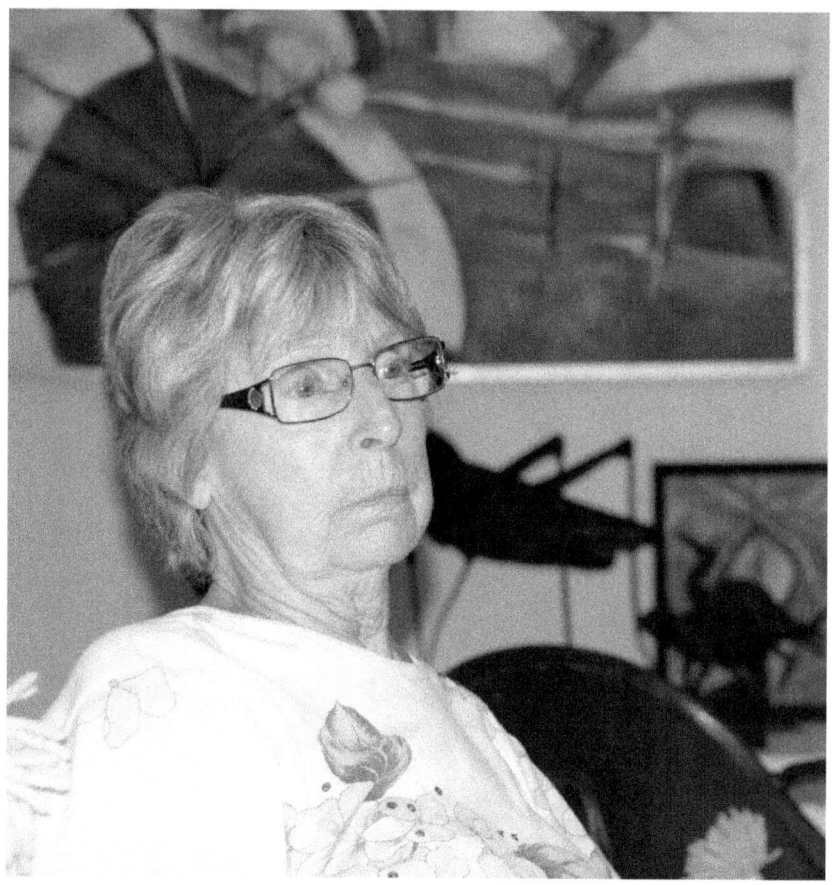

Estonia lies just south of the Gulf of Finland on Russia's west border. Its proximity to the Baltic Sea made it a perfect base for the communist Russian military and in 1940 Stalin made Estonia an offer it couldn't refuse. Stalin, never known for his subtlety, made certain that anyone who opposed the annexation of Estonia by the Soviet Union was dispatched without ceremony. When the Nazi's invaded in 1941, some hoped they would be the lesser of two evils; however, that hope soon died as Hitler's racial policies resulted in more Estonians being brutally murdered. With the fall of the Third Reich, the Soviet Union again took over Estonia in 1944. During these long years of violence and terror, Estonia, along with its neighbours Latvia, and Lithuania, was erased from the political map and countless numbers of people were either killed or fled. One of those who *can* still be counted is Mai Onno who escaped to Canada with her two aunts when she was fourteen years old. And what has all this to do with San Miguel? Mai Onno has lived and painted in San Miguel for over fifty-five years.

I am sitting in Mai's modest but comfortable home where we are surrounded by art- her paintings and the many beautiful sculptures of Mai's late husband, Lothar Kestenbaum. I had seen Mai Onno's paintings before I met her and must confess had not immediately made a personal connection to their energetic abstraction. To the casual observer, they are not easy paintings. But listening to Mai speak about her life, I began to understand that her work is a direct expression of her deepest self, a window onto a life which has been at times joyful, often difficult, and in many ways, remarkable.

"As a child I wasn't particularly interested in painting. I would sit in a tree and imagine myself as a great poetess, a poet or a ballerina. From very early on, I was propelled toward the creative. But life became very difficult during the war. It wasn't possible to go to ballet class. In 1940, the Russians marched in and occupied the three Baltic countries and all the intellectuals or anyone who was a power were slaughtered. It was a horrible slaughter. Then the Germans came in and in '44 the Russians came in again and the Germans retreated. After the war we had lost our country, we had lost our homeland, we had no documentation, we were displaced people. Estonia, Latvia, and Lithuania, the three Baltic countries disappeared. We didn't belong anywhere. There was a great exodus from that place. When we left, there were no more boats in the harbour. We found a small cargo boat, two women and three small children. My aunts got us passage on a large freighter but we were just on the deck. My mother had been lost already and my father stayed behind. Of course when you go through early life in a dramatic way, it reinforces the creative drive. It is a counterpoint to a reality that can be rather horrible and cruel."

Mai arrived in London, Ontario, Canada not speaking English, having lost her parents and everything that was familiar to her. But, being the determined individual she is, she quickly learned the language and became a top student. At the age of sixteen, a serious thyroid illness put her behind in school. "I think it was a response to all the trauma I had endured. I was uncertain about what I should do when one day I wandered into the H.B. Beal Technical School. I saw the art department was having an entrance exam and I meandered into the classroom to write it. I passed it with flying colours, so my art life began by falling into the right place at the right time."

In 1957, after five years of training in art school, Mai accepted one of twelve scholarships to study at the Instituto Allende in San Miguel. Other students she knew had preceded her so she says the prospect intrigued her. She recalls her first impressions of San Miguel. "It was an isolated place. In those days the only feasible way to get here was by train. You came by train through the United States, traveling 3 days and 3 nights. I took some Spanish lessons before I left but otherwise, I didn't make any preparation, in a way I wanted it to remain a mystery, so I was completely unprepared when the train chugged in at 2:30 in the afternoon and there was a dusty hole. A group of children held out their hands and asked to carry my bags. Then another cloud of dust brought a taxi and out popped Doreen and everything was all right."

Doreen Lindsay, Mai's guardian angel, was one of a number of Canadian students also attending school at the Instituto on scholarships. Others included Toni Onley, Joy Laville, and Don Richurt. "We were working shoulder to shoulder. We were all young. It was wonderful. The whole of San Miguel was only

15,000 people, a small village and the atmosphere was very different. We put up in the San Miguel Hotel which is gone now, at the end of Hidalgo street where Doreen and I shared a small apartment. It was a total culture shock, of course it was, but it was magic, a fairy land. That first year, I met my husband Lothar Kestenbaum who had come from Los Angeles on a scholarship but was already teaching at the Instituto. He was looking after this tiny house where we are sitting now for the Canadian owners and we eventually bought the house with money Lothar made from a show in Los Angeles. We lived here 'in sin' for two years, as they called it in those days, then in 1962 we got married and left for Rome. Lothar had been given a grant to spend two years in Italy. The second year we stayed in a quaint German villa just fifty kilometers from Rome called Villa Serpentara where many artists had lived, even Goethe had done some writing there. It was a great, great time."

Mai and Lothar returned to San Miguel from Italy, but shortly afterwards, moved to Santa Barbara and within a year to Milwaukee where Lothar taught at the University of Wisconsin and where they had their only son David. During those seven years, they maintained their connection to San Miguel and continued to spend summers in their little house which they gradually rebuilt. Lothar's resignation from the University of Wisconsin caused a sensation among his colleagues who were dumbfounded by the Kestenbaum's decision to leave the U.S. for the wilds of Mexico. Lothar was offered and accepted a position at the Bellas Artes, the federally funded art center in San Miguel and the family moved back for good.

I ask Mai to describe her work, suggesting she perhaps take one picture in the room where we sit, and tell me about it. Her reply is an illuminating insight into art itself. "You cannot take just one picture on a wall or anywhere because one's work is a lifetime's accumulation of thoughts and ideas and building an interior world of one's own. It is an accumulation of imagery from music, painting, theatre, dance, all the arts. Your own forms are permeated with all that knowledge. We have a disadvantage here in San Miguel because we can't run to a museum to see all the new exhibits. You have to rely on books. Occasionally you have to move out of here to renew your information, to refresh your thoughts and ideas. For a while I would go to Canada to care for my aunt, my foster mother and I would go to Toronto and I went to Mexico City to exhibits now and then. A big city gives a shock, an elevation to your self, half scary, half not, but bringing new ideas. When I have exhausted one idea, I move on to another theme which is carried on for a length of time. I do not duplicate myself which makes it hard for me to put on an exhibition. I have to find some unity because each painting is individual. I approach each painting as a new statement. Of course there are periods of work and themes that connect paintings."

"The organic form has always been the major theme in my work. The contemporary artist of today is encouraged to express himself immediately, to throw his art out in some emotional way but I think you first need to know the basics. When you undertake a creative discipline and you learn the techniques, you have enormous flexibility. I learned the basics through eight years of study and when I began to work on my own, I had to search for a means of personal expression. My husband had a powerful personality which he conveyed through his sculpture. His figurative and animal forms portray great drama. They make such a strong statement. Being younger and not established, I had to find a world that was my own and so I turned to the organic form. The natural world belonged to me, be it seed, or leaf, or flower. For years I did watercolour. Before that I used pastel extensively. Later, the organic form manifested in a long period of landscapes. As the years went by my painting became more and more simplified until finally it was distance and depth that I began to portray. When you look out at the Sierra Madre Mountains, you see that enormous distance and that is what I began to paint, without the mountains. Eight years after my husband's death I thought I could shake him so I tried the human figure which I had done before but without any dedication. After working with it for some time, I came back to the organic form.

And now I have gone back to the landscape but in a very different way. It took me a long time to throw out the image and use the brush to convey a certain state or emotion. So you see, you cannot explain anything with one painting. It is a lifetime's endeavor."

I am interested to know Mai's opinion about the artist's relationship with his audience. Does she think about her audience when she works? Her response is manifestly straightforward. "That's where integrity comes in. You have to do art for your own reasons, not for exhibitions, but because you believe in it. If you go away from the very solid image into a greater interpretation, I prefer that word to *abstraction*, then you lose the audience to a certain degree, unless they are willing to take time to look and to understand the work. The artist communicates something but where does he get this communication? He gets it from the world around him. You communicate yourself to your art and that in turn communicates to the one who sees it. Most of the time we have dedicated our life to our art, growing and maturing, making it clearer. The viewer can't just walk past. If he wants to see what is being communicated, he has to do some work too."

Finally, I ask Mai to reflect on how living in Mexico and particularly in San Miguel has shaped her life and her work. She laughs softly. "I'm not a very good example of anything. I've been displaced in so many ways, through the second world war, losing my country, being shoveled into a detention camp in Germany, with great difficulty being allowed to immigrate into Canada, and then coming to Mexico where you can live a lifetime but still be a foreigner. So I belong here and yet deep down I don't belong here. It is true that living in San Miguel made it possible for Lothar to teach and to still have time to do his own work. Living here made it possible for me to paint. It made it possible for us both to pursue the creative life. We could live comfortably on a small income, the climate is good, and there were fellow artists close by, people of like minds with whom we could exchange ideas. Especially in the sixties and seventies there was a nucleus of foreign artists who in turn attracted eccentrics, odd but brilliant people, so it was quite a wonderful milieu."

"As for the Mexican culture, although it was a culture I appreciated, it was not my culture. I was not going to use the pre-Columbian or the Aztec in my paintings. It would have been superimposing something that was not part of me. I still remained very much a European and a Canadian. I still am today. My influences came from the art world as a whole. But there is one definite connection. Over these many years I have absorbed the influences of nature, the explosion of light as it hits the trees and the flowers, the glow. What Mexico brought to me was the tremendous natural world, the sunlight, the plants, the landscapes, the enormous contrast between light and dark, the sun and the shadow, the intense colour, these have been my inspiration and my life here. I have absorbed it. It has become a part of me completely. So in this way, I belong."

During our many conversations, I have come to admire this intelligent woman. She may be nearing eighty, but there breathes a spirited girl just beneath the skin. Her images trumpet an elemental courage that has not been muted by the many challenges she has had to endure. Her paintings dare the viewer to come closer, exhorting us to respond to their candid vitality, to a profundity grown out of long dedication, wisdom and hope. At first, we may not know where to look or even what we are looking for, but as Mai Onno herself has said, if we are patient and do the work, the meaning is right there.

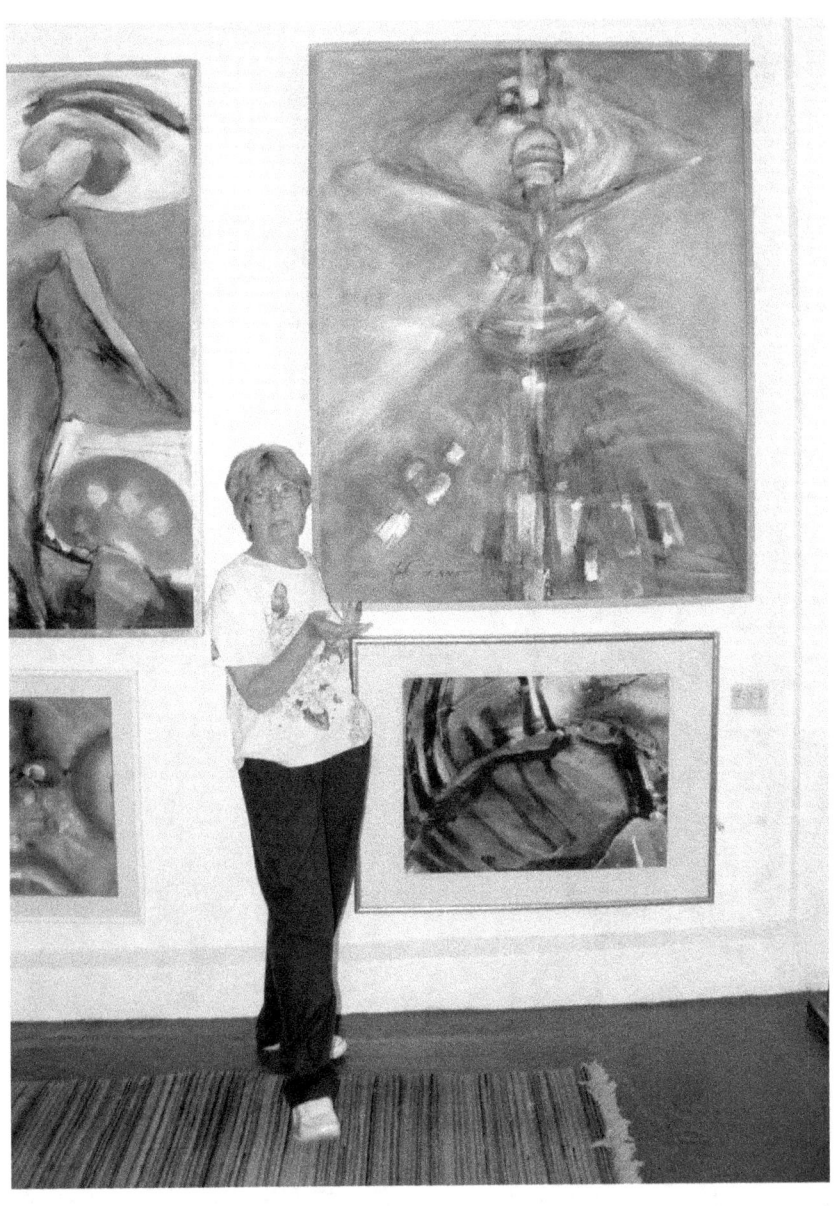

Erv Kaczmarek

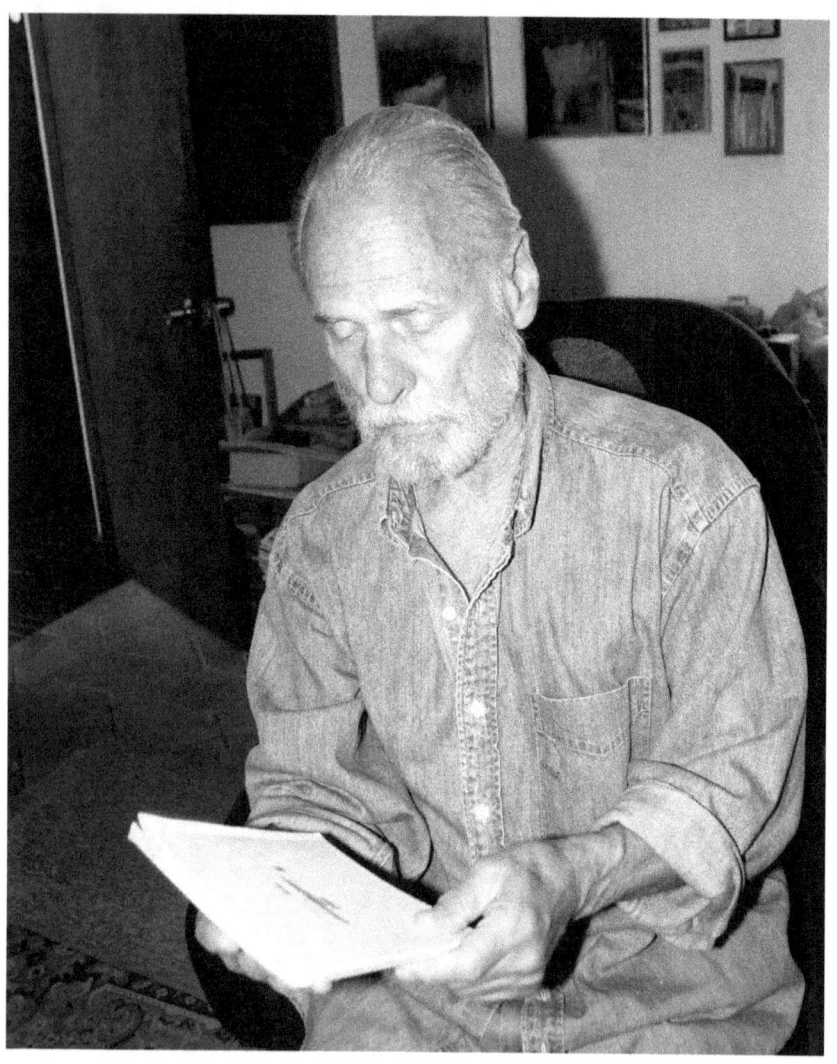

I am a little woozy having climbed to the top of Calle San Francisco, all the way up along the narrow prolongación past the Calvario church and I'm searching for a number on a white wall that is reflecting the bright sunlight and making me squint. Seeing the address, I stand on tiptoes to ring the bell and almost immediately am greeted by a small Mexican woman who ushers me through a compact entry hall lined with paintings into a cozy unpretentious room with many books and a comfortable well used couch. After the brilliant light outside, my eyes need a moment to adjust to the darker interior and I am happy to wait while the woman goes to fetch Erv. In a couple of minutes I am seated across from a trim, athletic man with close cut gray hair and a beard. His clothes are casual but they reveal a person who is careful with his appearance, or is lovingly looked after. I notice his hands are strong, familiar with work. Today he has pulled a muscle in his back and is feeling some discomfort but he insists we go on with our interview so I begin by asking Erv Kaczmarek how it is that he is in his seventies and has lived all his adult life in San Miguel.

"I was born in a Polish ghetto in Milwaukee in 1939 and lived there until I was a teenager. It was interesting growing up there. After the war people had jobs, people had money and they began to buy refrigerators and televisions and cars, all the amenities, things that people never thought they would have. My four grandparents all immigrated to the US around 1910. They beat the war although they knew it was coming. My maternal grandfather walked from Poland to Scandinavia, made his way to England and then to New York. Most of them landed in New York and moved out from there. I've never been back to Poland but I have two uncles who have done some research on my ancestry and they have sent me photographs that I have shown to my grandkids. After I moved down here my parents visited many times and my mom learned to speak Spanish. She loved San Miguel and when she traveled to Poland she found some similarities between San Miguel and places in Poland and oddly enough she said she found some similarities in the language between Polish and Spanish. "

Since reading Tina Rosenberg's 1995 Pulitzer Prize winning book, *The Haunted Land: Facing Europe's Ghosts After Communism*, I have admired the many Polish citizens who were persistently defiant while their country was under foreign control. As time wore on, Communist authorities chose to overlook some of Poland's noncompliance as you might choose to ignore an obstreperous child out of sheer frustration. In more recent times while travelling in Europe I have met determined Polish emigrants everywhere who are taking advantage of unrestricted borders and are looking to get ahead. In some countries they are criticized for appropriating local jobs, but if a physically demanding job needs doing, employers know that Poles are willing, dependable workers. Much as Mexicans have been accustomed to doing the heavy or tedious manual labour in the U.S. and Canada, Poles have been playing similar roles in Germany, the U.K. and other countries in the European Union. As employment opportunities in Poland increase, many expatriates will choose to return home just as Mexicans would prefer to live and work in their own country should the economy in Mexico ever be allowed to thrive. My observations have convinced me that ordinary Mexicans are among the hardest working people in the world. Unfortunately, the country's current economic conditions are largely determined by forces beyond the average citizen's control.

Erv continues, "It is hard to pinpoint why I became an artist. I did a year in an industrial college where there was one man, one of my teachers, who I remember well. At that time I wanted to be a drafting instructor and I had an English professor, Mr. Benson, who would come in every morning and write the names of philosophers, painters, poets on the board and he would turn around and say, 'If you guys want to know anything about these people, I suggest you go to the library.' So I started going to the library and pretty soon my room was piled with books and I started drawing. Benson lived around the block from me and we would meet in the park and we would talk and he said to me one day, 'Get the hell out of here and go to an art school'. I can thank him for that. I enrolled in a fine arts school and I did have some good instructors, people that had gone to the Bauhaus in Chicago when Gropius and Moholy-Nagy and others came over, and I took a lot of design courses but I was always torn between fine arts and interior design."

"It was during my second year in fine arts that I and others began to think that we weren't getting all that we needed and what we were paying for. It was an expensive school so we, with the help of four instructors, wrote a manifesto saying that we thought we deserved a better education. The administration turned it down and subsequently over half the students out of my class and some of the instructors left. One of the guys said he was going to Mexico so two of us agreed to go with him. We bought a '50 Chevy for a hundred bucks. A friend of ours had a sister who had come here to take classes at the Instituto. I had done six months in the reserves but the other two guys had to be enrolled in school to beat the draft so we came here to see if we could enroll. It was September, 1961, I was 22 and I knew in twenty minutes after we arrived that San Miguel was going to be my home. We slept that first night on the lawn at the back of the Instituto. It was huge in those days. We slept on the lawn and we walked around and we were amazed. It felt so good to be here. I just felt free and clean and good being here. The town was small and you could talk to everybody and you got to know your neighbours. It felt good and I knew I wanted to stay so I got married. I stage managed, I ..."

Wait a minute. You got married? How did that happen?

"You have to remember there were only fifteen thousand people here in those days. You knew everybody and everybody knew you. There were lots of parties and only two bars, the Cucaracha on the jardín and the Papillon. You could go in and meet a lot of other painters and writers. Some of those friendships lasted a long time. There was only the centre of town, not all the colonias like there are now, so you walked everywhere. The first class bus used to stop nearby and both Mexican and American guys would wait at the bus stop to pick up girls getting off the bus. I met my wife Lupe at an Australian writer's house in 1961 and we were married in '63.

Did you have to ask her family's permission to get married?

"Her mother had been dead for a few years and her father was a pretty heavy drinker. I met him and we talked and drank together but there was no question of having to get permission. It is probably why it came off and why it has worked all these years. We just celebrated our fiftieth wedding anniversary. I mean we didn't have to walk in opposite directions in the jardín or any of that stuff so it just happened and it has been pretty good."

"Anyway, I stage managed, I built sets, I house managed, I was in a theatre group that was sponsored by American Airlines and had top notch actors from New York and L.A. I did that for a while, I made fake antiques, and a couple of times I went back and worked at summer jobs in factories in the Milwaukee area. I did everything I could to stay. I worked as a buyer in a store here in San Miguel for many years and all the time I was working at other jobs, I painted. For the first three years I went to the Instituto on a scholarship where I had instructors like James Pinto and Fred Samuelson who were two of my painting teachers."

"James Pinto was a damn good teacher. I hung out with him, I played poker with him, I drank with him. He was Yugoslavian and immigrated to the States before the second World War and he came here in the fifties just when the Instituto was getting established and he was instrumental because he took an interest in students who were really serious and wanted instruction. He knew art history and European painting and he could talk about any painter in a way that made it exciting."

I ask Erv about James Pinto's large painting on the wall in the Instituto that reminds me of the paintings of Siqueros and Orozco, the square muscular characters striving bravely forward. David Siqueiros was born in Mexico City in 1896 and became well known as a muralist, as did Orozco and Rivera. He was a member of the Mexican Communist Party and frequently incorporated political ideas into his work. Erv knows exactly what painting I am referring to. "I think that painting is dated '57. Siqueiros was here in San Miguel and painted a mural in the Bellas Artes. Pinto and Siqueiros were kind of similar in manner although Siqueiros was a much bigger guy. They must have known one another."

Jose Luis Cuevas, a Mexican painter, engraver, and writer who was born in 1934, became an outspoken critic of Siqueros, Rivera, and other artists who produced art intended to make political statements. "Cuevas and his buddies used to hang out at restaurants in the area of Mexico City called the Zona Rosa, a name they came up with. A few of them are still alive. Cuevas has his own museum in Mexico City. They also came up with the term Cactus Curtain to describe those painters who painted pictures with political themes, women in robozos, old fashioned stuff in their opinion."

"I knew Jim Pinto a long time but he died in 1987 and then his wife committed suicide. Shortly before she died I saw her on the street and she said I should come over and get some things of Jim's that she wanted me to have and I didn't go and a couple of days later she was dead and the entire house and all its contents went to the state because there was no will. Here in Mexico it is important to have a will, otherwise your possessions can be confiscated by the government. I had been out of that group for a while so I was surprised to hear Jim had died. I guess when I quit golfing I lost touch."

Where did you golf here?

"At Malanquin. That course has been there for going on forty years. I have a funny photograph that Tom Horn and I took to make a comment on how slow they were to get the place finished. Tom is an author and we were friends from the beginning. Things out at the golf course were kind of shaky and Tom and I were sitting around one day and he said, I've got an idea so we decided to send this photo to every member." After some rummaging through drawers, Erv locates a photograph and brings it over to me. It shows a little boy peeing in a large hole in front of a row of four or five small cement buildings. "This is my son who was about five then, he's now forty-five, and below the photo it says, 'Help us fill the pool.' and we sent it to every member of the golf club and nobody could figure out who did it but it got some action. They finished the pool. Once I said to Tom, why don't we get a couple million dollars and make a movie of your book and he said let's get a couple million dollars and go out and get drunk. He has a son and a daughter here and he bought an old place outside of Manzanillo and one day he invited Lupe and I to go and use it but my teaching schedule didn't allow me to go. I stay pretty close to home." As we speak, the sounds of talking and frequent laughter drift up the stairs and soon I can smell food cooking. I am aware that the house is full of activity below us but very quickly I am engrossed again as Erv recounts his early adventures in Mexico.

"When I came here I really wanted to be part of the Mexican community. I read everything I could get my hands on about Mexican history. I had a great history teacher, Dr. Oseena, a medical doctor who came from Spain in the forties, a wonderful man who also taught at the Instituto and he suggested books for me to read. That was great. Stirling Dickinson had moved here from the States in the thirties and he was determined to make the Instituto a first class art school. After the war ended he established a scholarship program for Canadian and American students and he saw to it that the instructors here were good. When I finished my studies, Stirling asked if I wanted to stay on and study another year but I said I wanted to get my own studio. San Miguel was small enough that we had the time to get to know people and to develop our art. That's always been part of being here, the people. When the town was small it was more community oriented. Many of the Canadians and Americans that come here today don't have a lot to do with the Mexicans. It was nicer then, although I guess we all look back on the past with some nostalgia. A New Yorker I met once said to me, 'Erv, you've been here a long time. Have you ever gotten close to a Mexican?' and I said, 'Yeah, every night."

"I first met Stirling Dickinson at the Instituto but it was when I was playing baseball on his team that I really got to know him well. Stirling introduced baseball to San Miguel. He thought it would be a way of getting into the Mexican culture, to teach the American game of baseball to the local guys, so he bought some gloves and balls and eventually they even had uniforms. For many many years it was an all Mexican team. I had started playing on an all American team called The Mob that a writer friend of mine started. We challenged Stirling's team to a game and they wiped us twelve to nothing. We weren't very good and eventually our team disbanded so a few of us went to play for Stirling. I was on the team for three or four years. The only way you could talk to Stirling was after a game when he had had a few drinks."

I've heard he was shy.

"Hah! When you were talking to him you had to keep moving forward because Stirling would keep taking steps back. He was extremely shy. He played bridge. Beside the baseball, bridge was one of his loves, and orchids. I got to have some great talks with him. We'd go to towns within fifty or sixty miles to play on a Sunday. Most of the games were in cow pastures, you'd have to dodge the cow dung, then afterwards we'd go have carnitas and tequila and a few beer somewhere. We were in an industrial league in Queretero around '64, '65, '66. We played against some good teams and won the league championship two years in a row. The second year we were undefeated. We had this pitcher Lamar Herrin who later became a writer and taught at Cornell for years. Before coming to San Miguel he had been signed by the Cardinals then he got into some kind of accident and ripped up his arm but he still had something."

I look Lamar Herrin up on the web and find he has written six novels, has been published in Harper's and The New Yorker and had a successful career as a creative writing professor at Cornell University. There is no mention of his pitching exploits in San Miguel.

"Stirling was kind of sexless. He wasn't gay but he didn't ever marry. He came here and bought a piece a property for next to nothing where he grew and cultivated an incredible collection of orchids with the help of three or four gardeners. I ran into Stirling one afternoon not too long before he died and I told him his orchid garden was going to fall apart if he didn't find someone reliable to look after it but unfortunately that didn't happen and his collection has all but disappeared."

The phone rings and Erv tells the caller he is teaching Tuesday, Wednesday, and Thursday morning. He says his back is sore but he hopes to be in shape for class tomorrow. After he hangs up he apologizes for the interruption and explains that it was one of his students calling.

You do a lot of teaching?

"I am very informal. I call it unteaching. I have no rules. I go one on one with my students whatever level they are on although I prefer people who have had some experience. I help them with composition, with colour. My idea is to just do the work. You learn about yourself. It's like doing anything else. Just keep at it.

I realized not too long ago that I had better be doing things that I enjoy and that I want to do. I don't like hassles. I don't like showing or dealing with galleries. I don't make a living selling my work but teaching helps pay the bills. I taught at Bellas Artes for eight years and since I quit there, students have allowed me to teach out of their homes. It's been great because they are all very nice people and fun to be with. That's one of the reasons I stayed here in San Miguel. The fact that I meet people from all over the world feeds me and it feeds my work. Teaching is very fulfilling, otherwise I wouldn't be doing it, and besides, it gets me out of the house."

"I have had students from every country, Japanese, Chinese, Germans, Americans, a lot of Canadians, young people and old. I don't like to think of myself as teaching. I try to motivate. Gradually I introduce things and I make suggestions. I have had people in mid career change what they have been doing and they have been happy with the change. Painting should be personal. It should be yours. I should be able to see your personality in your painting. And it should be happy. I can't stand all the dark, angst kind of stuff that is being done today. Also it should enhance your life and it should make a better person out of you. You are going to struggle sometimes. There will be areas where you're in doubt but most of it should be a lot of fun."

Why don't you tell me about your work?

"My work is pretty much nonobjective but it is based on architecture and landscape. You can see there are horizons in 70% of the work. I painted the figure and I painted landscape but the stuff that appeared behind them started to become much more interesting so I discarded those realistic kind of things. I go back to chairs periodically because there is a certain humour there that I like to play with. I like the simplicity of chairs. Like this one." Erv retrieves a program with one of his paintings pictured on the front. It is a landscape with two chairs in the bottom left hand corner. The chairs are simple profiles, tipping back, seats facing one another. He says, "I had a retrospective at Bellas Artes a number of years ago, this painting hangs downstairs and someone almost took it home a couple of weeks ago but they couldn't fight the price, anyway this is very humourous."

The chairs have personality. They look like they're talking to one another.

"They are actually. They are talking and they are dancing. It is a fiesta." Erv coughs. "Excuse me. I have a reaction to the jacaranda and the mesquite." For anyone new to San Miguel in the spring when the jacaranda trees are in bloom, the clouds of lavender flowers that appear throughout the city can cause both delight and dismay. Many discover they are allergic to the pollen of the trumpet shaped flowers and must wait out the blooming period for about a month before their noses stop running. The mesquite tree also produces pollens that can cause allergic reactions and anyone with this particular sensitivity will struggle to find respite in this part of Mexico where it has been traditional for residents to plant mesquite trees just about everywhere. These drought tolerant trees produce pods that have been used as a food source for centuries and their wood makes an excellent slow burning fuel for cooking. Mesquite wood is extremely dense so any furniture made from mesquite will be heavy and durable. In San Miguel all sizable trees are protected although it is possible to obtain a permit to cut a tree down but there must be good reason and the city requires that a number of young trees be purchased and donated to the municipality in return for the loss of one.

Erv points to a small painting on the wall behind me, "Some of my paintings I work on for years. This one came pretty quickly. See this little figure here, it is Guadalupe, the Virgin and the title is 'Shoveling Snow off the Roof with Guadalupe' so there is the humour." Erv takes the painting off its hook so he can show it to me. "I used this piece of cloth back here, Oaxacan cloth, and this silver paper, and then I pasted on this hunk of cardboard." I who have been warned in museums to keep well away from the works on display am intrigued when Erv's confident hands touch the surface of the painting as a sculptor might caress a figure he had brought into being. The visual and tactile vigor of Erv's work is transmitted in the way he holds his paintings, as a father with a large family would clasp a familiar child. There is a wide swath of lime green paint down the left side and along the bottom of the image. "Stuff just started to come together but what took me a longer time to realize was the colour I needed here. I forget how many colours I tried."

That green is perfect.

"Well thanks. I finally reached the colour I was looking for. I started with collage about twenty-five years ago. I had a one man show at the Bellas Artes at that time and I had several people come up and tell me it was the best show they had ever seen here. Subsequently, after looking at the paintings, I destroyed quite a few of them because I felt they were not resolved. They were good starts and gave me the impetus and some ideas to go into but I painted over quite a few of them and I have done that throughout my life. Destroyed paintings. I am actually keeping more lately because in the last ten years I have felt so good about what I was doing and how my life was going so it has been easier but there are still times when it takes me a couple of years to get a painting just where I want it. I think I have finally learned how to finish things." Erv laughs. "So maybe I will have more shows. I'm not out shopping for one but who knows. I had a show this past year and sold about ten pieces right away which was great, considering how the economy is here and in the world right now, and then over the next couple of months the rest sold. It was in a great gallery. This month they are showing Alejandro Santiago's work. The story is he lived in Paris and he travelled a lot and when he came back to his village in Oaxaca all his friends had left to work in the States so he did a bunch of sculptures out of clay with some of the young guys in the surrounding countryside. The show is worth seeing. I think he's a great painter but I don't like what he paints. It just seems too easy. I've seen videos of him working and he's got fourteen paintings on the floor and six more over here and then he comes along with the same colour brush. He's got kind of a production company going and that's ok. That's cool. When the Bellas Artes opens again he's going to have a show there." Some music is playing downstairs and in the momentary silence I am conscious of it.

There is music in your paintings.

"Good, because I listen to music when I paint. I like both jazz and classical but I'm an old bebopper."

Erv and I exchange stories about our favourite musicians. We find we both like Keith Jarrett and Oscar Peterson. I tell him that I once saw Peterson play at the Banff School of Fine Arts, a school where artists and performers can go for a few weeks to develop their talents and share the results with others. He tells me about a similar centre in the States. "Are you familiar with MacDowell Colony? It's an art colony that's been going since 1907 in Peterborough, New Hampshire. I was up there twice for two months each time. Usually about thirty people are invited to go there to paint, compose, do architecture, sculpt, write. You have to apply but if you're accepted, it's free and you have your own studio, in fact the second time I was there I had a live-in studio which was really great. They bring your lunch to the door at 12:00 in a basket so you don't have to think about a thing except what you are creating. That's a place I really met people. I hung out with composers. There's a man who is a composer here in San Miguel who also went to MacDowell. He lives around the corner from me. I didn't know he lived here until someone asked me if I had met Jimmy Lewis and I said no and it turned out we had just missed each other at MacDowell. I preferred the company of composers because I liked the way they spoke about their music and played me stuff they were working on."

Our reminiscences remind Erv that he had a call this morning from Sylvia who owns San Miguel Art Gallery on the jardín, the main square. She phoned him because she is cleaning house and wanted to return a couple of paintings that she'd had stored for years. It seems that after fifty years Sylvia who is in her mid-eighties, is closing the gallery. "This is another instance of how San Miguel has changed. I went down to pick up the paintings and we sat and chatted for a while. We decided we could count the old timers that are left on one hand. I had a show there in '65." Erv goes to one of the neat piles of paper that are placed around the room to retrieve a bibliography and tells me he had his first show at the Instituto in 1963. He had a show at Bellas Artes in '64 and then in the Galeria de San Miguel in '65. "Then I had several shows in Oklahoma City and I met some great people who encouraged me in my career. I had a show in Celaya and in '67 I had a show in the Diego Rivera museum in Guanajuato but on opening night there was a downpour and the director was in a car accident so me and my wife and an oboe player and his wife sat up in the office and tried to drink all the wine. Shows have started because of people coming here to the house and seeing my work but I do very little self-promotion. I've done other things to make money. I'm not knocking on doors. Doing the work, the process is what is fun. I'm happy to do it for myself and a few other people, friends and collectors who buy my work. Another one of my ex-students was encouraging me to have a show featuring chairs but I don't know if I want to be pinned down to having to make thirty paintings of chairs. I was recently talking to a dealer who sat right there and I told him I don't have a brand, all my paintings are individually done, and he said he noticed that."

I'm not sure I agree. I do see your signature in your paintings.

"Yes, you can tell they are mine but I what I mean when I say I don't have a brand, I'm talking about say, Andy Warhol, that kind of thing. When I walk into a show and there are twenty-seven paintings with the same shapes and the same pallets, it gets pretty boring, I mean I don't want to bore myself. I want to get excited. I am looking for new things. It is not a big deal but there's no stamp on my work. I'm not an idea painter and I don't really care for political painting, although I respect the muralists. My painting is painting. I don't like having a show and then having a person come up to me to ask if I can explain this chair or whatever. It's nonverbal. I want my paintings to communicate joy. Mozart. Yeah, joy. If you look at my work going back forty some years, you'll see each painting is an experience. When I start, I'm not conscious of what it is going to look like when it is done. I like the surprise of seeing it when it is finished. It's another painting. Most of my favourite painters are classical painters because I love the way they apply paint. That's what I'm interested in, the doing of it, the process."

I'm not an expert on abstract art, but your command of colour and composition seems extraordinary.

"Well you have hit on two things, composition and colour. I'm really an edge freak. That's what I'm about, edges, colour, and shape. The collage thing happened and it was such a great feeling because it gave me a real start. You can see I have stacks of paper that I rip out and maybe five years later or maybe tomorrow I will get an idea for something." Erv brings a small canvas to show me on which he has glued a piece of paper and then applied some paint around it.

It's almost surrealistic.

"It's very surrealistic. My work is nonobjective surrealism. Last night I pasted on these two pieces of green metallic paper and then I will start working on those but this was the beginning of the painting. People use abstract wrong. Everything is abstract except maybe a classical portrait. Nonobjective is carried another step." He indicates a nearby painting. "This isn't foliage but it is. This isn't a sky but it is. If you look long enough you are going to see dogs or clowns in all kinds of paintings but this one is probably the furthest in recent paintings toward being nonobjective, no objects, no landscape. Even the top one on the right could be a landscape but it is fun to explore arrangements of material just for its own sake."

Has living in San Miguel affected your work?

"You can see just walking around that there are many things to stimulate painting. Colour for one. Not that it is going to lead me to portray an image exactly but it jogs something and I'm sure subconsciously I remember what I have seen. I left the figure quite some time ago because what was going on around it became more exciting for me. I painted landscapes for a while too but they also lost appeal. Now it is more what is in my head and in my heart. I was watching Gehry on YouTube talking about what he would tell children about his art. He was holding a piece of paper, folding it and he says, 'Look at that, it is so silly, it's beautiful.' I love that. When someone asked him why he had done something a certain way he told them he just felt it had to be done that way. That's how I paint. I feel that the thing has to be done exactly that way."

"People have asked me why I wanted to stay in San Miguel. In fact I was at a swim meet on Saturday with my daughter and a couple of her girlfriends and they were asking me why I stayed. I told them that Mexico was, and still is exotic for a conservative coming from a city like Milwaukee where in the winter at three-thirty in the afternoon it was dark and you didn't see any sky even in the summer. A young guy at the age of twenty-two would have been nuts not to throw himself into it."

I suppose you could compare it to going to Europe in the days when people would go to Paris to paint. It was wonderfully different and stimulating.

"My daughter and her friends brought that up too. The only reason was that Mexico was closer and you could get here in a '50 Chevy. I had never flown at that time. I'd thought of Europe but didn't get there until years later. When we were in Spain I could have seen myself living there and getting along but to get visas and all that, it just seemed more complicated."

In the early days did you have to get a visa to stay in Mexico?

"You needed a visa and it was only for six months. I used to do yoyos. I would go to the border on the train, get off and go in and get a new tourist card and hop on a bus and come back. I didn't get a hotel or anything, couldn't afford it. A couple of times I had problems. They started to get a little sticky but I managed. I fell into some things. I was fortunate. Of course there were bad times. There was one time I was really poor I remembered there was a lady who showed in the Galeria of San Miguel. She was selling the hell out of some pieces of wood with flowers painted on them so I went and bought a book on how to paint flowers and I was working on one of these when I hit myself in the head and said what are you doing? I'd rather starve or clean toilets, and I threw the damn book away." Erv laughs until he coughs. "We lived on a hundred dollars a month. My rent was eight dollars a month and then it was sixteen and then twenty-four dollars and then one day a friend of mine said, Come on, I want you to see a house. I said, Get out of here, I don't buy houses. But I came up to look at it and I knew that was going to be my house. My mother and dad had been here several times and they had said anytime you find a house you like that's a bargain, let us know and we'll help you out. So I called and mom had just sold her antique business so she had a little cash and I told her about the house and she said ok. I went up there and came back with twenty-two thousand dollars in fifty-dollar bills strapped around my waist. I was sitting on the plane and fortunately there was nobody sitting on either side of me so I was able to lie down but I'm thinking, what if this plane goes down man. I got through with no problems but I could have been thrown in jail. At that time you were only allowed to take five thousand dollars out of the country. So I bought the house and I had a two and a half car garage studio. The house was falling apart but we fixed it up. We loved the house, it was very funky but it was too big for us once the kids left. I have a few great memories but no big nostalgia thing. I paid my folks back month by month."

Has it been a good life in San Miguel?

"Very good. Look, with all the changes, the only bad thing is the traffic and sometimes the noise but you put up with that because it is still number one, a good place to live. It was a good place to bring up a family, my kids went to good schools, and to universities later. We have two kids. My daughter teaches at the University of Leon here. When the kids were in university, I said to my wife Lupe, we have to think of some way to make money so we started to make crosses and masks and we paid the tuition so that was another thing we just fell into."

"There are only a handful of us left from the old days. Leonard Brooks is gone. Mai Onno is still here but her husband Lothar died a long time ago. He was an amazing sculptor. He taught at the Instituto and we had a show together." Erv goes over to another corner of the room and retrieves a brochure advertising an art show from many years back. He is pictured on the opening page with his arms around his young son in front of a large painting and Lothar Kestenbaum, Mai's husband is on another page.

Whoa! Lothar was a real good-looking guy.

I am surprised to see a movie star handsome man, tall and dark in the picture Erv hands me. Erv too is an attractive young man. A third person, Kent Bowman, is shown on the last page of the brochure and Erv tells me he is dead but at the time was a great painter and jewelry maker.

San Miguel has attracted a lot of interesting people.

"You're right. I hung out for a while with the guy who wrote the book on Howard Hughes, Clifford Irving. He was totally interesting. He came here after he got out of prison for faking Hughes' autobiography. And there have been lots of others over the years. One of the most unusual was Neal Cassady. I played poker with him the night he died on the tracks here. I was involved with the theatre then and the lady that was running it became friendly with Neal. He came here with her for several months, maybe a year and he would play poker with us. He would usually play for an hour until he was bored and then he would get up and leave. History has it that he was at a wedding that night and perhaps that is where he went after he left us because we were playing cards on Canal Street and it was a straight walk down. The next day someone told me that he had been found dead. I found him to be fascinating. He was probably the first rapper. He would sit on a stool with a hammer and he would throw it up in the air and catch it and while he was doing that he would pick up on the conversations in the room around him and he'd include those in his rap. It was amazing. I don't think he was significant for his own accomplishments, he never wrote anything. His speech was kind of factory worker stuff. He worked on the railroad with Kerouac. Nick Nolte played him in a movie called *Heart Beat* and he had every move of Cassady's down perfectly. He must have looked at film. I know there was some talk that Kerouac came to San Miguel. Gregory Corso might have been here but Kerouac never was."

Suddenly a woman bursts into the room and gives Erv a huge hug. They are obviously thrilled to see one another and after the exuberant reunion I am introduced. Her name is Michaela and it turns out she and Erv have known one another for forty years. She has just returned from an extended trip away and says she finally gets it. She is never leaving San Miguel again. She and I agree that the world at large has changed.

"Believe me", Michaela says, "I have looked and I finally understand what Erv discovered a long time ago. He went to Europe looking for the next place and my greatest fear was that he would find it and leave us but he came back and stayed, and that is what I intend to do. Sometimes we don't realize what we have until we come back home."

I turn to Erv to ask the question, "When you left San Miguel, what were you looking for?"

He shrugs. "Whatever it was, I didn't find it. I was never looking to escape the rest of the world but I haven't taken a lot of interest in what goes on out there either, other than I read the newspapers once in a while. My best move was this. I'm apolitical. Politics are a distraction. Hey, I paint. I'm a fuckin' painter man. Everything I wanted was right here."

I leave Erv to catch up with his old *amiga*. We should all be so lucky to have friends and family who love us, a house full of laughter, and a room in which to paint. Here in the high desert of San Miguel de Allende, fifty years ago, Erv made a quick decision. He chose happiness.

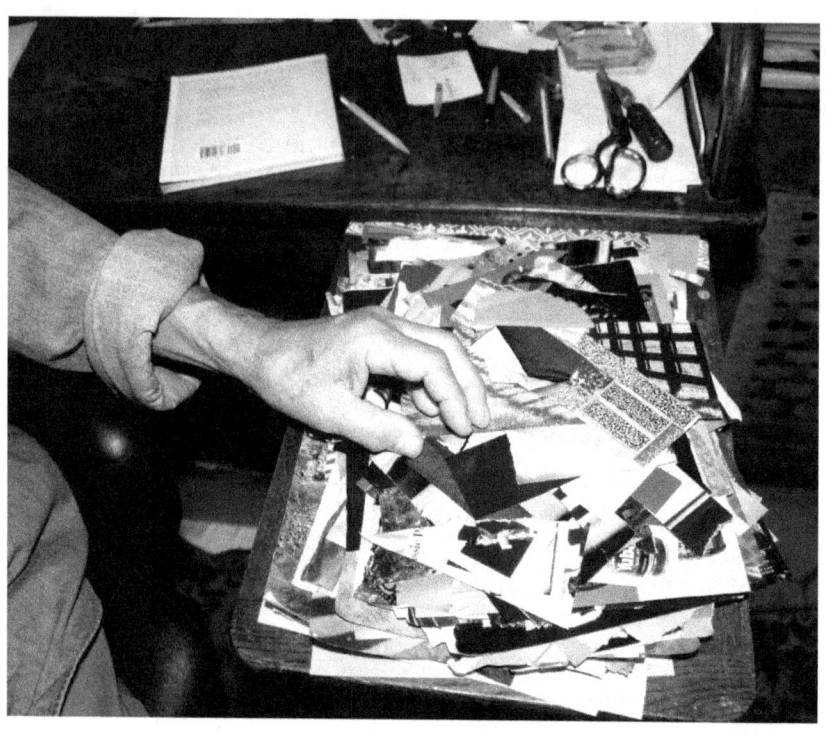

Keith Miller

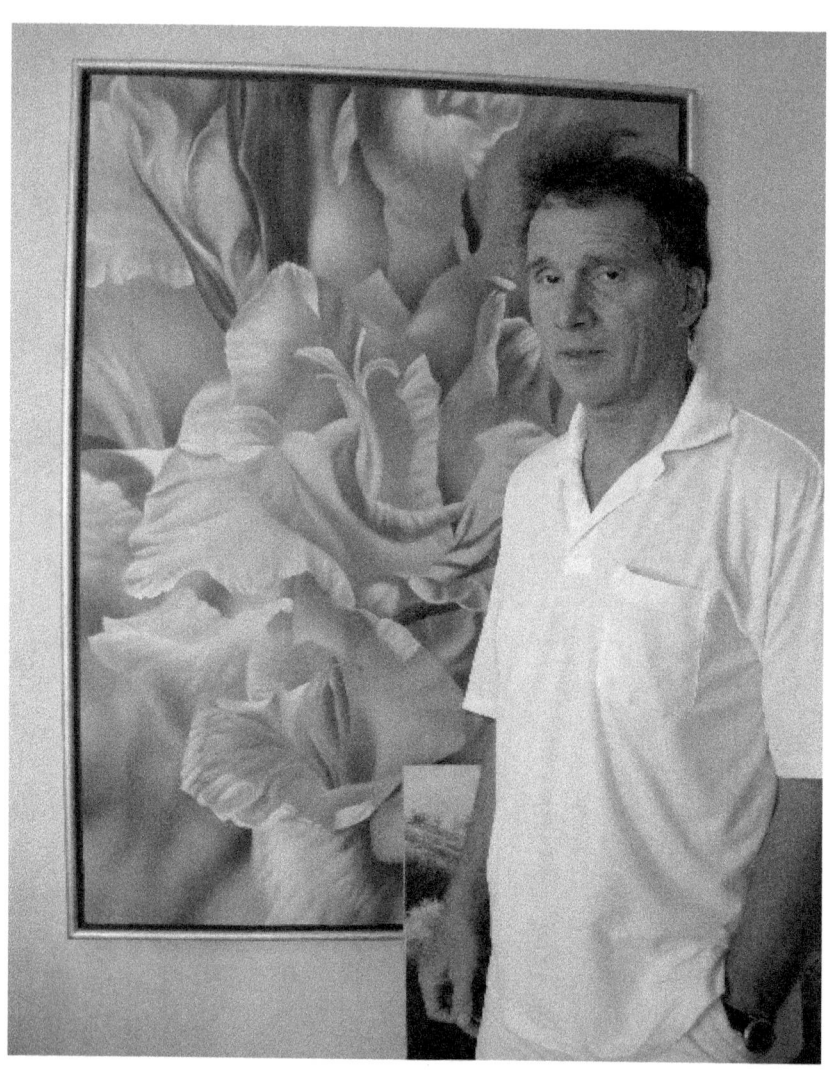

Any number of people will happily tell you why they love this out of the way corner of the world, but today I have come to ask Keith Miller why he decided to leave Canada twenty years ago to settle in the mountains of central Mexico in San Miguel de Allende. Keith is an artist, one of many who have made San Miguel their home over the past several decades. Now in his sixties, he is handsome and relaxed as he invites me to accompany him to his compact kitchen where he pours us both a coffee. His house is comfortably unpretentious, and we sit in a nook in the courtyard with one of Keith's dogs at our feet while we talk. My first question is an obvious one, "Why San Miguel?"

"I loved the idea of living in a foreign place, learning another language, and of escaping a growing dissatisfaction with where I was. It wasn't that I had any particular grudge against Canada. I was simply drawn to another way of life."

Keith was born in Chatham, Ontario on December 17, 1949 and was one of a pair of twin boys. "I remember that as early as age seven I was scribbling and drawing and because I enjoyed it and did more of it than my peers, I grew better at it." He was lucky enough to attract attention and praise and as time went on, everyone, including himself, assumed he would study art. "I don't know if you could say I had an artistic personality, whatever that is. Like most kids, I was curious about the world, architecture, cars, and so on. They just naturally became subjects for my drawings. And I suppose I was drawn to art because it is essentially a solitary pursuit and I think I was a little shy and I don't mind being alone or working alone. Temperamentally, I think art suited me."

Keith's formal training was at The Ontario College of Art in Toronto. He eventually did graduate but part way through his studies, he set off on what was to be one of many trips he has made to various parts of the world. His first experience in

Europe, particularly in Spain and Greece in 1970 left a deep impression. He confesses that the Mediterranean culture probably planted a seed which later flowered in Mexico. "The climate, the foliage, the architecture were all familiar to me when I ultimately arrived in San Miguel." He'd been teaching at Sheraton College for a number of years when in 1984, he and a woman he was living with at the time, decided to fly down and take a course in landscaping at the Instituto. "We saw an ad in an art magazine we subscribed to in Toronto. It was funny we decided to come here. I had always had suspicions about Mexico because when I was growing up in the fifties and sixties, Mexico was one of those incredibly exotic but dangerous places where gringos run afoul of the law for doing nothing and end up in jail and have their cars confiscated and are never allowed to see their families again. If you didn't want a prison term in Mexico, you didn't go. I had some apprehensions, but we got curious so we flew down."

"When I first came to San Miguel it was an isolated mountain town, dusty, sleepy and it got very quiet during the siesta hour. Things didn't get started again until after four p.m. It had a bit of a feeling of a place lost in time, and I hasten to add that I don't think that is the predominant feeling now. But from talking to people I think I caught the last moments in the mid eighties when you could sense what Mexico had been and what San Miguel had been decades earlier. There weren't good connections, transportation, or communication. There were very few cabs in town and if you wanted to make a phone call you had to go to a paseta, a long distance telephone office. Of course there were tourists in town, there were gringos who lived here, it wasn't the Wild West exactly but there was a bit of the atmosphere of old Mexico in 1984. At the time I thought this would be a great place to live. I could be in a foreign place where there would be other foreigners at hand if I felt kind of at odds or at sea with my environment because already there was a well established foreign community. Anyway, we quickly found a place to rent for a month, took the course at the Instituto which turned out to be an amateur thing for people who wanted to take an art course in a pretty place. We were both practicing artists already and so the course wasn't really useful but it did introduce me to San Miguel and when I decided to leave Canada for good, it was the place I came back to."

After its establishment in 1940 by American artist and writer Stirling Dickinson, the Instituto Allende enjoyed a lengthy heyday as a significant international art school but by the time Keith arrived, most of the noted instructors were gone and the art school went into a decline that eventually changed the nature of the institution altogether. Now the Instituto has been divided into two distinct parts, one which continues to offer limited courses in art and in Spanish and the other which has become the picturesque setting for lavish destination weddings. Every weekend, what housed the Instituto and was originally built in 1735 as the summer home of the wealthy de la Canal family, is transformed into a fairy tale creation of flowers and ribbons and starched white table cloths, a perfect place for dreams to come true.

Keith tells me he took a third trip to Europe in 1985 and in 1987 he set out for Japan, Korea, and parts of southeast Asia. He spent the next three years traveling, doing watercolours and many, many drawings. "I didn't do any studio work because during that time, I was an itinerant person, backpacking, staying in hostels and guest houses, traveling around with the Lonely Planet crowd. I enjoyed it and I had the energy and the patience to do it but at the back of my mind was always the idea that I wasn't going to live in guesthouses all my life. Eventually, I began to feel I had to get back to having a studio and showing my work and having a base. I wasn't eighteen anymore and I began to feel the need of a more permanent community. That's when the idea of San Miguel really rose up."

"Maybe I had changed too, but coming back in 1990 I noticed that the town had changed in the six years since I had been here.

There were more services, more traffic, more restaurants. It still wasn't a big place on the tourism map although it was getting a fair bit of press and more tourists were coming here. Many of the people I met in the early nineties are still here. Of course some have died or moved away. The problem is keeping up with the ones who moved here in the late nineties when the population mushroomed."

Keith expresses a sincere affection for his long time fellow residents. Many remain close and form what he jokingly calls, his "support group". "Although I guess as time passes, we support each other. In those early days, I enjoyed getting to know Leonard Brooks. I got to know Gary and Annemarie Slipper. I mention some of the Canadian mafia here. I was taken by their work and their life decision to live here. Socially, one of the great things about San Miguel is you've got a whole mixture of people from different socioeconomic backgrounds. You get the wealthy rubbing shoulders with the not very well off. You get the artists mixing with the retired CEO's. And also the people from different countries and of course, the Mexicans. It's one of those places that if I had stayed in Toronto I would never have met the variety of people that I have met here."

"What has been choked out somewhat now by the rising cost of living in San Miguel, is the bohemian feel that used to be here. I mean, can you have bohemia next to a five star restaurant? Even so, I think I can sense a bit of the old feeling when I get together with 'lifers' so to speak, that is people who have been painting for a long, long time or people who have been traveling for a long time. There are certain shared values that come up. It's the idea of a profession imposing certain values on people or a certain worldview on people, and I think that happens with artists as well. We're pretty diverse but we all have our war stories about trying to earn a living, surviving, trying to do well, not doing as well as we want to because secretly we think we deserve to be famous and rich. What person in the arts doesn't have some of these feelings? Politically, I don't think you find too many conservatives among artists. I think there is a shared feeling of camaraderie because the struggle we have all gone through is similar -presenting our work, trying to progress with the development of our work, while still trying to earn a living. I think we end up feeling we hold certain life experiences or attitudes in common."

Friends and acquaintances within San Miguel's artistic community have no doubt influenced Keith's decision to settle here and to continue working as an artist in this relatively small place although he emphasizes that a receptive community is probably not sufficient. "Anyone who intends to make art his profession must have a singular determination to overcome the challenges that being an artist presents. If you don't believe in yourself, you're probably not going to persist. One of the things you have to develop is a kind of internal engine that involves the ego and keeps saying, 'The work is good', and at the same time you have to learn to deal with the frustration when you believe you're not getting the recognition you ought to have."

Keith's desire to be appreciated as an artist is not difficult to understand yet I wonder why he, like so many other artists here, has elected to step outside the more mainstream art world. San Miguel isn't New York. What personal and professional sacrifices were made and what was gained in coming to Mexico?

"The influence on my work of living in San Miguel has been gradual and gentle and has seeped into me over time and into my way of looking at things. You hear clichés from people about how their sense of color has changed, and I guess that's true for me. With the climate and the bright light and the fact that we're up at 6000 feet, if you go out and work on location there is a lot of acute clarity in the air, it's not a murky, soft light. I suppose that my color sense did change, I mean my palate did lighten a little bit although I still enjoy doing dark moody paintings and I'm not as afraid of saturated color. One of my painting instructors at Sheraton was from Chile and she complained of the boring color sense that Canadians had, which is really true if I look at it now. People here don't hesitate to use color in their houses or whatever. I think gradually over the years, I became comfortable experimenting with a broader use of color."

"When I first came here I just went out on the street because I wanted to discover the town so I was working on the spot. By the end of that first year I moved more into the studio. The botanicals started in 1990 and there was a series of still lifes, working on tropical fruit so all of these subjects are alternated. I don't like to keep doing the same thing. Whatever the subject matter, what interests me the most is the light, the effect of light and shade. With the botanicals specifically, they happen to be semitransparent so you get the idea of translucency. If you want to explore light, and the effects of light, botanical subjects are ideal. That can be true in landscapes as well. I didn't always recognize it, but if I look back on my work now I see that I have always been preoccupied with the nature of light. I think that's what threads my work together. I know people can look at the variety of my work and maybe think it is a hodgepodge but to me it feels like an evolution."

"When I look at how long it has taken me to explore all those different areas it seems to me it has been a long time. Most viewers of art are casual observers and they don't have a perspective on the chronology of an artist's development. I put together a book called '*Another Mexico*' because I wanted to describe some of the background to my art."

"Anyone in the arts has to be somewhat self-indulgent and in a very pragmatic sense, San Miguel has nurtured my art because I've been able to earn a living here, I haven't had to worry about making contacts and connections all the time, the community buys my work, it has given me a beautiful place to live, a great climate, friendships that have been sustained over a long period of time. Once you have those things you don't have to be preoccupied with survival. Life here is very comfortable."

Keith admits that when he left Canada there was a cultural adjustment to be made. In our discussion I remark that more than one person has told me that it is difficult to be fully accepted by the Mexican people, although San Miguel has enjoyed a reputation as having a population that is tolerant, even grateful for the presence of foreign tourists and residents. Unquestionably the cost of living has risen dramatically in recent years and housing is particularly expensive, often rivaling prices in the United States and Canada. As the demand on resources, especially water, in this near desert environment becomes more acute, there are calls to develop a community plan which places some parameters on development. It is worth stating that San Miguel is not just a tourist destination for gringos. Large numbers of well-to-do Mexicans make the trip from Mexico City, Queretero, and other nearby cities for the weekend. Many have built holiday homes in and around the city. As in any community where change is apparent, the social dynamics are complicated. Keith believes that if newcomers to San Miguel want to become more integrated into the indigenous community, they have only to make the effort.

"I've gotten to know several Mexican families. For the most part they are hospitable and welcoming. It depends on how much effort you want to make and the degree of fluency you have in Spanish. Some people say they feel like outsiders but they don't take the time to learn Spanish with any proficiency. Others sometimes don't try to shift their sense of time and punctuality and all of these natural things if you're going to live here with less stress or annoyance. You have to make some adjustments in your head to be happier here even though as a WASP Canadian it still can drive me crazy if someone is late or doesn't show up at all. Certain things can still grate, but you get acclimatized."

Keith smiles and we both become aware that we have been talking a long time. He has appointments. I have to get going too. As I rise to leave, he pauses thoughtfully. "You know I look at it now and I think, not that I was terribly clever or wise about it or anything but, it actually did work out. It's one of those decisions that just did work out. I mean there weren't any big disappointments. It was very tough to earn a living in the early years but when I look at it, it really turned out to be the correct decision, not to go back. I know if I had stayed in Canada I would never have had the warm and varied group of friends that I enjoy now. Naturally I've known a few people who have moved away from San Miguel looking for happiness I suppose, but I've often thought, if you can't be happy in San Miguel, you can't be happy anywhere."

A contented individual by anyone's standard, Keith Miller has made a success of his life and his art. Many years ago he made decisions about his future that to some might seem unorthodox, even reckless, but he has managed to maintain those commitments with discipline and dedication. His art reflects the skill and beauty that result from fifty years of inspired practice. Two of his most endearing qualities, his sense of humour and the curiosity that was evident from childhood, are still very present today. The belief in one's self that every serious artist must possess, is manifest in Keith's open engagement with the world and his trust that good does prevail. San Miguel helped no doubt, but the quality of his life and his art, in my estimation, derive principally from the quality of the man.

Marion Perlet

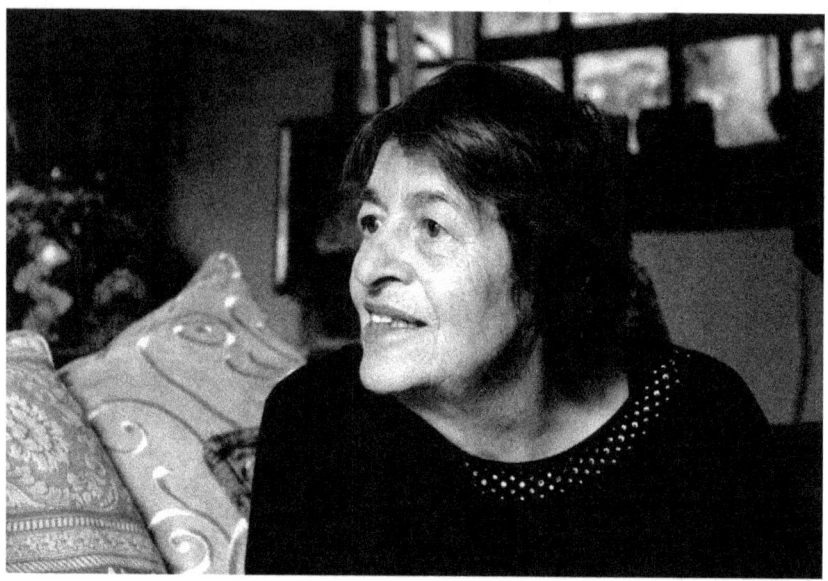

Marion Perlet first caught my attention in the bank in el centro. She strode across the large room wearing a broad brimmed straw hat as though it were a crown, the wide pants of her suit sweeping after her in an effort to keep up. Her companion was Toller Cranston and when he introduced Marion, he insisted it was she who was the truly gifted painter. I asked if we could meet to talk about her life and work, and she graciously agreed.

Marion Perlet lives in a house on the side of a steep hill overlooking the city of San Miguel. I arrive in the early afternoon and as we make our way up the stairs from the kitchen, Marion explains she is recovering from a near fatal heart attack and must not exert herself unduly. After a slow climb, we emerge on the terrace where she points out the four churches she can see from this vantage point. "My mother came to visit me here in 1998 just after I had built this house. She spent morning, noon, and night up here. She loved it. She was ready to move in but I said that's not a good idea. You know I was scared of my mother. The following year she had already purchased the plane ticket but before she could come back to San Miguel, she died, bless her heart."

Tell me about your mother.

In her deep voice, German accent still evident but firmly woven into her English like a colourful thread, Marion Perlet paints a picture. "I want to tell you and this is the truth, my mother was very artistic. My mother was an opera singer. She studied opera when we were little. My father was forty and my mother was nineteen when they married. We were stationed in front of the concentration camp in Dachau. There were big iron gates and I used to ask my mother, what are those dark clouds like rubber burning. We didn't know what it was. My father wasn't Jewish but he was against the regime and someone turned him in. He died in the concentration camp. We were bombed out and were living with some farmers and somebody brought some mail and my mother was crying. I was holding on to her dress. I was two and a half or three years old, no more, my brother a year younger. I remember we went with a horse and buggy with a table and some chairs and a mattress to Munich. There was nothing else. All the houses were down, just piles of rubble. You know when I was little we were bombed out so much and had to run for our lives. Life was so difficult, not only for us but for everybody." At this last, Marion's voice rises, revealing an anger undiluted by the passage of time. I wonder how it was that a creator of such sublime images was born out of such devastation.

"When the Americans came in 1945 to Munich they took over Germany. Munich has many beautiful buildings and one of them the Americans made into a school. It was a cultural center for the poor children who really didn't have much and my brother and I went there and we went to the painting class. It cost nothing. Students from the university would donate their time. The teacher would read us a story and then we would paint it. Right away the younger teachers asked us if they could keep our pieces. My little brother and I became stars because we won almost every month the first prize. We got books and our paintings were hanging on the wall with a big golden star of excellence. We were very proud of that. My brother was extremely talented. My brother was playing the piano when he was four with little fingers like this." Though Marion is seeing her brother's small hand, the one she raises is her own strong one, a working woman's hand.

"My mother was strict. We weren't allowed to go out, she gave us so much homework. I had to make the lunch on the gas stove. She taught me to make up the dinner, fried potatoes with onions everyday because we didn't have anything else. We were the poorest from the poor. I had my communion at the church and they had to give me a dress to wear. My brother got a candle and my mother was singing the Ave Maria. My mother wanted me to be a singer. I was cultivated in art I must say, through my mother. My mother was a painter too but I never saw her paint. I guess she was exposed to someone when she was a little girl who taught her fine manners. We didn't have many visitors because we didn't have any family but when my mother's friends came, we were not allowed to speak unless we were spoken to. We were not allowed to move. We sat with a ruler on our hands. You know how the Germans were old fashioned. I was brought up like that. I come from somewhere else."

Although it is midday, the church bells begin to ring. I presume there must be some significance to the time of their ringing but I have yet to ascertain what it is. I do know from personal observation, that every evening at sunset, as the sun slips below the horizon and the light is at its most pellucid, someone rings the bells. They are rung again to announce the dawn. I am grateful that attention is being paid; that there is a witness to the steadfast but changing relationship between earth and sun.

As the peal of the bells fades, Marion continues her account. "We could never go anywhere because we didn't have any money. I was tired of standing on the street looking in, into the windows. I said, Mother I can't take another day. It was dark and grey for me all the time. I just wanted to get the hell out of Germany. My mother didn't want to go but I said, What are you waiting for? Let's go somewhere else, so we applied. I'll tell you the truth, I would have preferred to go to New York. That was my dream but the quarters were all full. The only opening they had was Canada. You remember we had to have a sponsor and I guess we knew somebody who knew somebody. In Germany my mother had tried to work as an opera singer but it was no good. She blamed us for it but she had stage fright too. She did have a beautiful voice and she obviously was very smart because she sang in all those languages. All my life I heard my mother sing."

We sit in silence for a moment, then, "I came to Canada when I was seventeen and a half. Remember they speak French and English and I didn't speak either. I worked first as an au pair. I got off a couple of nights a week and I had one day completely off every other week. And those are the days I went to school to l'Ecole des Beaux Arts. I had my first exhibition in Montreal in a very good area. I was only twenty-two but they said, No, you are ready. I was making no money so when I had three hundred dollars it was like thirty thousand dollars for me. In those days you got the whole week's groceries for fifteen dollars, you remember? The paintbrush I used was so poor, the hair came out in the painting. We sold it with the hair. I never made enough to live on it. I always had to work some shitty jobs that I hated, to survive. But I was not one of those that asked for a handout. I worked in a laundry. For a while I worked on the boats on the Great Lakes. I never worked so hard in my life. Pots! I remember when I went up there in my little white dress and white stockings and there must have been a hundred and fifty pots and three hundred plates. I had to wash them by myself!" Marion laughs, a great burst of sound rich with memories. "My God and that was three times a day! God it was a lot of work. We used to come to Montreal. I used to jump the locks in Montreal. You know how dangerous that was. Totally verboten. I would take a taxi and one night I went with my mother to the Kon Tiki. We got completely smashed and we had to come back because I had the night shift. My mother said, I am going to come with you. I'm going to help you. Honey, we flooded the whole galley somehow. We had to mop it up. I think we finished at midnight. My mother, my mother… I had all those lousy jobs but I figured it out, I had to have these jobs to get time to paint. Every other year I had a show. I did sell my work, but not enough. It wasn't enough."

Suddenly Marion exclaims to the dog lying nearby, "Pushka, what are you doing? Mommy just bought that for you this morning." The pale yellow dog is happily tearing the stuffing from a little toy. Marion tells me she would take it away but the dog is not completely tamed and could bite. For a moment I am uneasy but the dog has no interest in me. San Miguel was once plagued by hundreds of dogs in various states of ill health until the municipal authorities removed them. As one long time resident told me, the dogs disappeared overnight. Still, there are a number of homeless dogs remaining and Marion has always had a soft spot in her heart for animals. She never married and has no children but has filled her house with dogs and cats. When she first came to San Miguel she was given a purebred pug by a friend. Since then she has taken in strays. She asks me what kind of dog I think her dog is. I guess, a Heinz 57. Marion explains, "I saved this dog. Her mother broke my heart. She was white and she had a brown patch, a feisty dog. When I came back from Europe, I saw the mother crawl out from the empty property next door. The mother crawled out, with the ribs sticking out and the mange and I cried for the misery of it. I fed that thing and then one day they picked her up and took her away.

Then the maid told me the dog had a baby. The baby lay three days without water or food. I took that dog but she is a very extreme dog. I never had a beast like this. She's actually quite dangerous. You know that I gave her up. She was too aggressive, too territorial so I put her on a dog farm. She was there three weeks. She escaped and she came back to my door. My other dog, the one that I wanted to have, I had to put down because he had a fungus. One year I tried to save that dog. The blood and the hardship I had to go through." She stops to draw my attention to a bird that has landed a few feet away. "Do you see that cardinal on that bush. Sometimes I see a lot of them flying over me. You know I feel they are good luck. I couldn't live in a big city anymore. I like the peace and the quiet."

Marion remembers her life in Montreal and then in Toronto as a series of difficult jobs and a prolonged struggle to market her paintings. "I was young. I thought I was going to be a great artist but boy did I get the horn on my head knocked in a few times real good. But you know I didn't care what anybody said. I did it anyway. You see, when you are chosen to do this, you are going to do it because you need to do it. For me, it's my salvation. Look, I like to paint because I get lost in my work. I must say I am on my highest level as a human being when I'm working, at least in my case. Some people do other things. Whatever they like, you understand, I don't care. But for myself, I know what I like."

How did you and Toller Cranston became friends.

Marion's face lights up as she remembers her first meeting with Toller during the time they both attended l'Ecole des Beaux Arts in Montreal. "We met in engraving class. The machine was over there where the palm tree is. There were thirty students and only one printing machine and everybody was always running to get to the machine and I was running and watching only the machine and we BANGED into each other! He flew this way and I flew this way! I said to him, Go ahead please go ahead. Then I had a look at his work, and I said hmm, not bad. We were both inspired by Beardsley. We loved Beardsley at this time. Well, we had to start somewhere. I lived around the corner in one of those grand Victorian apartments along Sherbrooke Street with real crystal chandeliers and Roman columns. I lived in one part and rented every other room out. I asked Toller, Come, I live around the corner, I said. It must have been at Christmas time because I had black German chocolate hearts, they were special for Christmas and I served mint tea in my grand salon. Toller was only sixteen and I was twenty-four and we were poor but we lived like lords. We had a style of living and he loved that. He lived outside of Montreal and sometimes he would come at eleven o'clock at night with his new piece and show me. We were like brother and sister. When we two worked, everything burned in the kitchen. And it was all his fault because the two of us, we forgot everything." Marion and Toller have remained friends to the present day. Both now long time residents of San Miguel, they maintain a connection that can only be described as family.

Montreal is a long way from San Miguel de Allende. What brought you to San Miguel de Allende twenty years ago?

"After eighteen years in Montreal I moved to Toronto where I lived for about fifteen years. I first came to San Miguel in 1987 because some artist friends of mine, Annemarie and Gary Slipper, good Canadian artists, traveled around the world. On their travels, they went to San Miguel. After they came back to Toronto from their large journey we had a dinner and they talked about it. They had decided to sell their house and move down here and they said I should come. I said, how can I go to San Miguel? I'm working fifteen hours a day. Well somehow I did get the money but under great hardship and I came here for three months."

"There was a taxi strike when I arrived. I came on the bus in a turtleneck sweater and blue jeans. Bloody hot and dead tired and not a single taxi would stop for me. I had to hire two boys to carry my suitcase and the handle fell off. But I tell you this. San Miguel and the people were very good for me. I loved the Spanish architecture. I loved the cobbled streets. Now, after twenty years I hate to walk them but I loved them, I did. When I sold my first painting in San Miguel I had a big party. I went and bought a roast of pork and chilies, and ten chickens. Everybody got drunk, I'm not a drinker, but everyone had fun. Half of them are dead now. Some artists, rich and poor, and I was really happy. I found a gold bracelet, broken, on Aldama Street and I said the streets are paved in gold here. The next year I came back, I rented an apartment on Recreo and it was expensive for me. But I sold some paintings and of course that wasn't enough but I lived in a beautiful place. I had my first studio in my life and a little house and I spent six months here and six months in Canada for about eight years. Finally I decided to cash in my life insurance and all my savings and I bought the land here. Eventually I managed to pay for this house, which I don't think is exactly shabby. You know, I did this all on my work so I'm very proud of it. It is hard enough to make a living as an artist, let alone a woman artist. I had to go through all of it. That's what made me what I am today. You have to have hard knocks if you're hard of learning like me. I'm a late bloomer. Things come late to me in life but that's all right. Better than never. You know what I mean? At least in my lifetime I'm enjoying. I'm ten years already in this house but I'm already twenty years here in San Miguel. It's a miracle."

The sun is growing warm on the terrace and I can see Marion is beginning to tire. We make our way down the stairs in the cool interior to Marion's bedroom. It is here we say good-bye, in this small intimate space filled with lovely things, many of them having belonged to her mother. There is a window opposite the bed with a view to the hills beyond and I am reminded of Italy.

Some months later, Marion and I are meeting for a second time. On this occasion, we sit in her spacious salon surrounded by some of her larger paintings that cover the high walls. There are other works here too, paintings by Toller Cranston and a chair by Pedro Friedeberg. Since our last meeting Marion has recovered much of her energy and is busily preparing to go out to a gathering of prospective clients. "Now we have to go to these big dinner parties. We have to entertain our clients. You don't want to ask them because we are so proud but you are going out of your way to please them, to make it really perfect. It's another creation, another extension of myself. And I give it gladly. Of course I hope and pray but I cannot be disappointed when nothing happens. They are the Medicis and I am the Marion Perlet, right?"

The phone rings in the adjoining room. "I am waiting for Toller to call me." She hurries off and I overhear her speaking to someone in Spanish and English, the two languages intermingling to produce a stream of sounds. She returns and explains, "That was the gallery. They called to tell me they had sold one of my books." The book to which Marion refers, *Marion Perlet, From the Outside Looking In*, was published in Mexico in 2008. In large part, it traces Marion Perlet's artistic life and as such, it is an achievement in which Marion takes great pride. She and Toller collaborated to write the text which is embellished by a great many colourful illustrations.

Knowing that time is short, Marion suggests that I ask her a direct question.

All right then... What motivates your painting?

Marion relaxes. She is on familiar ground. "My motivation is my life. And whatever I paint, I am at that time. That's why I don't like too much commissions and things like this because I'm really very selfish about my personal feelings. Of course, when I am travelling, when I was in Italy I was into the Renaissance.

Now I came back from Turkey I am into the dervish and the Turkish gardens and all that, just because it inspires me and I'm still in my heart, I still have feelings for it and why not take it out. I will move on from that but this moment will be bringing me to the next moment. You understand? We don't know. Sometimes I'm in love with my work. Maybe it doesn't last very long. Sometimes it lasts a long time. Like these two pieces up there. You know, everybody wants to buy them but these pieces have a price, a price that I want because I paid a price. These paintings didn't come easy. That one there is called Europa and that I painted twenty years ago or more." She points to a picture of a woman lying across the back of a bull, holding onto its horns. It is a sensual work with strong forms, the two figures equal in their importance. "It was the turning point. It was the first piece where I was forty-five, I quit my bar job and worked in the studio. I quit everything in my life, like the job, no more security, nothing. All my friends said we won't let you starve. But I was very nervous. I had to either make it or break it. So this piece is, I'm taking my life by the horns and … Life is hard. It looks gentle that bull, but it could be the devil. Life can be wonderful but it also can be damned hard. Anyway, so I went beyond myself because as you can see I'm quite whimsical, decorative. I like design, esthetic, that's the word, because I like beauty. See I don't like anything ugly because why would I want to look at something ugly. There's enough suffering out there. I know all about it and I see it every day. I don't need it hanging on the wall. But once in a while after you do so many beautiful pieces, you need to do something really painful. Just for once you have to let it all out. It's a personal piece. But in my case, (she chuckles) it's like, I'm going to hell and I don't know, I try to be faithful and believe in myself and believe in God and believe in the universe and everything. But sometimes when things are very hard, it's very hard to believe in that. I'm a Catholic, a Roman Catholic, not a fanatic but I do pray to the universe. I'm grateful for everything every day. It is very important. The other thing that is very important, I have to say, I'm completely self-centered, right. It's only me, me, me. What I mean is, I get up and I have a journey every day and I have my rhythm in my life. I like to get out early. I go to bed at eight o'clock at night. Ah, there are some exceptions, but I like my rhythm. Eight o'clock to bed, it doesn't mean that I am sleeping already, but soon after. So anyway that was the turning point. That was a whole series of these very aggressive and bold pieces. And they were beyond me, believe it."

Do you ever tire of painting?

"I still get a lot of joy out of my painting. When I wasn't feeling well it was very, very hard but the work that I did was about my life. You understand? They came from way deep in. I do find I need variety. I get bored. I get tired of this thing and I move on. Then I'm tired of everything I'm doing. Even in my work, I do experimental pieces. I do something completely beyond me, different colours, different mood, just to try it. It's very difficult because you are used to using the red and the black and the white. As I get older I am getting softer but I still want to paint some incredible works. I do. I have still a desire to do a power work. When some of these are moving, then I don't have any pressure so I can paint truly as God said I should do it. I can take all the time in the world and make it into a jewel, make it something worthwhile looking."

A dog begins to howl somewhere nearby. Marion stops and listens. "That's my baby. That's my Minky. I'll open the door for her. She can go up to the terrace. Do you mind, because she's going to howl like this for hours. She's very bad." Marion goes out and the howling stops. She returns and sits down facing me.

"Anyway, back to that. I'm taking it easier and I'm trying to, what is very important is my state of mind. I like to go for a walk in the morning, but quiet. I don't like to talk right away. I need to be quiet for a long time. I need a lot of quiet time. I find in the silent I can hear myself better. Do you know? I don't give in so easy anymore. I don't do to please people. I'm thinking of myself. That's the difference. I still... but I do say often, no. I just can't. I want to. I make some exceptions because I absolutely have to, but not too many because it's just too much for me. Like today I have to go out at five. See I don't want to go out at five because by the time I come home, who knows what it is, seven or eight. You know what I mean? I'll be really tired. I don't like it. I need to relax. I need to be quiet. I want to go in my room and watch the news. I have to make my list for tomorrow. I am very busy tomorrow. I have a lot to do tomorrow. I have people coming here so I have to prepare.

What do you think living here in San Miguel has given you?

"You know what, that was my best move in my life. In Canada I was just a labourer. I knew a few words in English. Nothing. I was seventeen when I came from Germany. I was the moving force behind that. My brother's dead now. My mother's dead. My father's dead. Everybody's dead. I have no family. I'm completely an orphan now. I would not say I have a lot of friends but I do have a handful of friends that love me. I didn't know it until I had my heart attack. I guess I am very loved but then I try to be a good person. I try. I try. Not perfect but working on it to become perfection, which is a lot of work." She smiles. "Well, I'm going in the right direction."

"There is something unique about San Miguel. You can come here and reinvent yourself. You can be anybody you want to be. Sooner or later the truth comes out because nobody is stupid here. They are not from the moon and they get your number, don't worry. Here there are mature women. Fifty, sixty, seventy, they have lost their husbands. They want to be independent. They come to San Miguel. We have two institutes of art, over forty art galleries, we have more than one hundred restaurants, music festivals. We have veterinarians, dentists, doctors, a hospital. The Mexicans are good people. I was inspired by the architecture, I liked the climate, I liked the light. And you are mixing with millionaires and the poor together. Nobody really cares. Before, I never had a good life. You know this is the good life. This is the best period in my life."

Marion is anxious to get ready to go out and although Toller hasn't yet called, I realize I must bring our conversation to an end. When I thank her for being so candid, Marion says, "I hope it was alright." and I reply that she has been wonderful. "Really?" she asks. "Yes", I say, "you speak like a poet."

"I am a poet in my art. I cannot say it, but my paintings have a meaning. You know I am a symbolic painter. Like this painting is called *The Fruit of the Sea*. But what it really is this young man here is stranded and she is coming out to bring him back to life, to nurture him. She's going to save his life."

The phone rings again. "The phone is ringing all the time. What is it today? It's like the devil is after me because I am busy." Once again this dynamic woman is up and rushing off to answer the phone. I can only marvel at Marion's resilience, the determination that constrains her physical and emotional vulnerability. In many respects, her undeniable fortitude belies her tender, feminine nature and as I wait for her return, I recall my travels alone in Morocco, where I encountered a belief system in which gender was one's most significant and defining attribute. Such circumscribed classifications are too limited for Marion Perlet. She is a human being first and last, a painter who expresses herself fearlessly in her life and in her work. From a young age, she has fought to be independent, to do what she wanted to do, which was, more than anything else and in spite of all the obstacles, to paint.

Walking down the hill that leads from Marion's gate, I pass little tiendas displaying laughing skeletons. The Day of the Dead is only two days away. Each year at this time, Mexicans remember their loved ones by constructing altars on which they arrange mementos of those who have gone on to the next world. For one day, these departed relatives return home where they are honoured with joyful celebrations. To members of other cultures it may seem a bizarre custom, but here in Mexico it is an ancient ritual, the greatest sign of respect one can pay to those who were once an important part of one's earthly life. I recall Marion telling me she has built an altar to her mother every year for the past ten years. "I have her picture upstairs with a flower. Normally I have a whole altar for her but my maid isn't here and she didn't do it so I just gave her dry roses with the orange flower. It's a personal thing. When the police called me from Canada and said my mother was dead in the apartment, it broke my heart. In my will it says they have to bury me with my mother and my book and a few things. I'm going to another world. I will wear my white robe that I bought in Egypt. I liked the desert and the temples and the mentality. It's the mystery. When I came to San Miguel I had the same powerful feeling. I am very lucky. This land is a blessing. I traveled a long way to get here."

I have just been to the bank to withdraw some pesos for my trip to Mexico City tomorrow and from there, back to Canada. Unexpectedly I bump into Marion on the street and she tells me that she too is planning a trip. In less than a month she is leaving for Europe to, as she puts it, see the great works of art again. "They feed me", she confides and it is obvious that she is relishing the preparations with the enthusiasm of a young girl planning an important birthday party. Her health is excellent Marion tells me and I have to agree I have never seen her looking better. They say that a passing acquaintance with death can often have the effect of making life sweeter and in that way we receive recompense. Marion and I talk a little more about her itinerary and then we both have commitments that call us away but as I turn towards home I am buoyed by Marion's light heart.

Marion Perlet died on her travels in November, 2013. Buen viaje querida.

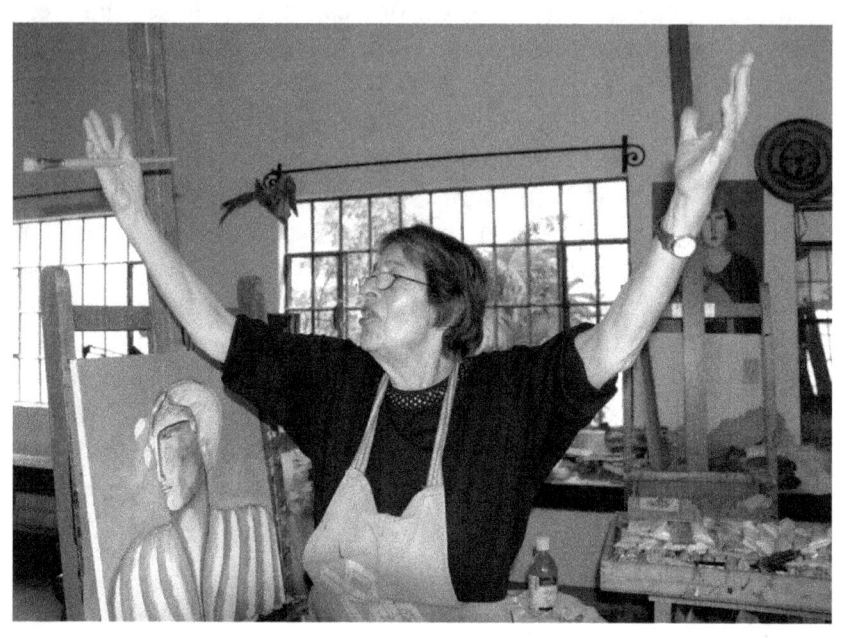

Toller Cranston

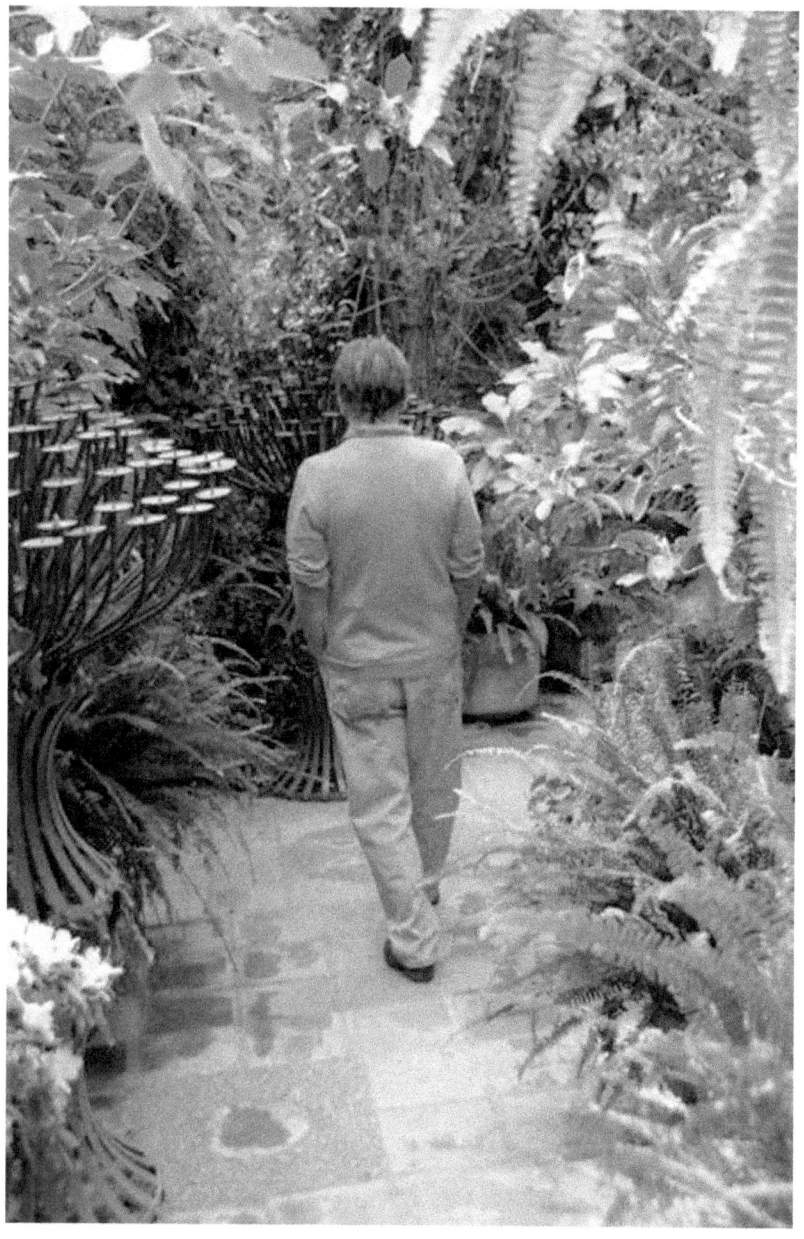

I happened to run into Toller Cranston at Juan's café on Relox and he invited me to join him for lunch. He had ordered steak and it looked delicious when it arrived. "Marion lets me order whenever we go out to eat because in the past, when our food arrived, mine always looked better." And indeed it is the case now when I compare my food and his. I explain to Toller that I have not finished the piece I am writing about him. I have been putting it off for many months and am dissatisfied because I cannot get a handle on him. Toller looks at me from under the wide brim of his hat and remarks, "I take that as a compliment."

Today I am trailing a mountain lion. Tousled tawny-coloured hair glinting in the sun, compact athletic body in constant motion, tail flicking, Toller Cranston leads me on through the lush vegetation surrounding his spacious home in San Miguel. Although we have met a number of times, I still have little more real understanding of what lies behind those penetrating eyes than a mouse could tell you of any of its cat acquaintances. Toller is a private man, yet he luxuriates in the attention of an audience and by his own admission, has always thought of his life as being lived on a stage.

Toller Cranston is best known to baby boomers and anyone else who takes an interest in ice skating, as the Canadian who changed the skating world forever. He eschewed the standard athletic jumping that was the rule for male figure skaters in the nineteen seventies, and introduced a more evocative, modern dance equivalent of figure skating. To see him for the first time in those days was surprising, and unsettling, not least because for that generation, the divide between genders was still very distinct. To see a man being so overtly emotional in his gestures and expressions, even in a skating competition, was definitely treading new ground. I recently watched a film of one of his early performances and was delighted, overwhelmed once again by his beauty and skill. In his twenties, on the ice, Toller Cranston was unequalled, the personification of confidence and contemporary style.

It may be the dual nature of the man that shields him from the world. On his most public and accessible level, Toller Cranston is a star, a former Olympic medalist, a prolific painter and publicist of his own work, a person on a grand scale. To see only the outer appearance is to overlook the humbler version of himself that is extended but is frequently obscured by the celebrity atmosphere that is everywhere evident around Toller. In San Miguel de Allende where he has lived for more than twenty years, he is known *of* by many, but is an intimate of few. His closest friend is a fellow painter, Marion Perlet, a woman he met at art school in Montreal when he was in his teens. They have had their differences, but he professes a love for her and she for him that is based on long acquaintance and on a genuine admiration for one another.

There are parallels between Perlet's and Toller's work but whereas her creations tend toward contemplative dreamscapes, Cranston's paintings are fantastic images that leap off the canvas much as Toller leapt off the ice. Even in a large space such as Toller's home offers, they can be overwhelming- the detail of pattern and colour reminiscent of Russian folk art but with more overt theatricality. Toller maintains a great admiration for the Dutch painter Pieter Bruegel and certainly the human drama and the surrealistic semblance typical of Bruegel's and other's work are present in many of Cranston's compositions. After a brief tour of his home I am invited to sit in a large beautifully furnished room surrounded by his paintings and by some of Toller's many decorative acquisitions from Mexico and the world. Small talk is quickly put aside and Toller proceeds to trace his artistic beginnings much as one would get on with an assignment for which there is a dead line. As the afternoon unfolds, he relaxes and I have the pleasure of seeing his keen intelligence and humour revealed.

"The first thing that I remember about my artistic life was doing a crayon drawing, an abstract in grade two in Galt, Ontario, a city we now know as Cambridge. Basically what the kids did, this is all too boring but the idea was to draw black lines all over the place and where the lines intersect and form shapes, you colour them. I remember mine was absolutely and totally different beyond words which was only in black, turquoise, and purple and it was like a paisley design, eastern, Indian, it probably would have been understood in New Delhi but this was grade two in southern Ontario. The dye was cast at that time. My mother was an artist, I guess. She painted. She actually was pretty good but would not have had what was ultimately necessary for me which was an adherence to discipline. She was too artistic for words but all over the board. I used to do too many artistic things but I no longer do them because I know that to actually achieve anything in art, the competition, which is a competition of artists that have lived for the last twenty thousand years, the competition is so steep you can't afford to be all over the board. You have to concentrate so I'm quite narrow even though someone else might think I am quite broad because I do many different things but it's under one umbrella. The response to my grade two effort wasn't good but mistakes are only mistakes if you don't learn from them or derive a positive end. This was a lesson in life. I remember a skating family in Montreal who had two young daughters who were very talented and the mother became insane, like Gypsy Rose Lee's mother, a skating mother beyond description. At the age of thirteen or fourteen the older child died of cancer and that was a tragedy but what it did at a terrible price was it jolted relationships with other people into a focus that wasn't there before so there was a positive result that transpired after this tragedy. My mother... it is hard to talk about it because it is as though I didn't even know her, well, I did but I didn't, I am convinced she was psychotic, genuinely so, and also very resentful and jealous of what I was. Tragically she hatched a child who was everything she wanted to be: artistic, famous, talented and more than anything else which was her Achilles heel, dramatic and flamboyant. The cruelest cut of all, Julius Ceasar, Shakespeare, was that her fame was directly because she was my mother. It wasn't her own.

So that was that and now we are in grade eight, and I remember this as clear as day. The first little project that we did in school, I was one of three boys in the art class. Boys didn't do art. They did industrial arts, beat nails, and sawed. So we were told to go home and do self-portraits of ourselves." The phone rings and Toller goes off rapidly to answer it. I listen to the insistent sound of the marching drums and trumpets that every resident living near Parque Juarez knows well. Each afternoon a group of young men and women practice in preparation for the next parade which, in San Miguel, is never far off. When Toller returns, he continues his narrative without pause. "I lived in suburban Montreal and this was a late September day. So there I was sitting in my little room with my stuffed cobras and things and the light was coming in at a very oblique angle and it was yellow and red, sunset. In the mirror my face turned yellow and red so I thought I had done an absolutely fantastic job with my self-portrait which was in yellow and red but when I brought it to school I instantly got a detention and had to write out lines about being disruptive because I was against the grain. Against the grain in French is *a rebours,* sort of against nature. That was important ultimately because I was always against the grain although it was my natural inclination and I could never understand why people were upset with me. It never entered my head that I was doing anything wrong. I didn't know that I was different, something that ultimately became a strength. I was a child of destiny. It was so clear to me. A force was propelling me but I didn't know what it was and I often didn't know what I was supposed to do."

Toller smiles to himself. "The mistake in discussing one's past is beginning with *what if.* I auditioned for the art school in Montreal, Ecole des Beaux-Arts which is a fine school. A thousand applied and only fifty students were accepted.

Fantastically, and this was great, the teachers who were involved in admitting the students, were looking not for finished work but for potential. Real creativity. The school taught me everything and it taught me nothing. The very first day I went to Ecole des Beaux-Arts, we went to a sculpture class and there was this mad Italian with freaked out hair and he was doing sculptures with wire and clay donuts that went twenty feet across the room. I was making, this isn't a joke, dolls out of paper. That was important because I was not a sculptor, I was two dimensional and decorative but the best thing was they encouraged individuality, do whatever you think, be yourself and I was doing paper dolls with flowers in their hair, I suppose quite fantastic in their own way. Another pivotal point was in my third year before graduating I failed sculpture but I was a little more confident at the time, and told the teacher, 'You know, I'm not really a sculptor so I really don't think I should be doing this. This is not who I am and by the way, I am having an exhibition in Toronto next week. Would you like to see some of the pictures?' This exhibition was the big time with three famous famous artists in Quebec, Ulysses Comtois, Jacques de Tonnancour, and Robert Wolfe. I had gone to the bank and borrowed two thousand dollars, don't ask me how a seventeen year old managed it but I got the two thousand dollars for the frames. One thing I have always been guilty of and I encourage other people to do it but they often don't because they don't have the ability is, think big. Do it right." To make his point, Toller reminds me of an art exhibition he hosted in his house not long before. I attended along with a large crowd of resident San Miguelians and tourists. The artist was an older man who was a beginning painter, one of Toller's students (and a client) who Toller encouraged to have a one man show. "Every single painting sold because it looked serious. It didn't look amateur. So, after I failed sculpture I left the school with their blessing and did what I wanted to do which was to paint. The exhibition in Toronto was a great success. I sold every painting and I became rich. I had $6000 in my pocket in 1967. When you think about it, it's quite fantastic. Think big."

"My magical mystery tour re my painting career afforded many many adventures, highs and lows, incredible, way beyond anybody here for its colour and texture, mad things that happened to me. But the basic discipline, subject matter, work ethic, and hunger to succeed would never be appeased. It was always in fast forward. My work which you have seen over there, I don't say it is better because artists aren't allowed to say that because something done at an earlier age could be much more intense and visceral than something done better with an acquired technical ability but is in fact less. But there has been no difference, from the time I was two to the time I am in my sixties."

"The next thing was a huge advantage. Because of my skating career and my voracious appetite to learn, I developed from the age of seventeen a desire to see the greats of the world so I was aware of every great museum in the world and would have seen them many times. As a suburban Montreal boy I was familiar with the Louvre, the London National Gallery, and many more. That was a huge luxury because I saw what great was. I saw the high water mark. I'm not against exactly, the Group of Seven. I almost feel they are more historically important than artistically important because they painted things that simply weren't being painted. But I was not seeing Tom Thomson. I was seeing Fra Angelico. That education started to distill my artistic sensibilities. Like the skating, I was almost self-taught, self-invented."

I find myself interjecting to ask Toller how he was able to continue the intense work on his skating while he was exploring the art museums of the world. He doesn't hesitate. "My skating was a religion."

"Most people would have been overwhelmed by it."

Toller reminds me. "I wasn't most people. I said I was a child of destiny but don't ever think that the world was my oyster. I left home at the age of 16, never to return but you see, one of the most important things was that I had a master foreman at the controls, Ellen Burka. I was in the hands of a master. I learned about the adherence to work and discipline. I learned, as de Vinci did, if I may use him, about something many people today don't have a clue about, refinement, beauty, grace, and sophistication. That was, by accident, my reality. I had a great desire to see and learn. I have never mentioned this before but in the Olympics in Saporo there was an eight hour wait in the airport. The whole team was lying on the floor asleep and I hired a taxi and went to see the National Museum of Tokyo. A zillion years later, I mean it is insane but it is also true, talking with a friend here, I became aware that there was a flaw in my artistic education. I realized that I hadn't seen the Prado in Madrid which is in the top three, no top four, no top three museums in the world. I flew from Mexico City to Madrid, got off the plane and went to the Prado. I consistently do this. Usually if I know I am going to see something important, I will study for six months. I don't want to go in and say wow. I want to go in and see something I know. I want a confirmation. The Cairo museum is a wonder of the world but there is one thing that perhaps puts it on a lower level than the Louvre for example. The Cairo museum is only Egyptian art. The Louvre is everything. The Met, according to Kenneth Clark is equally important. He did the book *Civilization* which I still read almost every year because it acquaints me with the greats and with the significant periods in art. I don't have the knowledge of Kenneth Clark but he fails on one level, and it is the level that I don't fail on because he is an academic and I am an artist. I have a deeper, an overawed response to something. He is guilty of being too intellectual, too scholarly. In my opinion, art is joined to the human condition and passion or emotion. I don't think one can discuss artistic endeavors on a high level without emotion. Vincent van Gogh's work is a good example of emotion frozen in art."

"The creative process in an artist is the most uniquely fascinating aspect of being an artist. Most artists, although it is so dangerous to generalize, work with more spontaneity of concept and idea rather than being too thoughtful. That being said, after a work is finished, whatever it is they have done can be traced to the source of influence or source of creation. In other words, it is not quite as casual as you think. One of the most interesting, not the best, there is a difference, but most interesting artists, was Henri Rousseau. Henri Rousseau is an artist who hit me straight between the eyes because I am thrilled and fascinated by naive and at the same time, sophisticated art. He was a customs official, absolutely blue collar, but why is he painting lions and sleeping gypsies? Where did that come from? It did come from somewhere. As a matter of fact he was influenced by the Botanical Gardens in Paris and other images he saw at the time."

I am curious to know whether you think the personal lives of great artists matter outside the context of their work. Do we need to know for example, what kind of person van Gogh was or Picasso?

"I don't know if Leonardo de Vinci or Picasso or other artistic genius' can really be judged in the same way we would judge ordinary persons. How nice they were or how much you like them is unimportant because what they do is historically important. Something that I read in a biography of Marcel Proust impressed me. He said, *'The thing that I abjure the most is the criticism by people, of the private lives of genius'*. The private life of Rembrandt is completely unimportant to us in the 21st century. His contribution is his artistic achievement, not was he nice. That being said, years ago Marion had the most fantastic and personal revelation about Rembrandt. She and I were on our way back from Egypt and in Amsterdam she went to the Reich's museum and discovered Rembrandt. She had been aware of Rembrandt her whole life but on this occasion, she really saw his work for what it was. She realized how beautiful his paintings were- not the physical beauty so much as the humanity. She told me that on the steps of the museum she cried. Rembrandt and Bruegel were Dutch and they understood Dutch life. They portrayed the life- peasant weddings, children's games- that they were so familiar with. For those artists their paintings reflect a celebration of a culture and an intimate understanding of that culture. I suppose for, let's say, a Canadian, Bruegel is easier to grasp because it is so visual and joyous and colourful. The Rembrandt palate for some is somber but is of course, positively glorious within those hues. The thing about Rembrandt that seems to astound, is his ability to paint casually but meticulously the flesh, you can see the blood under the skin, and his ability to capture light, which was a preoccupation of Dutch seventeenth century masters. Vermeer was even better at it than Rembrandt."

"Rembrandt and Bruegel, and this becomes a very esoteric subject which is fun to talk about, were deeply interested in humanity and capturing the truthfulness of people's lives. In the Kunsthistorisches Museum in Vienna there are two Rembrandts hanging in one corner of a room, an old man and his wife. In seeing them there, I discovered I couldn't see one without being aware of the other. They had emotionally or chemically grown together. The beauty of one was contingent upon the attention of the other. This is different from what one experiences in Rome where you might see saints hung upside down and slaves stabbed and who knows what. The subject matter is so unappetizing that you can't really get to the mastery of the painting because you just can't look at that. Rembrandt, for some, might have painted themes that were not particularly appetizing, like the Prodigal Son, but the humanity of those paintings is unsurpassed."

"Picasso who was deeply and patriotically Spanish, was bent upon something quite different, which was to become extremely inventive and radically creative within painting and artistic mediums that were precedent setting. The ingredients to the genius of Rembrandt and a genius like Picasso were very different. As a rule, an artist builds upon the achievements of artists that have preceded him. Heironymus Bosch painted before Bruegel and sometimes it is possible to mistake one for the other. Picasso was unlike anybody else. Incidentally, I am not Breugel or Bosch, alas. And not Piccasso, alas. But being creative in my own way is very important to me. The word that should be chiseled on my tombstone is 'neo', new. I was new as a skater and even though this isn't what you would call new (Toller indicates one of his nearby paintings), it is a neo interpretation of things that we already know."

"The *way* that people paint is also important and an inspiration to me. Take the Canadian painter Lauren Harris who you might think couldn't be further away from me. I like the tactile way he applies paint, particularly when doing snow. I learned from Lauren Harris that snow has every colour of the world, there is an iridescence to it. I have been very influenced by that and yet you wouldn't necessarily see the similarity unless I pointed it out. The neo means having absorbed and understood artistic styles and movements and then taking bits and pieces from all things and redoing them in a neo way, in an original way which in fact, isn't original. A lot of it has been inspired by others which binds me to and links me to the history of art. We are talking about tradition within art as opposed to someone who flaunted tradition like Jackson Pollock. He didn't make love to his work I don't think, and the understanding of art in the context of Pieter Bruegel was the antithesis of what Jackson Pollock was. Bruegel's works mirrored culture, structure, classical composition, magnificence in how they were painted, attention to detail, enmeshed and mired in discipline. Pollock was all against that. I'm a great fan of Pollock yet his initial approach was different. Pollock would not have had a structured or academic drawing underneath the picture. Paintings of Bruegel and Rembrandt were steeped in academic knowledge and masterful technique that is so obvious. One can't see that in Pollock because it doesn't exist, which makes it extremely new and interesting."

"Andy Warhol, whom I met, was on the cover of Interview Magazine which was the hippest and the hottest magazine in New York. He was out there and brand new. I don't think I am brand new. I learned from seeing others. Nobody would have taught me about colour yet I have an impeccable sense of colour because I taught myself through my own experience. One of my strong suits is that I have an interest in and an appreciation for all forms of art. I'm an Aries, Taurus. Both the ram and the bull will charge and not backtrack. I have always charged into anything artistic, full steam ahead without looking right or left or wondering what is going to happen. Aries is the god of athletic ability, war, individuality, aggression, colour red, stone diamond, the hardest but the purest of stones. I'm all those things but more one dimensional since I'm on the cusp. The Taurus sign is the painter sign, the same sign as Adolf Hitler whose birthday I share, April 20th."

"Thank goodness you don't have an army."

"I sort of do with all the people on the property. But you see you can interpret the signs of the Zodiac positively or negatively. Aries is the most dominant, it's the, my way or no way sign. What sign are you?"

"I'm a pisces."

"You almost made it... Depending on what I choose to do, it could also be writing, I have a reservoir of creativity. I am unique because I became world class in two things. Da Vinci was never the figure skating champion of Italy."

"The beard and the robe would have gotten in the way."

"Rather than saying hurray for me, I realize it is a unique privilege. I am humbled by the knowledge of what has preceded me. I know that I am not da Vinci but I have a creative energy propelling me forward, even against my will sometimes. I have one thing, a terrible albatross that most people can't relate to. Even as I am sitting here, I am squirming a bit because I still have energy to go back to my studio and work longer and unless that energy is exorcised each day I am frustrated and not in harmony with myself. I think that comes from Olympic training coupled with a natural inclination to be that way. I often have a visual metaphor in my mind of dying and making my way up to the pearly gates and the angels directing me to the escalator going down to the smoky regions, saying, 'But you really tried hard. You're going to Hell but nobody tried harder.' And I did. A member of the French figure skating association and a former competitor of mine, told me once that he watched me performing in Soporo, my second Olympics. He said, 'Watching you skate around the ice ended my skating career. The look in your eyes made me realize I could never be like you.' I was intense, probably too intense. The greatest artists can do what they do seemingly without effort. On the other hand, that's what I was."

"Because of my experience, I couldn't say education, but experience that became education, the history of art and the knowledge of art is very important to me. I would guess that very few people in San Miguel would have more knowledge about the history of art than myself because one, they wouldn't have travelled as much, and two, it is extremely important to the development of my work. I want to know what has transpired before me. I want to be absolutely familiar with abilities and techniques of all artists so I can make my choice. I always think of it as a kind of weapon. The books I have are aggressively acquired because the more books I have read, the more knowledge I have. That knowledge of art is a crucial ingredient to what I do."

"The culture of the artist, whether it be Italian, French, Russian, or whatever, stretches my artistic vocabulary. Art and culture, although related, are not the same thing. Deus ex machina is Greek for 'god from the machine'. Basically what it means is that someone or something can cross your path unexpectedly, thereby changing your life forever. Many years ago I had a reading with a tarot card reader who lived in San Miguel but has since died. She said to me, 'You have to get out of Canada. It is not the right country because the culture is too new. You must go where the earth is ancient and it is there you will become the person you are supposed to become.' If one talks about tradition and culture, one does not talk about Egypt and Canada in the same breath. Like the Jackson Pollock, the brand new, almost without culture, is exciting and innocent and spontaneous and wonderful whereas a Bruegel is rooted in the understanding of a culture. In fact the Bruegel and Rembrandt paintings in many ways, are as Dutch as they can be. The paintings push a cultural button for Dutch viewers that ignites joy. I don't think we have any Canadian artists that do that for us and if we do, it is limited. An artist that comes to mind is William Kurelek who came from the Ukraine and painted rural life on the prairies. Cornelius Krieghoff doesn't do it either. He was French Canadian, a coureur du bois. Frederick Verner painted buffalo. The Group of Seven, I suppose might be considered but Canada is too new. None of them harpoon our culture like Bruegel did for the Dutch."

When I look at your paintings, I see little evidence of San Miguel. Has your work been influenced by living in Mexico?

Toller's answer is immediate. "Not at all. Well look, when I say not at all, we are influenced by everything we see and feel. First let me say that people make the mistake of thinking bright colours mean Mexican. There are bright colours in India, Persia, Russia, China and they are much more refined than in Mexico. Mexican colours tend to be folksy, meaning lime green and pink and orange, not ruby red and emerald green. The colours that I think distinguish the jewel qualities of Russia like the enamels of Faberge, have more depth. Why did I come to San Miguel? Because San Miguel is a major art centre. It attracts very high-end brains, quite fantastic. I'm not old San Miguel but I got here early enough to be on the ground floor, just as I did in the skating world. I wasn't the last word in skating but I was pivotal. If I had come ten years later I would have been ten years too late, and the skaters were better than me ten years later. As for San

Miguel, there are those people who think that you choose to come to a place and that is one way of getting there but the place could summon you as well, or invite you, or your own personal destiny could get you there. For me, I would have been made aware of San Miguel years before I came. Gary Slipper and his wife encouraged Marion Perlet to come to San Miguel and I guess in a way encouraged me to come to San Miguel. Importantly, I didn't have any preconceptions so I couldn't be disappointed. In 1989 I arrived and was taken to the Santa Monica hotel on the park which at that time was owned by an American woman and had a personal touch. I was taken for a drink around sunset and in the process I decided to stay there, even though I had been booked to stay somewhere else. I remember saying I like it here and I want to stay here so I was put into room #1 which was white, nice but not fancy. The next morning over breakfast I asked the owner of the hotel, could she recommend a realtor? It happened there was one around the corner so before I had even set my foot on the ground of San Miguel, I got into a car and began to look for houses. Of course, I was a realtor's worst nightmare. For three years I looked at houses. I liked things but I wasn't biting. My realtor finally said with terrifyingly frightening politeness, 'What is it you are looking for?' and I replied, 'I will know it when I see it.' By chance, Marion happened to live across from this property and one day she told me it was but wasn't really on the market. I arranged to see it and when the door opened, I took one look and said, 'This is it.' For a year I tried to acquire the property until I ran out of money. There was a point, and this has happened to me several times in my life, when I told the lawyers, 'Oh by the way, if you can't come through with this deal I'm going to have to kill myself, just so you know.' It's true, because I had given them cheques for ninety percent of the asking price but had no receipts, no security. I had sold everything I owned so basically if the deal fell through, I would have to kill myself. I saw it as a racecar going down a highway out of control but for some reason staying on the road. Anyway, somehow I acquired it having never done anything by myself in my life. All the papers were signed except my name wasn't yet on the deed and unless your name is on the deed in the municipal hall, you don't own the property. I decided to go see a lawyer, one of the tough guys in town. After all this time I was convinced there was a great conspiracy against me so when he didn't show up at his office, I went to his house and sure enough, there was the book of deeds on his table. I signed the deed across the entire page like d'Artagnan with his sword, and the place was mine."

"Incidentally this positively fabulous property was a veritable ruin and dump but strangely it has never changed in my eyes. I have always seen it as being wonderful. I remember showing guests the cactus patch or the falling down buildings thinking everything was wonderful. I thought it was beautiful the way it was. I've made a number of changes but I would never change the essence of the property and the charm of it and the layout. The negative space or the flow of air here is very special. A lawyer called me the other day and asked if my place was for sale and I said, 'Well not really but everything is for sale for the right price'. Life is about chapters and there is nothing about San Miguel that I don't like but like Adam and Eve, after a while people can opt to leave paradise even with the conscious knowledge that you can never have anything better. That is one of the great human flaws. Men frequently walk conspicuously and knowledgeably to their own deaths. So if you wanted to write me a large cheque, I would sell this property knowing that I was making a mistake, that I will never experience anything better than this, but I hunger for change. Change is a rebirth, it is creative, it is embracing a new chapter, and for that I would do it."

Cranston makes no secret of the fact that he is always at risk of living beyond his means. His house and gardens are filled to capacity with decorative objects. Where one beautifully painted plate would be enough for most of us, there are fifty. Where one glass ball would suffice, there are a hundred. The large furnishings are sumptuous and beautiful. During my first visit,

Toller sat on a pale yellow suede couch. He had forgotten our appointment so was still dressed in his painting clothes and when he got up to change nearby, I remarked that he had left a paint stain on the fabric. He dismissed its importance saying the maid would remove it, and so it was. The next time I visited, all evidence of the paint was gone. As we talked people came and went. They were usually introduced, employees, renters, clients, sometimes staying to listen to Toller's conversation, sometimes passing through. His large expenditures necessitate constant production and courting of the market. In every corner of the many buildings that dot his jungle landscape, there is evidence of his voracious visual appetite. Curiously, Toller's painting studio is a stark exception. It is white, entirely bare, an empty space waiting to be filled. He admits that he applies the same discipline to his painting as he did to his skating career. He paints until he exhausts himself. "A good day for me is when I can go to bed so tired, I fall asleep immediately. I need to push myself to that point or I feel dissatisfied with what I have accomplished."

"If I ever do sell, I can't imagine the act of dismantling this property. Everything is in its rightful place. Can anything be in a better place than where it is? But the reality is, if I sold it, all I would be left with is money. Can you imagine? It would be gone in a week. But I would consider it. I would have to leave San Miguel because after living here as a first class citizen, I could never have anything better than this. In fact there *is* better, but not for me better. This is as good as it gets. I have a horrible acknowledgement. It happened once in skating and it is happening as we speak. This is the most fecund and enriched period of my life. This is when it is really good. Like all things, skaters, artists, you and me, we live in a circle. We don't live forever, we don't live in a linear way. I can say this to you but it's almost a secret. I am on top of my game. I have endless energy. My memory is at its height. My knowledge and experience is fuel for me, but I know that it can't last. Sooner or later it will end. It all has to end. Nothing lasts forever. Some artists, as they age, paint out of desperation. They believe that just by painting another painting they can live forever. I am so weak in some areas but part of me is very resilient. I accept that my life will end."

"Marion and I, joined at the hip as we are, have no idea what we are going to do with all our work. There is a ton of stuff in this house. I'm different from the popes and the kings and pharaohs because I think it would be perfectly ok to live my life as I have and the day that I die, to evaporate like mist in the wind. Contrary to what people might think, I'm not afraid of being forgotten. What I think I want with the few people I have left in my life, and truly they are dropping like flies because I am outgrowing people and just don't care any more, I would give all my possessions away. That is one thing the Medici's found out- you can't take it with you. Tutankhamun took it with him but most don't. I believe in thinking big but what am I going to do with all this stuff? What if you bought this property and then you decided you had to do something with all this shit and you decided to have a big bonfire. You could be burning paintings worth millions. Or not. I would rather give it back to people and let them enjoy it as I have. I don't want to go down in history, a legacy. I have lived my life in a huge circle, even with figure skating, with circle-eights, I have spent my life going in circles. I'm very aware of that so I accept the cycle, the beginnings and ends."

It is easy to admire Toller Cranston for his obvious talent but his personal discipline and commitment to hard work are what really distinguish him. Some time ago I was interested to learn that so-called child prodigies have been observed to practice ten times longer than other children and Cranston is an excellent case in point. His dedication combined with his natural ability has brought him well-deserved renown. He was the Canadian National figure skating champion from 1971 to '76. He won the World bronze medal in 1974 and the Olympic bronze in 1976 but quite beyond these successes in competition, Toller Cranston changed skating for good. Much as painters like Cezanne,

Picasso, and Pollack were pivotal figures in the art world, Toller was equally significant in the world of figure skating. Is he satisfied with his achievements? As he himself has said, a bronze medal isn't the gold. Today there are ever more canvases to be filled with paint and finished ones to be sold. At present every artist in San Miguel is struggling to maintain his or her financial stability as tourism fluctuates and the world economy flounders. Despite the challenges, Toller manages to preserve his energy and ambition. The determined look in his eyes that cowed his fellow skaters is still there. Toller Cranston may be aging but the horizon beckons and I have the feeling that this particular lion is destined to be forever on the hunt.

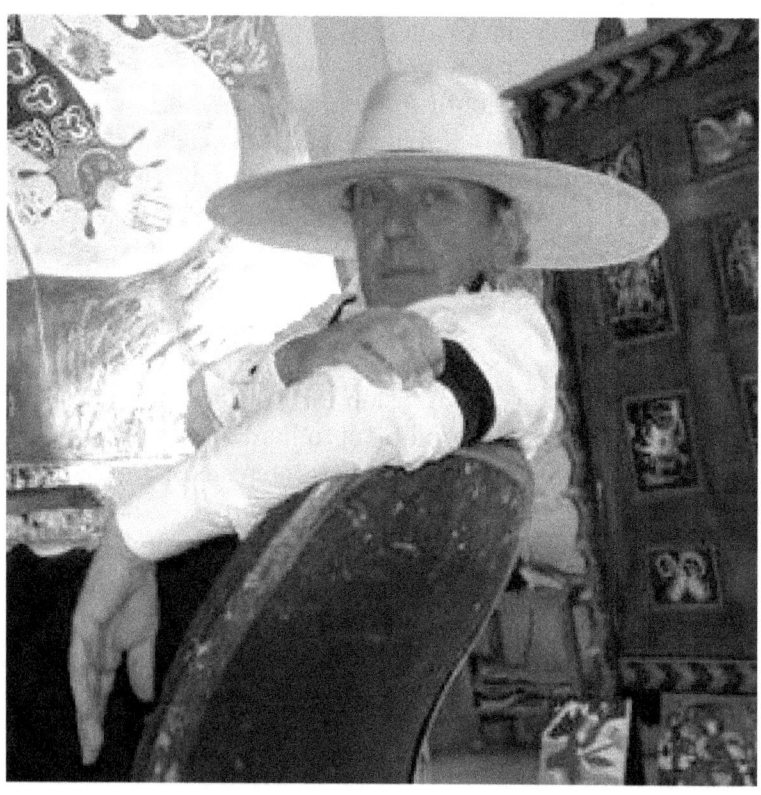

Mary Rapp

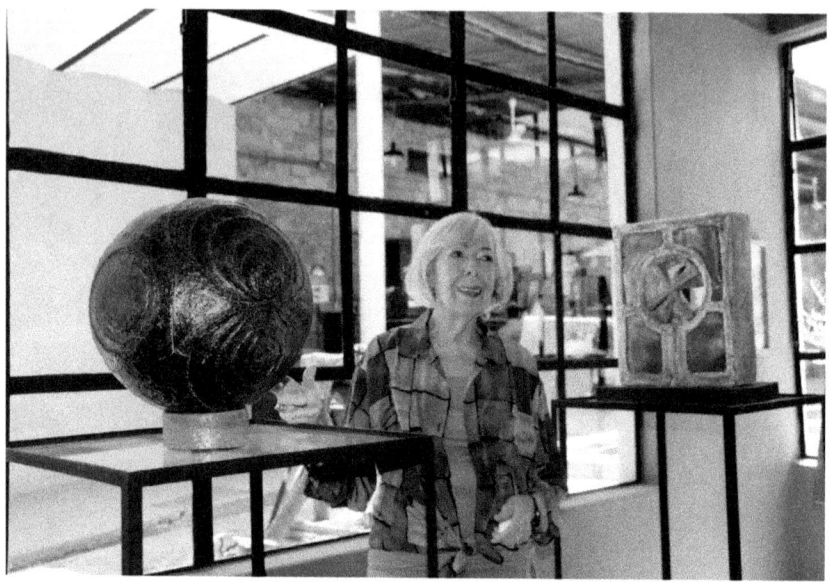

Did every baby boomer who read Jack Kerouac's *On the Road* have the same reaction I did? I was seventeen in 1965, and in my first year of university when an enthusiastic fellow student whose name I don't remember, offered to read the book aloud to me. Every day we met in the dining hall and after we ate lunch he read for half an hour or an hour depending on whether we had classes to get to. A casual assent soon became a fascination as Kerouac's words reorganized me cell by cell and I realized that all the rules that had once applied to my life had become optional. Anything was possible.

Although I have been a life long fan, I was never cultish about Kerouac but if I had been, I would have discovered that he was friendly with a young man named Lucien Carr who was friends with Allen Ginsburg and William Burroughs and that Kerouac may have come to San Miguel de Allende in the fifties and another friend of his, Neal Cassady, the Dean Moriarty character in *On the Road*, had died on the railroad tracks here, the cause variously listed as hypothermia, renal failure, drug and/or alcohol overdose, no one is too clear. Because he introduced and influenced many of its central figures, Lucien Carr is credited with having founded the group known as the Beats. When he was twenty he was famously imprisoned for stabbing and killing an older man who had persistently pursued him for over five years. After serving a two-year sentence Carr was pardoned and began a successful career with United Press. He died at age 79, having lived an improbably long and stable life for someone with such fateful beginnings.

Earlier on another continent, Max Beckmann was born in Germany in 1884 and became one of the country's most notable painters. He served as a medic in the First World War, an experience that left him deeply affected, its influences visible in all his subsequent paintings and sculptures. In his youth he was considered avant-garde and over the course of the next fifteen years he gained a considerable reputation in the modern art world. His fortunes changed dramatically with Hitler's rise to power. Never a fan of the new art forms, Hitler had Beckmann fired from his job as art instructor in Frankfurt, had his paintings, almost six hundred of them, removed from all German museums, and declared Beckmann a "degenerate artist", a term that sounds implausible today but had profound implications for Beckmann. With his stature as an artist and his ability to earn a living gone, he left Germany in 1937 and fled to Amsterdam with his wife. He continued to paint powerful, unsettling paintings of people looking off to the edge of the frame as though searching for some meaning to their existence. After the war Beckmann emigrated to the United States where he taught at the Washington University Art School in St. Louis. Just three years later he died of a heart attack in New York. He was sixty-six. Since his death, Beckmann's international reputation has grown and he is now considered one of the most important artists of the twentieth century.

What have these two legendary men to do with Mary Rapp, a long time resident of San Miguel who maintains a relatively low profile, living quietly on the outskirts of el centro with her husband Gil? Remarkably, Mary Rapp was an intimate of both Lucien Carr and Max Beckmann. Seeing her today it is difficult to believe that Mary is eighty-eight years old. She is youthful, animated and, as a long-time friend has described her, always, always elegant. I find myself feeling in turns, amazement and admiration as we talk in her studio at Fabrica la Aurora, formerly a textile mill, now the home of high end stores and galleries. It is here that Mary lives and works. The scale of the building with its high ceilings and roughly plastered stone walls is in contrast to the slim, poised woman beside me. She would look more congruous in the lobby of the Waldorf Astoria than in this spacious room surrounded by her bold sculptures and paintings. I discover that Mary's physical beauty has been a fact of her long life and while it has undoubtedly opened doors, it has not protected her from the heartaches that life assuredly exacts. Notwithstanding what she describes as a challenging sixty-five year marriage, she is a strong, irrepressible spirit who, in her own words, "can't stay depressed for long". I begin by asking her how she became an artist.

"I was born in St. Louis and lived all my childhood there. My interest in art started very early, in fact my mother had a letter that I had written when I was very young and it was mostly drawings. I really think the explanation was that I was nearsighted, couldn't see the world very well at all. I think I started drawing to bring the world closer to me so I could examine it. I wasn't aware of that at all of course. They found I was nearsighted when I was in third grade and from that time I didn't draw as much until later when I was in my early teens and then it became an obsession that has lasted all my life. I was very lucky to live in St. Louis which has a remarkable art museum.

My mother took me to a program they had for children and I decided right then that that was what I wanted to do, particularly sculpture. They had an enormous hall full of monumental sculpture, huge and wonderful things and I was so impressed with all of that. I guess that helped solidify my intention. My first serious class was when I was about sixteen with a teacher who didn't think much of my work. Well I think at that point I was preoccupied with drawing females with a lot of detail, with their hair and what they were wearing which I guess was my own concern about how I looked and how I wanted to look and what I saw in other people and I think he was pretty bored by that and I don't wonder. After high school I enrolled in Washington University Art School which was about two blocks from home and not what I had in mind. I talked the family into sending me away to school to the Pennsylvania Academy of Fine Arts in Philadelphia and at that time Walker Hancock was supposed to be teaching but suddenly he was drafted, this was during the second World War, so Paul Manship an extraordinary person from the century before basically, took over his class."

Paul Howard Manship was born in 1885, won the Prix de Rome as a young man in 1909 and became a prominent sculptor over the course of his career in Europe and later in the United States. He produced hundreds of works but perhaps his most famous are the Prometheus Fountain in Rockefeller Center in New York and the gates to the central park zoo. "He did all those little finials on Sixth Avenue too. He was a charming bon vivant and he would show up impeccably dressed in his grey flannels to instruct on Thursdays. I was always trying to do very serious things, kind of political things, and he would say, 'art is supposed to be beautiful', and he would chuckle and take us out for pizza after class so it was a marvelous experience in every way. He really knew anatomy and we were obligated to go to the anatomy classes and I learned a tremendous amount at the Pennsylvania Academy. It is surprising I learned as much as I did because when I entered the Academy I had just fallen seriously in love and that was my real concern."

Was that when you fell in love with Lucien Carr?

"Yes. We met unexpectedly and it was love at first sight, for both of us. That was an incredible encounter. We were in St. Louis in a strange place, a park, at a day long picnic in celebration of something I don't remember what, and there were little paths throughout the semi-wilderness and we encountered one another at one of the crossroads and that was it."

What was the attraction between you?

"He was absolutely gorgeous, blond, blue eyed, the perfect specimen. It was sex I suppose. We were seventeen years old after all. We were together for almost three years and I came to know him very well. As time went on I became terribly worried about him, I was having nightmares about what was to become of him and finally I just couldn't take it anymore and I left. Three months later he killed Kammerer and I felt so bad about that. Lucien was, at that time a very troubled person, quite neurotic. He had had David Kammerer tracking him for years, since he was fourteen. Lucien's mother allowed this man to take her son to Mexico because he was fatherless and she thought it would be good for him. She was very naive. David Kammerer's relationship with Lucien was difficult yet one of some dependence because David was a brilliant man and had been Lucien's teacher. There's an interesting account of their relationship in a book by Kerouac and Bill Burroughs called, *And the Hippos were Boiled in Their Tanks*."

The mention of William Burroughs, a man about ten years older whom Mary and Lucien used to meet in the bar in St. Louis, prompts me to do some reading on the man. I confess I never read his most famous book *Naked Lunch* which was popular among members of my hippie crowd at the same time I was reading Kerouac. Burroughs had been to Harvard and studied medicine in Vienna. He was a very gifted intellectual and is talked about as having created a new literary art form but what I'm left with is the fact that he was a heroin addict, shot and killed his wife in Cuernavaca while pretending to be William Tell, and lost his only son to alcohol and drugs. For all his cleverness, I doubt anything could compensate for such tragedy.

Mary explains that Lucien met Kerouac through Kerouac's girlfriend Edie. All three were attending Columbia University. "I only met Jack once when I happened to be staying at Edie's apartment and Kerouac came looking for her. I was asleep when there was a knock on the door at five in the morning and when I opened the door, there was Jack in a sailor suit. He asked for Edie and when I explained she was away and had let me use her apartment, he asked me if I wanted to go for a walk. We walked to a children's playground not too far away and he drew pentagrams in the dirt and tried to summon the devil. I remember it was the Saturday before Easter. I don't remember what we talked about." Both Kerouac and Burroughs were arrested as material witnesses in the killing of David Kammerer. When Kerouac's parents refused to do so, Edie's parents posted the bail for him on the condition he marry their daughter. The marriage was annulled a year later.

"Lucien and I were in love but towards the end, he was becoming more and more unpredictable. It was very dramatic when I left him. Had he been a little more stable, I never would have gone. His brilliance, his quickness, and even his volatility were part of the attraction. There was never a boring moment. We spent hours wandering the streets of New York talking, going to French movies. He was addicted to French movies and spoke pretty good French. I was in Philadelphia studying and Lucien had moved from St. Louis to New York. My poor father who was paying my way didn't know I was spending my weekends in New York. A couple of years ago I discovered that there's a description of me in one of Ginsberg's books where he is discussing Lucien and me and Lucien tells Ginsberg that he is worried that he is having a negative influence on my work. I was surprised because I never met Ginsberg but he obviously knew about me through Lucien."

Allen Ginsberg was a student at Columbia University when Lucien Carr introduced him to Kerouac and Burroughs. Ginsberg first attained notoriety with his poem *Howl* which was banned for its explicit language and its open references to homosexuality at a time when homosexual acts were illegal in the U.S. Ginsberg became a spokesperson for free speech in the 1950's when his book was banned as obscene. The subsequent trial and the ultimate lifting of that ban made Ginsberg a person of considerable renown. There is no doubt he was responsible for the breaking down of many barriers that needed to go but he didn't embrace chaos either. Ginsberg had a partner of forty years, Peter Orlovsky, and maintained a relatively modest lifestyle which was shaped by his practice of Buddhism and his commitment to social justice. The success of *Howl* and his other works allowed him to devote his working life to writing poetry and his public readings continued to be popular until his death at the age of seventy in 1997.

My conversation with Mary shifts to her first meeting with Max Beckmann. "A couple of years after my break with Lucien, I transferred to the University of Chicago during the Hutchins days when they were doing the Bachelor of Philosophy. I spent a lot of time at the Art Institute looking at the fabulous collection there. I never did finish my degree. Instead I went back to St. Louis where I met my husband. We had been married for about six months when I read that Max Beckman had accepted the post to teach at Washington University. He was coming from Amsterdam where he had spent the war years as an artist exiled from Germany and I thought he was a magnificent painter. I had seen only one of his paintings. It is called *Departure* and it must have been in New York. But I had seen others in photographs and I wanted very much to study with him. Unfortunately he was teaching only advanced painting and I was not enrolled in the university at all. I had written a couple of little articles on art for a suburban paper so I found out where he lived and I went and knocked on his door. It was audacious of me, I can't believe I had the nerve to do it but I did. He answered the door very suspiciously with the chain still on it. I guess he had heard America was full of crime. I told him I was a newspaper reporter which he didn't quite understand so he called his wife to translate. I was invited in and I asked him all the usual questions about why he was in America and so on, and then I told him I had wanted to study with him but I wasn't enrolled at the university. He and his wife talked for a moment, to me it seemed like forever, and then she said, 'He will take you.' And I replied that I didn't have any money and they talked some more in German and then she said, 'He says that's ok.' For some time I thought he agreed to teach me because of my talent but I now realize that he couldn't have known whether I had any talent at all. He must have accepted me because he wanted to paint me, which he did because I am in about six paintings. In those days, I would get on a streetcar carrying my still wet paintings, go to his studio and he would comment on them then pick up a paintbrush and apply corrections with black paint. One of the first paintings I took to show him was of adults riding on a merry-go-round. He looked at it and said, 'Women don't go there?' and I realized all the people in the picture were men. He liked to have fun with me but he was always very insightful. I went on digesting things he said for many years afterward."

"Usually, after some discussion of my work he would say, 'Now we drink,' and we would get into another streetcar and go to a very gaudy bar that he liked and drink Scotch. He didn't speak English and I didn't speak German so we communicated in bad French. Eventually we got so we could speak fairly fluently, we joked that we spoke in "Scotch". It was a nice friendship. He was aware of the dark side of life but my experience of him was very joyous. He had a good sense of humour and made many jokes and liked teasing me about things. He was interested in what I thought about everything. After listening to me comment on something he would say, 'Well you know a few things, but not everything.' I was twenty-two at the time and of course looking back on it I didn't know much about anything. I remember I was trying to stop smoking and he offered me a cigarette. When I refused, he said 'Mary, life isn't so important that you can't smoke.'"

I have seen pictures of you from that time and you had a unique quality. Do you think it was your appearance that captured Beckmann's interest?

"I think I must have had something at that time with the long black hair, a certain look that attracted him. Max had a personal iconography of people that he painted that he thought of as archetypes and I think I must have in some way fit that mold for him." Mary gets up to get a paragraph she herself wrote about Beckmann. She reads, 'The most striking aspect of his character was his identification with mythic concepts and figures. I think the people he embraced as friends and lovers in his life bore a marked resemblance to these mythical figures that only he recognized. In some way unknown to me I must have passed the test and entered into that fellowship because I do appear as a model in several significant paintings of or about women, probably the most famous being *The Fisherwomen*.'"

"It is probably what gave me the courage to go and see him. I had seen paintings he had done of people and I felt I looked a little like those people and I thought maybe he would accept me because of that. But I didn't know how much of an education it was going to be. I think our friendship continued for a lot of reasons. This was his first experience with America for one thing, and I was young and interested in art. I think the combination fascinated him, and the fact that Gil and I were newlyweds and Gil was interested in art. Max met my husband and did drawings of us both and we are in a painting he called, *The Rapps* and in his diary he refers to me as Mary Rapps so people who are writing about him have looked for me as Mary Rapps. I finally put up a web site that ended the confusion. As a result, I was contacted by a woman named Lynette Roth who was working on a book about Max' years in St. Louis and she came to interview me. An archivist from Munich also found me so I made a trip to Germany a couple of years ago and had a truly wonderful time. I saw a lot of Max' work that I didn't know. He had three big retrospective shows recently, one in Basil, another in Leipzig where he was born, and one in Frankfurt. I couldn't go this time because Gil isn't well and I can't leave him but there are pictures of me as a young woman in the Leipzig and the Frankfurt catalogues."

Beckmann's paintings often have a profile of him included somewhere in the frame. I get the sense of a person trying to discover what life is about.

"This is exactly right. He describes it as looking for his true self. He was terribly concerned with the architecture of the painting and of the space and did some remarkable things with it. Some of his compositions are so complex and interesting. He was a major influence obviously and yet my work is not like his. I don't know how many painters have shaped me. I have looked at paintings all my life and it is now so well digested that I really couldn't identify who made the biggest impression. I know what kind of paintings affect me most deeply, like that wonderful Rousseau of the sleeping figure with the lion. I love that. The mythic part has always appealed to me. And I like abstraction although I wouldn't be satisfied doing it. I always have to go back to some figurative references. Most landscapes I see around me don't interest me that much unless they have some really striking compositional aspect in them. My paintings always include the human figure, perhaps because I studied anatomy very intensely. While I was in Pennsylvania I studied sculpture and for many years I did only sculpture. I did portraiture in sculpture as a source of income for many years, until I came down here. That got to be more of a job than a pleasure because often I was working for a committee doing a sculpture of a deceased bank president from very bad pictures."

How did you make your way to San Miguel?

"We first came here in 1964. Friends had talked about it and the Instituto still attracted many artists. There were some good instructors here in those days. Stirling Dickinson had done a lot to build up the Instituto as a reputable school and the American woman who married into the Canal family did a good job of managing it after Stirling left. We didn't stay long that first time. It was many years later in 1990 that we finally moved here for good. Gil and I made a lot of moves for reasons related to his work but it was my decision to move to San Miguel and I have never regretted it."

Can you tell me a little about the places you lived?

"When I was pregnant with my first child, my daughter, we moved to Birmingham, Alabama. I didn't have a lot in common with my neighbours and Gil was away a lot so I was lonely. Not long after my daughter was born, our beautiful collie was poisoned. We were miserable there and so after looking around we found Fairhope, Alabama. We were in Fairhope the first time for almost ten years. My son was born there and I made some good friends, friends I still visit."

In present day America where capitalism is king, Fairhope on Mobile Bay in southern Alabama sounds a little like a village out of a fantasy. The town was founded in 1894 as a single tax colony by a small group of people who wanted to ensure that the residents would have an equal share in the common property. They purchased the land together and divided it into long-term lease holds so that all interests in the land would remain equal.

"Over the years Fairhope had attracted a lot of interesting people because of its history and also there was a progressive school there in the John Dewey tradition called the Marietta Johnson School of Organic Education. The town is located on the bay and when it was being developed it had been gorgeously landscaped. Now I suppose it is more of a resort, still very lovely. As much as I liked Fairhope, I was never politically comfortable in Alabama with all the segregation problems and so later we moved to Memphis and were there when Martin Luther King was assassinated so we lived through a lot of the turmoil. It was traumatic. Many times during our marriage I would try to get established in the local artistic community, opportunities arose but my husband would have to move for career reasons and so we would pick up and go. We were like turtles, carrying our furniture on our backs from place to place. We went from Memphis to Atlanta and then back to Fairhope. Gil said he wanted to go back there where we had been relatively happy and we lived there for another ten years until Gil's health began to decline. He was a heavy drinker for many years. In 1990 when our finances got to the critical stage, I made the decision to move to San Miguel. You can have live-in care here which is marvelous with Gil's health as it is. He has been blind for the past ten years and recently has been suffering from dementia. In terms of my work, San Miguel has been very productive for me. I have met wonderful people and I have made lots of international contacts."

"I am a pretty independent person who has always needed to be strong. I wouldn't call myself a feminist although I do believe in equal pay for men and women. I am definitely an optimist. My husband has struggled with depression and it would be impossible if we were both depressed. I can't say I feel very optimistic about the state of the world right now but in my own daily life, I feel very fortunate. My work still excites me and keeps me entertained. I never know how a painting will develop when I begin. I enjoy seeing things through the eyes of an artist. Sometimes I am just doing the necessary chores, shopping, what have you, I may be picking up groceries and the colour or the shape of the fruit will catch my eye and I will think, 'Oh, I must use that.' I love having the freedom to create what I want without worrying too much about sales. I never get bored with the artistic life and the work I am doing. I am still discovering things that amaze me. It's never dull. It has not ever become routine for me."

What are you working on now?

"Right now I seem to be doing a series of farewell pieces and I think that is influenced by Gil's condition. I'm suddenly aware of how old we are. I do have aches and pains when my aged skeleton seems to be saying, 'I don't know about all this'. At my age I guess what I'm doing has to do with end of life feelings but who knows, my mother lived to be almost one hundred."

Will you have a show when these are finished?

"Oh yes. But I'm just getting started."

A couple of weeks later, I arranged to meet Mary at her studio once more so we could review my completed article together. When I arrived she was busy sorting vintage photographs that had been left to her husband by one of his relatives, a man who had explored Mexico in the thirties pulling a very unusual looking metal mobile home behind his car. I thought the car and accommodation looked like something out of an old sci-fi movie. Mary confirmed that there were real risks driving in Mexico in those days. The roads were crude or non-existent and there were still banditos roaming the open land. The photographs before us were enlarged black and whites and they captured the dusty difficult lives of the people who lived in Mexico at that time. I was surprised to find I couldn't easily distinguish between the people in the photographs taken eighty years ago and the people who struggle to make a go of it in the countryside today. The clothes were a little different but the faces and the circumstances haven't changed.

Mary put the photographs aside and invited me to sit in a chair near her so I could read to her aloud. She made a few corrections as we went along and I was interested to see her intense concentration even while we paused occasionally so she could greet visitors to the gallery who came and went. It was clear that this woman may have been a young beauty but her intellect was equally persuasive when it came to attracting the attention of the exceptional men she has known. She smiled as she listened to the section about William Burroughs and said, "He was mad as a hatter. I remember he was obsessed with planning the perfect crime. He would plot robberies of various descriptions but my job was always the same. He'd say, 'Mary, you'll drive the getaway car.'"

I am about to leave when an English gentleman wearing a white shirt and cream coloured dress pants enters through the open door carrying a shopping bag in one hand and an elegant wooden cane in the other. He takes two potted plants from the bag and tells Mary they are about a minute away from being pot bound. They must be transplanted immediately. She thanks him and invites him to lunch on Sunday. He accepts, "Shall we say two o'clock?" He bows slightly before going out and I have the impression that this must be an engagement they have had many times before and that I feel faintly cheated that I have never had such a man in my life whom I could invite so comfortably to tea.

To pass Mary Rapp sitting at a table in the cafe in the Fabrica Aurora you might be inclined to think she is just another pleasant looking elderly lady, someone's great aunt or a well-to-do visitor, in Mexico for a few days vacation. Since I first came to San Miguel twelve years ago I have frequently found myself in the company of any number of individuals who turned out to be persons of considerable accomplishment or fame; a Russian pianist, a television personality, a best-selling author, a senator, a used car salesman who can sing like Louis Armstrong, one never knows who one will meet in this extraordinary town. It is best not to judge by appearances. Mary Rapp is a woman who has lived a life full of adventures and how would you know unless you asked?

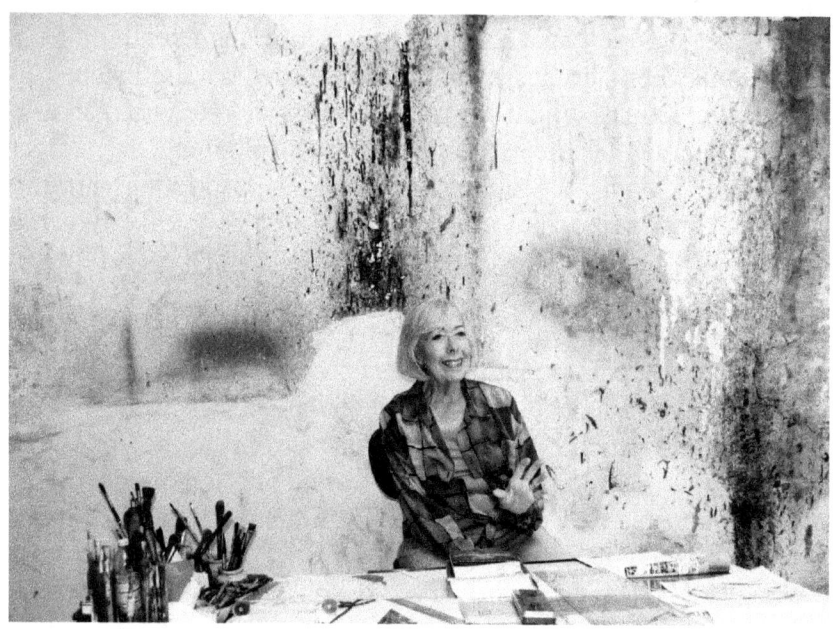

Tim Hazell

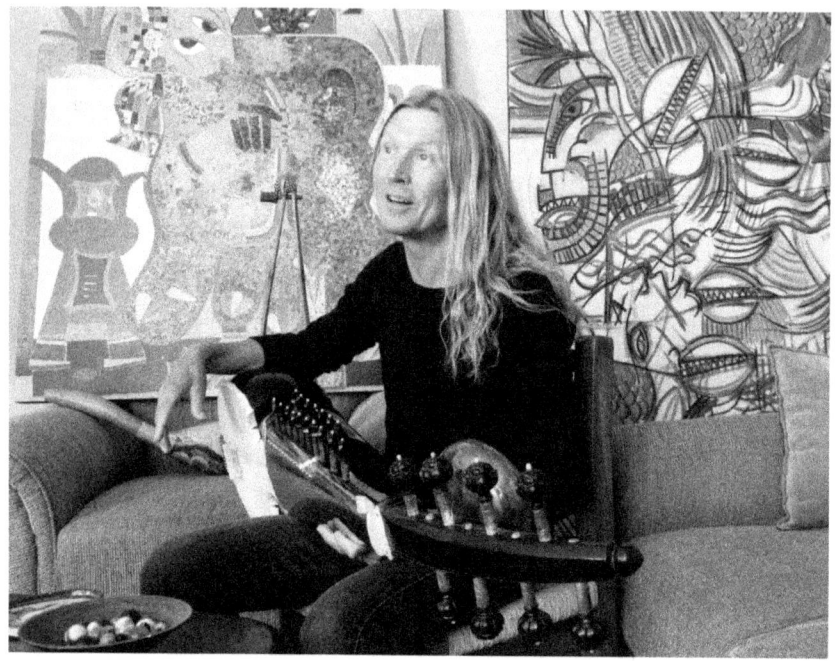

Few of us have artists as friends and even fewer of us know an artist personally who is wealthy, thanks to his art. Most artists live in obscurity and an artist's life, with only rare exceptions, is one of financial hardship. Tim Hazell has had his share of trying to make ends meet but today it is safe to say he is one of those uncommon individuals who successfully makes a living as an artist. In San Miguel among his fellows, he is known primarily as an interdisciplinary artist for he is a painter, a poet, a writer of books, a composer, a performer, and a teacher (www.tim-hazell.com). He does many things to support himself, embarking on ventures that originate in his imagination and are brought to light by his own initiative. If wealth can be defined as having resources in abundance, and if independence is taken to be self-reliance, then Tim Hazell is a good example of a man who has both.

I saw Tim for the first time when he opened the door of his home in a Mexican colonia of San Miguel to welcome me in. His youthful features are classically Scandinavian and on the morning in question, his long blond hair hung loosely to his shoulders. He has a trim athletic build that he maintains by running, an activity many would deem imprudent in a city of cobblestone streets and unexpected gaps in the sidewalks. I judged this unconventional looking artist would be difficult to get to know but nothing could have been further from the truth for within moments we were chatting comfortably about his connection to San Miguel and to its Mexican inhabitants. Tim invited me to follow him into the living room where we were surrounded by his extensive collection of musical instruments from a variety of time periods and cultures. He sat on the floor, I on the couch opposite, and so began a fascinating conversation.

Tell me more about your relationship with the Mexican community here. You were saying that San Miguel can appear to be a middle-class American ghetto unless you make an effort to look beyond that.

"When we first came here from Toronto, we were going to take a three month vacation, the first we had ever had outside of Canada. I met my wife in Montreal and we had spent thirty years in Canada when we came to the point where we wanted to just get away. We worked full time in the arts. Now we are doing a lot better but I am used to being on the edge of always having to work. When we came here in 1990 we were only going to stay for a short time but I immediately became involved in the music scene and because of that, we decided to extend our stay bit by bit, to see what would happen. I was working at a place called Pancho y Lefty's and doing whatever I could do. I was modeling on the side, anything that didn't require me to have my government papers because that took a while. I was paid through the local system of distribution of salary. I had to learn the language well enough to check my money and to go to the person who paid me and to deal with the other musicians so they wouldn't be leaving after two weeks and go somewhere else. It is often hard to keep people focused down here. I ended up at *Mama Mia*, a restaurant in town, and I was there for a long time. I was constantly having to deal with the Mexican community out of necessity. I started to show my paintings again in 1993 at a gallery run by Eugenia Lewis, a well-known Mexican artist. Louise and I had to seriously reinvent ourselves in order to be able to hang on here, as does anyone who really wants to live in a new culture. If we had gone to France, for instance, I would have tried to integrate with the French speaking population, not try to live on my own. I kept having opportunities come to me as a result of the Latin population, not the foreign population which tends to be retirees in San Miguel."

"The two countries that have been really good to me are Mexico and the U.S. Some time after we came to Mexico I got a National Endowment for the Arts grant to do a mural for the city of Metropolitan Nashville, involving the children. This was for the Centennial Arts Centre and the kids could work for a long time doing the basic under painting, or work for ten minutes and say I don't want to do this anymore, as they chose. Myself and another artist finished off the final details and it's there in a community centre. I got another grant the following year to use rap music as a vehicle to teach rhythm to black children from eight to twelve. After I got my Visa and O-1 classification, I worked at Watkins Institute of Design teaching portfolio preparation and aesthetic design and then on the side I worked at a number of other things such as unloading toys at Goodwill and stripping paint off buildings. To get to my various jobs I must have taken fifty buses in the course of a week. Often I was the only white person in the place but I have always been comfortable with that. So when I came back to Mexico with the

O-1 classification, I immediately got a position as professor of drawing at the Instituto. I became Director of Art a year later. Most of the students were women which shows how this culture is changing, and most of them were Spanish speaking so I had an assistant to help with my lectures. I'm only conversant in Spanish. Becoming fluent is a lifetime's endeavor. When I stepped down from my position at the Instituto, I was independent. The ongoing effect of having my papers has been to be frequently performing in front of the foreign population but tending not to have much contact with them apart from that."

Fifty years ago, artists came here from Canada and the U.S. with the intention of integrating into the Mexican community. Many of them married Mexicans and became citizens. Now most of the non-Mexican population comes to San Miguel not to have a Mexican experience necessarily, but to live in a small enclave with a good climate and an affordably high standard of living. Is there still a Mexican community of artists and musicians here that exists independent of the non-Mexican residents?

"Naturally there is a Mexican community here and there are artists and musicians who are expats who interact with that community. The rest of the non-Mexican population that is here now wouldn't have existed in San Miguel fifty years ago. If you weren't an artist, you wouldn't have been living here. The lack of integration today and how that has fragmented the community somewhat, has partly to do with the need years ago, of integrating simply to stay out of trouble. You couldn't walk into immigration and just get handed your right to stay here. I remember instances when the Director of Immigration had to be bribed with paintings. Maybe you got permission to stay, maybe you didn't. There was an element of risk and bravado in hanging on here. When I came, that still existed to some extent. I can only imagine in the fifties and sixties what was going on. If you crossed into the heart of darkness, if you came here to such a different place, more like India than like going to France, you had to be prepared for what I like to call reverse discrimination. I think we need to have a little bit of that coming from where we do. Also people like Leonard Brooks would have had to have a tremendous desire to put down roots here, like Gauguin going to Tahiti. In the old days you wouldn't have come here to retire. It would have been too difficult and too scary."

"Today, people come here because the climate is good, and usually they can afford a nice piece of real estate. It's a little cheaper especially when I think of how Louise and I live because we know our way around, we know the right markets to go to, although I don't think the people living in the up-scale areas really care about that much. They aren't going to the markets and they wouldn't eat the food even if they did go. What the expat community does, more than the Mexican, is support the scholarships. They give grants to the artists who are working. They buy the art. They are very valuable to have. The fabric of San Miguel has changed drastically in the last ten years but that isn't necessarily a bad thing. It's more cosmopolitan than it was. Being a successful artist here now, you have to be good. When I came you could say you were writing your memoirs, put a beret on your head, have a cappuccino and you were an artist. Now you've got to be really good."

Would you say when you moved here, your painting changed? You weave a lot of elements from other cultures into your work. Has that always been the case?

"When I was working in Toronto I tended to gravitate to cultures that were historically interesting to me. Egypt was one, also the Middle East, Asia, Africa, China, Sumer, and Japan, but there wasn't anything going on in my immediate external environment that I could identify with. A lot of the stuff I was doing then had some resemblance to what I am doing now because I was always headed instinctively to another place. I wanted the feeling of a living archeology around me. When we came here I immediately felt that the pallet that I had carried around in my head and used, I guess through force of will, was suddenly all around me everywhere like a hallucination. I just opened up. I didn't have to sit in my studio and try to imagine what it was like. It was right there. I was lucky enough to be invited to do a recording with a group here called Collar del Viento, The Wind's Necklace and we recorded in the studio of another Torontonian named Ken Bassman who co-produced the project. The group was formed as part of a program organized by Guillermo Mendez, a very interesting person, to encourage children from the Mexican community to learn to play native instruments that were collected from Pozos by Dr. Morton Stith. We were members of a committee that inaugurated the poetry room at the Biblioteca in 2002. I brought Collar del Viento into the poetry reading because we were going to study native poetry from the Americas so the music seemed a natural extension. I was fascinated by the instruments and then I got to meet the adult group Caracol de Fuego from Pozos." Tim gets up to retrieve a photograph. "Here we are in concert. I was asked to join after sitting in with them on a number of occasions and I was allowed to wear the native costume. I jumped at the opportunity. This is one of our dancers, Coyote, who is the sweetest man. He is wearing traditional Chichimeca dress. This is a living archeology, the real McCoy. This is why we are in Mexico. Here is another picture of myself and a colleague, Nestor Vargas in front of Canada de la Virgen, the pyramid that has recently been excavated and is just fourteen miles from here. We're in the sacrificial square of the Toltecs with the ancient instruments in front of that huge pyramid. That's San Miguel for you." Tim speaks with the enthusiasm of an explorer who has encountered an original civilization and neither fears it nor wants to conquer it. He clearly loves Mexico, not simply for its irrepressible present but for its long and complicated past.

"I was lucky enough to get involved with the natives, learn their mythology. Their religion became a cornerstone for me because I have always had faith but had never been able to articulate my belief system which is essentially totemic, shamanistic. There is Christianity in there but it is melded into Huichol ideas about creation. So in relation to my own work, my own growth as an artist, it was an incredible opportunity because this is an Indian nation. The native peoples are not off in enclaves. All the Mexicans to a greater or lesser extent, are Indians. There are 62 living languages spoken in Mexico. N'ahuatl, the language of the Aztecs is spoken by over a million people. What an opportunity for an artist when certainly in North America, the Indians are largely living on reservations. To my knowledge, Caracol de Fuego is the only group in Mexico that has integrated a non-native member. It has influenced my painting, my poetry, my music."

"My brother is a very successful architect in Toronto. My other brother was production designer for the X Files for four years and has worked with many well-known film people and has done all kinds of great work from Vancouver. So the conversation that they are having is a conversation that has a response from the culture that they have chosen to live in. We just took off artistically when we came here and I think it is the result of having that conversation with the right culture for us. My wife is French Canadian and we've been married now for more than thirty-five years. She has always symbiotically been with me in every way. We both spoke French when we came here which helped because I was used to her Latin feeling about interacting with life. That Latin element coming from Louise's side of the family was perfectly congruent in this culture. I saw a continuum here and never felt that I needed to be bonded with other people from either Canada or the United States. It has just been a very nurturing experience and fundamental to my career. I have had incredible opportunities. I don't think that would have happened had we stayed put, not because it can't happen to other people but I don't think with our sensibilities, it would have taken root in the same way."

Mexico was conquered by the Spanish five hundred years ago. Have the Mexicans suffered the same loss of identity that the native peoples further north have experienced?

The difference in Mexico, when you look at the conquest, and there were many conquests in Mexico not just the Spanish but the Aztecs overthrowing the Toltecs, the Chichimeca invasion, and so on; the difference is that Mexico is used to being drenched in blood. It is a characteristic of the country. When the Spanish came to Mexico, Mexico was an urban civilized place. Tenochtitlan was one of the wonders of the world. It's estimated that Tenochtitlan, which is now Mexico City, might have had a population of more than two hundred and fifty thousand. It had canals, and public toilets, and zoos. I think one of the things that enraged the Spaniards when they came, and what prompted them to thoroughly destroy everything, was the shockingly high level of civilization they encountered, equal to anything they had in Europe. Because it was an urban population, there was tremendous exploitation but the average soldier who came during the conquest, and following it, integrated with the population. What happened in North America with the hunter/gatherer societies that were widely dispersed over large tracts of land was different. Their traditions were oral, they were the traditions of a people on the move. Because of that they were easier to subdue, they were easier to contain, they were easier to eliminate. Here, even though the Spanish were putting thousands of people to work in the mines, including Mayan princes, the local population introduced a new generation as soon as the old one died. It just wasn't possible to become anything but 'la raza nueva'. The Spanish ended up being the new race, the integration of Spanish and Indian blood. Many Indians can't remember what their lineage was because preserving that knowledge wasn't encouraged by the church. It's changing now. There used to be a feeling that being native was kind of an embarrassment, unchristian. There was also a feeling that the Spanish were evil because they were of the conquest. I'm pontificating because I'm not Mexican but there is a duality that exists here, a darkness, a complexity in how Mexicans react to things that is born out of this tug of war. Is Malinche good? Is Malinche bad? How does Malinche relate to the Virgin of Guadalupe? (Malinche was a Nuhua woman who became Cortez' mistress.) How do these cultural elements relate to the old religion? How do they relate to Catholicism? Certainly the music and the traditions that exist in Mexico are very strong. The feeling of national pride is very strong. You ask a Mexican who he is and he has an immediate answer. It doesn't matter whether he makes an enormous salary or he is making twenty dollars a week, which many Mexicans do. They know their place, they know their traditions, their festivals, their saints. They may be carrying a banner that has the Virgin of Guadalupe on it, meanwhile they are dressed like Aztecs. There is an underlying continuum of tradition here which has largely been lost in other parts of North America, perhaps with the exception of some groups in British Columbia although I don't think even they were civilized to the same extent. I mean the Mayans were the ancient Greeks of the new world. I do have to say that on the one hand there is some reluctance to openly celebrate the old traditions while at the same time there is a tremendous unity with those traditions. That's why I say Mexico is an Indian nation. It is absolutely."

You mentioned that when you taught at the Instituto, many of your students were women and you think this reflects a changing culture. Could you elaborate?

"The students that I was working with and knew well were going to have careers, they were going to limit the size of their families. Their parents were from backgrounds obviously that could afford to pay for four years of university. They represented what today in Mexico you see replacing the agrarian population. People come to Mexico and wonder why some families on the farms have so many children. They simply don't realize that with a large family, things get done. But these women were after a career in the arts, they were aggressively after things that would have been exclusively male, would have been considered unfeminine even thirty or forty years ago. It was an interesting energy that surprised me because when I took on the job at the Insitituo, I didn't know what to expect, who my students would be, what being a professor there would be like. It was an incredible experience for me. Underneath the floor of one of the drawing studios, in a building that dates from 1726, was an Otomi graveyard dating from the tenth century, with the skeletons curled up with the pots and everything else. Again there was that feeling of layers being allowed to stand. In North America it is such a shame, especially for the youth, not to have a chance to see the older sidewalks, the older layers of the patina. It's all swept away and replaced with new stuff. You benefit from occasionally being in societies that first of all value other things besides materialism and secondly, are visibly part of traditions that are thousands of years old and are still given credence. You have to accept fundamentally that there are other societies with completely different value systems and infrastructures that function perfectly well. The old rationale that if it isn't from our industrial society it isn't worthwhile, that obviously everyone must be striving toward an opportunity to put on that tie and get rid of all that quaint stuff and become really modern, is complete nonsense. It makes us the adolescents of the world. It is an attitude we need to change if we are going to be taken seriously. You walk up to a woman here who has collected her cactus paddles for the day, she looks at the person with the two cameras and she's not impressed. Real respect for other cultures is a fundamental leap of thinking that frighteningly few members of society find it natural to make. They better start making it because the Third World is on our doorstep and it is being misinterpreted. It is stereotyped. We have plenty to worry about in our own societies today which are full of cracks and hypocrisy. Let's let the world in, seventy-five percent of which is the Third World. More people should come here. More people should look at the clockwork mechanisms of Mexican society and ask questions about why it is so different, why it doesn't have to be like where they came from. Hopefully that will happen."

Tim's words came back to me recently when I was enjoying the pageantry of a celebration in San Miguel in which men, women, and children dressed in brightly coloured native costumes danced to traditional drums. It was exhilarating to see these ancient customs being practiced with such reverence and joy. I was surprised then to hear the person beside me say that the Indians would be better off learning how to use computers rather than to waste their time with outdated rituals. I think I will let Wade Davis, the Canadian ethnobiologist respond as he so eloquently did when asked about the significance of other cultures.

"We (Westerners) reflexively think of ourselves as the cutting edge of history. And if the measure of success is technological wizardry, we would no doubt come out on top. But if the criteria shifted, for example, to the capacity to thrive in a truly sustainable manner, the Western way of life would come up short. We, for example, celebrate the individual at the expense of family and community. In most of the world, the community still prevails, for the destiny of the individual remains inextricably linked to the fate of the collective.

Consider the manner in which we impact the natural world. *Extreme* would be one word for a culture or civilization that does little to curtail industrial processes that threaten to transform the biochemistry of the atmosphere. This is not to say that we are wrong, but rather to suggest humbly that our way of life, brilliant and inspired in so many ways, is obviously not the paragon of humanity's potential. It is only one possibility. These other cultures are not failed attempts to be us; they are unique manifestations of the spirit – other options, other visions of life itself.

Some people say: 'What does it matter if these cultures fade away?' The answer is simple. When asked the meaning of being human, all the diverse cultures of the world respond with 10,000 different voices. Distinct cultures represent unique visions of life itself, morally inspired and inherently right. And those different voices become part of the overall repertoire of humanity for coping with challenges confronting us in the future. As we drift toward a blandly amorphous, generic world, as cultures disappear and life becomes more uniform, we as a people and a species, and Earth itself, will be deeply impoverished."   Parsell, Diana. "Explorer Wade Davis on Vanishing Cultures." <u>National Geographic News</u>, June 28, 2002.

I don't know what it is about airplane travel but I have had the misfortune to be belted in beside men eager to tell me about their mines in northern Russia, their dams on the rivers of British Columbia, their bear hunting kills, their off-shore tax shelters. I no longer have any illusions about Davis' message being heard by the people doing the most damage. I used to believe each of us could make a difference, as the words of that little Sunday school song assure us, "You in your small corner, and I in mine." Experience has made me a skeptic.

In Juan's Café I happened to pick up a book from the Artes de Mexico series, No. 161, Ano XIX. This one was titled **Vida y Arte de Los Huicholes, Segunda Parte, El Arte**. It turned out to be a book published in 1973 about the indigenous peoples who live west and a little north of San Miguel, the Huicholes. In it, the author Ramon Mata Torres writes about god's eyes, which, on the surface, are simple weavings done on two sticks. I used to make them with my classes of elementary school children. To the Huichole people, a god's eye is an offering. Torres describes one god's eye he found in a cave. "The rhombus had four colors and was an offering a father had made for his four-year-old child. The colors, from the center out, were black, blue, white, and red. Black is the color of Tatei Aramara, the Pacific Ocean, where the great serpent is, the serpent that devours man. Blue is the color of Rapawiyeme, Lake Chapala. It symbolizes the south and is the color of water and rain. White is the color of clouds. The pieces of cotton placed on gods' eyes or in prayer bowls are pleas for rain. They represent clouds. Red is for the east, the region of

Parietekua, where the god peyote abides. It is there that the most sacred places of all are found: Tatei Matinieri, Tuimaneu, Kauyumari Muyehue, Wirikuta and Reunar. The colors of arrows, prayer bowls and gods' eyes for the most part represent gods or sacred places. According to the Huicholes, with colors one prays and converses with the gods."

It is no small thing this connection to nature, to beauty, to the human story. The realization that these and other objects such as I see in the local market are not mere crafts gives me such pleasure that I ask myself, not for the first time, why it is that to have a sudden insight into some aspect of existence usually gives rise to a feeling of exuberance. Perhaps the act of flinging open a door in one's mind allows us to recognize that the mental territory we had previously inhabited was stuffy and confining and that by being in possession of this new awareness, our vision has expanded to admit fresh possibilities. In a so-called modern world where the horizon seems to have moved forward and down, I believe artists, more than any other community, invite us to embrace a broader perspective.

Some artists have described their creative activity as an escape to a place of refuge. For others, the desire to take up art as a career originated in childhood. Where do you think your creative drive originated?

"I was born in Sweden but we lived in England and in Poland as well. My father was English and a diplomat so he traveled a lot. I hardly ever saw him. My mother was Swedish and came from a very aristocratic family. She was naturally creative. She was able to paint, she wrote, she conceptualized very well. She created a beautiful environment for us. There was never an emphasis on acquiring things, rather we had input and discipline that encouraged us to do something interesting and to live up to her expectations which were formidable. She was quite a woman. We came to Canada when I was five. My parents separated and my father went back to England in 1965 so my mother had to support the family. She became a very successful private nursery school teacher. She was named nursery school teacher of the year in Quebec. I worked with her for ten years, going to the school three times a week doing art and music. I saw her do things to make a living that involved making beautiful things. Often the night before school, the living room floor would be covered with collages, or other projects she was planning to use with the children the next day. It just never occurred to me that it was going to be a hobby to do something like that. I started to paint when I was eight. I never did anything arts related that wasn't serious. My brother was an architect long before he put a label on it. My other brother gravitated toward working with his hands, did everything related to set design, and now makes a very good living in the film business. We all got that I think, from seeing the example of a person who had to struggle very hard with four kids but found personal satisfaction and a way to support us all, in being creative. My sister Joanna is not involved in the arts at all, yet she is a champion rower and I think athletics is an art form too. She's one of the most creative people I've ever interacted with in terms of what she gets out of life. I've learned a lot from Joanna, as I have from my wife Louise, about being a more complete human being, because I take creativity for granted. Every profession is honourable if you put into it what you want to do, give it integrity, give it discipline. The person who picks up my garbage has the face of a poet. What is dishonourable is to do something half way and try to convince people you have done a good job. Being in the arts, living the way I live, as 1% of the population, I better be prepared to justify it. I better be prepared to say I am contributing something valuable to society. If I can't do that then somebody else should be where I am. Maybe that kind of attitude came from a family where the creative process was visible. There was nothing mystical about it"

My husband drives to work every day past two pieces of art. One he says looks like a pile of beer cans but the other is a sculpture of a group of people trying to erect a large obelisk

by pulling together and he likes looking at it as he goes by. It has meaning for him. Do you believe that art has to have a meaning?

"I do. Even if it is deconstructivism, it has to mean something. In that case even a pile of beer cans is valid as long as it is an attempt to reflect a process in a serious way. The problem with a pile of beer cans is that too often it doesn't do that. It is merely something that is flung out thoughtlessly. John Cage was fundamental in contemporary music and one of his compositions consists of feeding hay to the piano. Even so, the man was profound and could back up everything he did with a great deal of thinking and dedication. Art is always comprehensible if it is good. The problem with art that borders on chaos, to me, is that most of the time there is no central idea behind it and therefore it doesn't communicate. The artist might argue that's because you don't get it, but the fact is great art communicates, but it's that one pile of beer cans, not the other hundred, that's doing it."

I ask Tim to talk about his own painting for a moment. We agree that we like the large piece on the wall in the room where we sit.

"This is a light hearted painting. It is the result of a number of happy connections that I made within the pictorial space. It might not have been a success but I really don't have time to spend on one piece. If it doesn't work, then the canvas is gone and I have a new piece going because I can't afford the luxury of being too contemplative. Most of the time I am so busy trying to paint, doing research, writing, trying to think about the music that has to be completed. I tend to be very on when I am working because I am always bathed in it anyway. If I was to take a break and then try to conceive of something like this, it probably would be more difficult for me to pull it off, but I'm just all over the place anyway so I don't even think about it. I have my coffee, there's the canvas, get to work. You've got to provide for your family. What are you going to come up with this time? Ideas are what I work with."

As the morning becomes early afternoon, I wonder aloud whether living in San Miguel these past twenty years has met Tim's needs. Does San Miguel still provide him with the stimulation he desires?

"I value San Miguel immensely. I like this house. I like the simplicity of it. Its not ours, we rent it. As a facility it suits me fine. I would like to live by the ocean a bit more. Most of the projects I get now are international. I don't depend on San Miguel for the kind of work I am doing in Nashville, for instance. I think San Miguel has become more cosmopolitan which means that if I am living here, I am easy to look up. The climate is good. It's a little too cold in the wintertime for me but we'll always have a foot here. I have another composer I'm going to be working with from New York who has won an Emmy and has worked with everybody from Paul Simon to Pavarotti. If someone of that caliber says they are going to work with me, the project is automatically slated for a larger forum. San Miguel integrates itself perfectly with the United States. There is a lovely strong flow here between the two cultures, more so than with Canada. We have been lucky enough in the last three years to have grants come in from the U.S. that have changed our way of living. I'm working on my second book with a music journalist who's up in the States doing research and I'm down here plugging away. It hasn't stopped me from living in San Miguel. I would like to go to places like Indonesia. I'd love to visit India, but I think that will come without my being dissatisfied with anything. It will come because I am naturally assuming that any artistic product shouldn't only be of interest to people in one particular place. If I have any chance of a future at all, what I do should be of interest to other people in other cultures."

"I went back to Canada last summer to scatter my mother's ashes. I had a very good visit with my family but I was glad to come home to San Miguel. You know Mexico is a heck of a place. It is teetering on the verge of disaster. It always will. It will never be unified. It will always have problems. It will always be lurching forward. It will never be a linear place but on a spiritual level and a cultural level the advantages here are profound."

Do you feel an obligation to put something back into the culture that has given you so much?

"Louise and I have always been involved in projects that required resources of faith in the outcome, that needed interaction with people not necessarily for immediate remuneration even though most of the time we have been together we have really had nothing except what we could go out and try to get for ourselves. I believe most of the artists here who are doing really meaningful work with their own creative processes are inherently inclined to want to give back to the culture because it is an extension of how they feel about their surroundings, how they have embraced the Mexican community. They want to be integrated and want to be taken seriously by it, not the other way around. I think when one looks at the possibility of remuneration in the arts, when you are going after those grants, you have to satisfy those people on the committee that you don't just have a lengthy curriculum. You absolutely have to have that, but the project has to be historically relevant, culturally relevant, possibly too has an emphasis on how it is going to educate people, enlighten people. What are they going to get out of giving you that money and it better not simply be because it is going to help you produce a lot of work and live better. They expect that you are interested in that but there has got to be more to it. People who think they need only consider their own desires are short changing themselves and in the long run they are not going to benefit from the work that they do. They might get away with things for a while but to get something out of life that has a deeper meaning, you've got to be willing to give back. Maybe there is another artist out there who has great ideas, who could use that shot in the arm to write that play, or there's some kid that needs a square meal. Those of us who have been doing this for a while can make a difference. There is nothing like the thrill of helping someone and also putting food on your own table. We don't own anything, we're custodians, so we have an obligation to give back."

If I needed any further proof that Tim is true to his word, I had only to attend a recent concert in which he and Ed Osman's son Turkkan played a composition they had been collaborating on for some months. There beside Tim on the portable stage in St. Paul's church stood the beautiful young man whose image I had first seen in his father's painting. "Pure love," Ed had said. As I listened to the compelling, rhythmic music, I witnessed a father's creative energy embodied in the son. At the intermission, it was announced that the evening's proceeds would be used to further Turkkan's musical education in New York. Tim Hazell assured the audience that the talented violinist, at the age of twenty-one, had been a full partner in the creative process and that the two would continue to work closely together. Walking home on that warm spring evening, my small corner of the world at least, was perfect.

Leonard Brooks

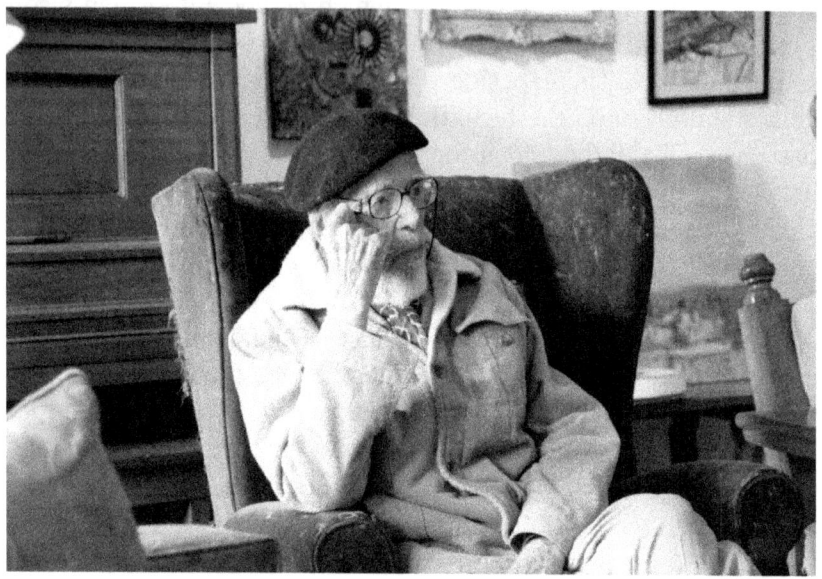

I attended an art opening last night at the Fabrica Aurora, a former textile factory that operated for ninety years and was once the largest employer in San Miguel. In 1991, after a so-called "free trade" agreement with the United States allowed large amounts of cotton from that country to flow into Mexico, La Aurora was unable to compete and the factory was forced to close. Ten years later the Fabrica opened its doors once again, the owners having converted the former factory into high-end stores and art galleries. The opening I was attending was a retrospective of works by Leonard Brooks, a Canadian who came to San Miguel more than sixty years ago and because I had recently interviewed Leonard, I wanted to be present for this auspicious event. Leonard has told me he likes to stay clear of collectors and galleries in order to preserve his energy so I am delighted to see he has come in person to witness the occasion.

He is handsome in a dark green jacket and the customary navy beret, and looks youthful despite his ninety-seven years. The paintings include early oils depicting the streets of San Miguel, some watercolour landscapes, one of which I would love to own but it is beyond my means, a variety of still lifes, and some wonderful collages. My favourite painting is of a vase of flowers on a table beside a sleeping Siamese cat, Leonard's much loved Nobby, with an open paint box in the foreground. It has a friendly informality that is emphasized by the relaxed brush strokes and ocher colours. In front of one of the collages, I ask an interesting looking Mexican man why he has come this evening. He tells me that he is an artist and that ten or eleven years ago he showed his work to Leonard Brooks and Leonard suggested he try collage, that his painting style indicated that he could be successful doing collage and it had turned out to be true. "No one had ever looked at my work that way. Once when we were discussing one of my paintings, Leonard asked me, 'What do you think is the most important point in this painting?' and we talked about what it was and why. He is a great artist. A very generous man." It was not the first time I had heard such praise for Leonard Brooks from a fellow artist and I am heartened to know that here in central Mexico, out of the limelight, this elegant man has lived a large life of genuine significance to those who matter most, his neighbours.

Some months earlier I had been invited to Leonard's house for the first time through the good graces of a mutual friend. Leonard had agreed to spend some time speaking with me although his sister-in-law Beverly who lives with him, had cautioned me on the phone not to tire him by staying too long. On a spring morning I was admitted to the extensive, jungle-like garden by Alfredo Arzola, Leonard's driver, caretaker, friend, and as I was to learn, a gifted carver and painter who Leonard has nurtured since Alfredo was orphaned at the age of fourteen. Beverly herself welcomed me into the main house and led me into a spacious room where a wall of large windows cast a filtered light onto a slim figure at work at an easel. His true proportions were hidden by many layers of clothing and when he shook my hand, I noticed he wore fingerless gloves. He greeted me warmly and invited me to sit beside him on the overstuffed couch in the centre of the room, our backs to the windows and facing the crowded bookshelves that lined the opposite wall. There was a table, a couple of comfortable chairs and everywhere were paintings - on the floor, on the walls, perched on top of ledges, and leaning against the stone of the large fireplace. A snoozing Siamese cat lounged in the sun. The room was cluttered but the impression was of industry rather than neglect.

I quickly discovered that a conversation with Leonard Brooks has little chronology. Whatever linearity this narrative now contains, is the result of my own editing, because from the moment I entered the room, Leonard lead and I followed. He is accustomed to being the maestro and to being sought out by those wishing to document his achievements. His great age gives him a special status, a rare historical perspective, and the right to say fuck it whenever he wants. But in all the time we spent together, there was never a hint of arrogance, just the evenhanded tolerance of someone who has lived a very long, very full life, and besides, where does one begin in such a landscape?

Leonard Brooks was born in England in November, 1911 and came to Canada when he was just a year old. His father returned to England to fight in the first World War, taking the family with him. After the war they came back and settled in Toronto. At the age of eighteen Leonard went to Europe on a cattle boat. "I wanted to get out there and be an artist the way Orwell and all those guys did in those early days. I went to Paris and London and lived somehow. I had no money. Slept in the parks, made some friends. Earle Birney, the Canadian poet was a great friend of mine. We met again during the war and he later came down and stayed with me here in Mexico. I went to Spain and when I got back I was broke so I went into the Toronto Star and sold them an article on bull fighting. That's how Hemingway got started. I walked out of there with 35 bucks and I thought my god I could be a Hemingway!"

"I've always liked to write and I have always loved music. I've been playing the violin since I was a child. I cried when I first heard a violin and begged my parents to get me one and they did. I had lessons but it was my own dedication that made me a decent violinist. I became a painter by kicking around with artists and by doing it. When I was a young man there was a teacher at school who took me aside and said, 'You have brains. Use them. Do what you want to do, but do it.' It was very important because I was rather lost. All life is difficult but if you start believing you are an artist, then you should hope to god you are left alone so you can go and do it. You have to find your own way. Artists, musicians, writers, all of them generally know at an early age that that's what they have to do. My mother and father were not involved in the arts. They say one of my grandfathers liked to draw but we all came from ordinary people in Bristol. I really don't know why but I've been driven all my life by this business of being a creator in the arts. And I've done it pretty damn well. I am amazed myself that I was able to do it."

Leonard met his wife Reva in Toronto and they married in 1936. He was working as an independent artist and he credits her with helping him get a job teaching at Northern Vocational School. He taught there until 1943 when he joined the Naval Reserve, first designing sets for Navy shows and then when he complained loudly that he had signed up to go overseas, he was sent to Ottawa and finally to the front as a war artist. "I went on every ship. I was the war correspondent for the government so I could go anywhere. I did literally hundreds of paintings and drawings. Now they are all in Ottawa." Leonard rises and goes to the bookshelf to retrieve his biography written by John Virtue in 2001. He opens it to some pictures. "Here is the kind of thing I painted for the Navy. Here I am going on board a German submarine. That picture is in the war museum. That's in Scapa Flow, the British naval base. That's me there and those are the

Germans waiting for me to come aboard. They had surrendered but I thought they were going to blow us all up."

When the war was over Leonard returned to Toronto but he didn't want to resume teaching. Instead he applied for a veteran's grant to study in San Miguel de Allende. His intention was to stay a year. "When Reva and I came to San Miguel there were no other Canadians. An American, Stirling Dickinson had come down first and there were fifteen American veterans here when I arrived but most of them were crazy. The war had driven them a little mad, but there were two or three nice guys and gradually we became part of the Mexican scene."

"In those days San Miguel was a quiet village. I guess some places had electricity but the house I lived in had nothing. A Mexican artist in town gave it to me practically rent-free and we lived there and I was very happy because I could paint all the time. I would go to the U.S. or Canada occasionally and give lectures or have exhibitions so I could afford to live. Then I started writing my books. I was always testing myself. I knew the Reinhold Publishing Company had published books about art already but I wrote to them and said they should write a more serious book of instruction for a more literate audience. They sent me a letter that got lost in the snow in Canada, that's a long story. It was eventually found. Anyway, it was from the publisher and it asked me to come to New York so I went and I met with the editor of this big company and he said, young man we like your idea do you think you could do this and I said of course but I wanted an advance. So I came back to Mexico and wrote it and it became a best seller. They asked me to do another on watercolour and another on oil. They were beautifully done but now those books are very scarce." He goes to the shelf again and gets a lovely hardcover book. "This one won Book of the Month for its design. I wrote this with all my paintings in it so they have been seen all over the world. It was published in 1957 and was called, *Watercolour – A Challenge*, and I did seven more books for them. They are all out of print now. So that was my writing career until Nobby took over." Nobby, Leonard's cat has become a published author himself with a book about his life as the companion of a distinguished artist.

Because Leonard Brooks is the last of his generation in San Miguel, he is without peers in the artistic community. I ask him to recall some of the members of his former circle of friends and he mentions James Pinto, Louis Ribak and his wife Beatrice Mandelman, Lothar Kestenbaum, and Joy Laville. There were many friendships among the musical community as well. "I played the violin all my life, professionally for a while. Little kids came here for lessons and their parents and the government finally asked me if I'd open a music department at Bellas Artes. I had that for thirty years. Some of my students have become quite famous. They're in Jack's book with photographs of them that Reva took. Tom Sawyer lived here for years, and Ken Harvey from California came and we played chamber music all the time, over in that corner there. We used to love playing. Tom and I used to drive over to Guanajuato to play in the violin section and we'd come back late at night. I stopped playing the violin three years ago because I wanted to save my energy for painting." Nobby meows and climbs up on my lap as Leonard continues. "None of those people are here now unfortunately. I met Diego Rivera."

What was he like?

"He was a powerful man. Siqueiros, the great painter and I became close friends. I met all the great artists. Siqueiros did something for Reva. He took many of her photographs and painted from them, so the Mexican government honoured her - something they wouldn't do in Canada or elsewhere." Leonard goes into the hallway and beckons me to come see a poster hanging on the wall displaying one of Reva's classic black and white photographs. It is of a Mexican woman looking into the camera with the same guileless honesty that one is accustomed to seeing in photographs by Diane Arbus. "Look at that. They had an exhibition of Reva's work in Siqueiros' house after he died. Imagine the Mexican government doing that. There's a great tradition, a respect for the artist. I met every president of Mexico. Mexicans are very fine people in the way they honour their artists. You mean something. You're a maestro."

Suddenly a huge smile lights Leonard's face. "Oh look who is coming." He reaches out to greet his housekeeper Carmen who is carrying a baby only a few months old. "Carmen's daughter had this little baby. Isn't she lovely? She must think, 'Here's that old guy again.' He laughs with delight and kisses a chubby little cheek. "Her mother is a girl we brought up in our house. They come in here, these men and women, some of them that I've brought up, with their beautiful little babies and the whole cycle begins again. That's part of the joy of being alive, the rebirth. Like those flowers out there in the garden that are just beginning to bloom. It's all very complicated." Leonard and I enjoy the baby a little longer until Carmen takes her out to the kitchen and I ask Leonard to tell me more about his art and the influence of San Miguel.

"I have been through different periods but I had my own style. Over the years I tried experimenting. I had a good basic training although I never went to art school. I learned from kicking around with artists in Paris and London and by doing it. Today there is terrible mediocrity in the art world. You can hang up a piece of string, an installation, and call it art. These young painters come to me and ask me how I paint like I do and I say, *paint*. They want to do something but they don't know how. They go to art school and they are told, don't learn to draw, don't learn to paint, but that is a bunch of crap. It's stupid. It is like writing a book with blank pages or picking up a violin for a couple of days and then making squeaky noises. Last week there was an article about four shoes hanging in a room and the critics went on about it, writing pages of jabbery words, talking absolute nonsense. I don't envy the young artists today. You need a basis of civilized thought. You can't dump centuries of great art. I don't talk about it too much because it sounds like old hat. The painting does the talking. A good painting doesn't need explaining anymore than it is necessary to explain a good book. I have a little Delacroix reproduction of a flower beside my bed and I look at it every morning. It talks to me visually. Delacroix painted his thoughts about that flower and I can feel what he thought. No words or critics could change this for me."

Leonard draws my attention to one of his own paintings resting on the fireplace mantel. It is a street scene, heartbreakingly perfect. "That's where I lived, on the end of Canal. I got Alfredo to drive me down the other day and I did a quick drawing and then I painted it. Today that house is painted bright colours but when I lived there it was still painted white, in the colonial style. That's the way old San Miguel was. In some ways it had more dignity I think."

I ask Leonard to tell me what he is thinking when he starts a painting like this one. "I'm thinking of the formal composition, the classic things to please your eye, the balance, the colour, all the things that make a good painting. That's the enjoyment of painting, like playing the violin. If a figure is not in the right place, I'll move it. It has to balance. You don't have to know about that as an onlooker but if you are looking at a good painting, you feel it is complete. If you look at any of the great artists' work they have that. They themselves may not even know why. They have a sensitivity. Like that one I'm doing of the lilies. Yesterday I put in that little bit of orange. I'll work on it for a few days until finally it will feel whole. I've torn it out of myself. That's the pleasure of it for me. It makes me feel good. That's the joy of painting."

He indicates a picture just behind another one of some calla lilies. "That one behind the lilies I did fifty years ago. I really love those flowers from up the hill. I could have sold that many times but I won't sell it. It gives me a lot of pleasure. San Miguel is a good place because it can still make you feel that way."

"So that was it, between the art and writing and the music I had no time to realize I was getting older and I think that is what kept me going, what keeps me going now. I get up early and come down here and work. I try to preserve my energies. I sleep a lot. I had trouble with my heart and had a pace maker put in. I had cataract surgery so my eyes are good. I paint without glasses. I'm doing pretty well for my years. Of course I miss Reva. She looked after me. She believed in me and helped me so much with her own creative drive. She had Alzheimer's in the last few years before she died and I wish I had understood that sooner... I've been a lucky man but I've always had to fight for it. I had a touch of drive and ambition and I had the brains to educate myself." Leonard is silent for a moment, before he speaks again. "I don't have very long to go. I paint everything now as if I won't be here tomorrow. It will be the best thing I ever did, you know, not for anybody else but for myself."

He has been a gracious host but I am aware of the hour and the need to respect Beverly's request. As our conversation draws to a close, Leonard invites me to take a tour of his home. "Reva and I built this house about 35 years ago. It is a beautiful piece of property. We are talking about making my studio a museum after I'm gone. Come out this way. We'll go for the grand tour."

Leading me through his large garden, in the diaphanous light Leonard Brooks looks more like a heroic Bilbo Baggins who has seen enough of the world beyond the shire, than a man of flesh and blood. I find myself overcome by sudden sadness, yet a short time later as I make my way down the cobblestone street, I am persuaded to believe it is true what they say about there being magic in San Miguel.

The Road goes ever on and on
Out from the door where it began.
Now far ahead the Road has gone,
Let others follow it who can!

Let them a journey new begin,
But I at last with weary feet
Will turn towards the lighted inn,
My evening rest and sleep to meet.

From The Old Walking Song; J.R.R. Tolkien; *The Fellowship of the Ring; George Allen & Unwin; 1954*

Leonard Brooks died in November, 2011 at the age of 100.

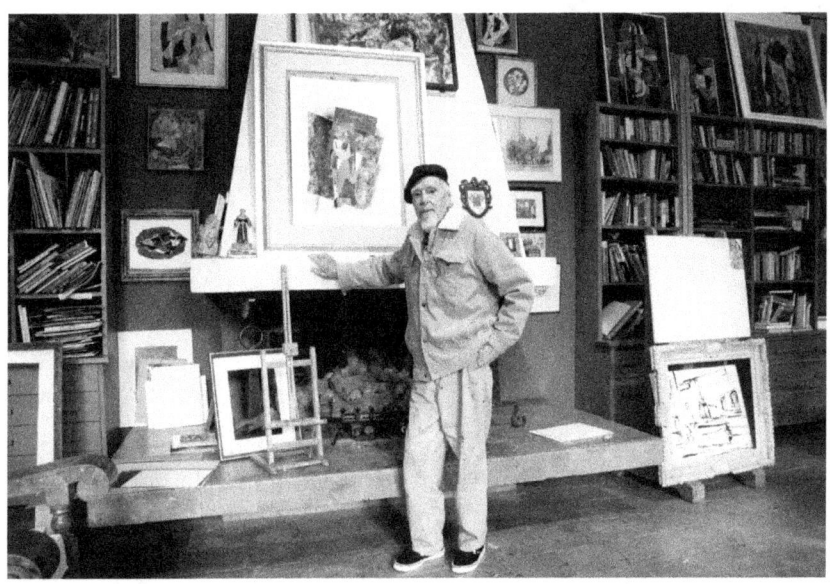

Tom and Donna Dickson

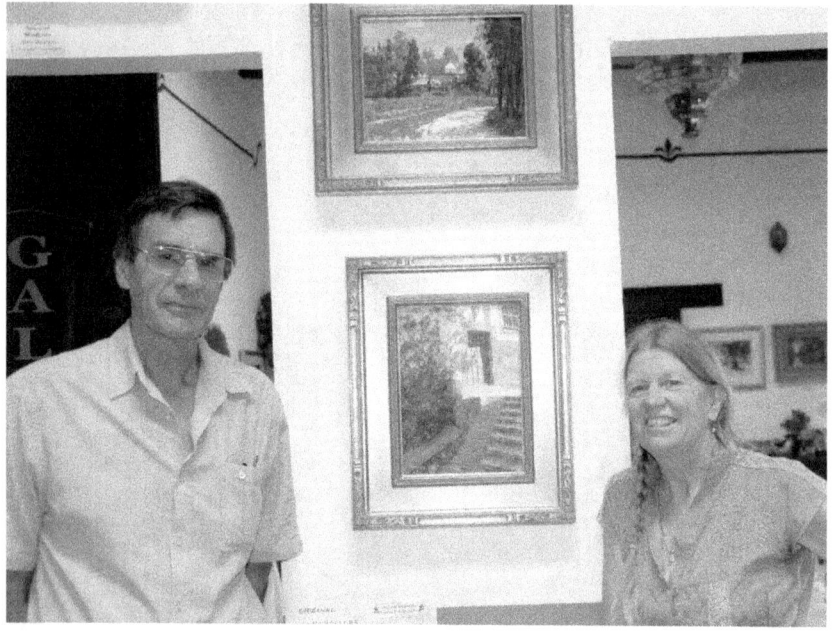

I was at a party some time ago where I got into a conversation with a man from the United States whose views largely differed from mine. We talked for most of the evening, exploring big topics like his expectations for his daughter and materialism and other related matters. After some lengthy time, his wife approached, was introduced, and reminded her husband it was time to go. As they departed, she added, "See dear, not all Canadians are boring." Not long after, I met an attractive Mexican woman carrying her young son in a Baby Bjorn pouch that sells in the U.K. for sixty pounds (I looked it up.). The woman and her brother are successful developers here in San Miguel. I mention her because when I told her I live in Victoria,

British Columbia she gushed, "Oh, that must be so boring!" She may have confused her adjectives as I do in my attempts to speak Spanish. Maybe she meant to say that must be so beautiful. In any case I was left wondering how to respond because I have never considered my place of residence to be responsible for my being boring, or for my being bored. I will confess I have been guilty of stereotyping Americans so I can forgive the fact that Canadians are understood by many to be miserly, dull, and from some inaccessible part of the world that is snow bound through four seasons. Such are the uncomplicated minds of human beings.

Tom Dickson is Canadian. He is a nice guy, shy and self-effacing, happily married, honest, and down to earth. He is also agreeably attractive, well educated, well read, and his politics are left of centre. In all aspects he is just what one would expect of a Canadian but like so many people one encounters in San Miguel, Tom is more than he appears. His genius is in his painting and both he and his wife are the furthest thing from boring that anyone could imagine.

I first saw Tom Dickson's paintings by chance in a local gallery. His was not the major work on show and it was only when I entered an adjoining room that I came upon two small paintings that stopped me in my tracks. Though art is on display everywhere in San Miguel, and art is available in most large centres around the world, seeing the work of a master outside a museum is still rare. The owner of the gallery was not encouraging when I asked about meeting the artist. "He doesn't like interviews and seldom gives them", she said, "but I will tell him you are interested. He may or may not get back to you." I had to be content with that and let the matter rest until a couple of days later I was pleasantly surprised by an email from Tom suggesting we meet. He also let me know that his wife Donna is an artist as well and so I arranged to speak with them both. On the appointed day, Donna was just making her way up the steep hill as I got out of the cab in front of their door. She was immediately warm and welcoming and we exchanged greetings and remarks about the vertical ascent that helps keep them fit. First time visitors to San Miguel are often surprised at how much climbing is necessary when touring the city on foot, in fact I am convinced that it is possible to go uphill coming and going, but am told by my surveyor husband this is physically impossible. In addition, walkers must always keep one eye on the stone walkways where it is usual to come upon missing sections of stone or large gaping holes. It can only be assumed that personal injury lawyers have yet to discover San Miguel. After introductions and a brief tour around the house and their respective studios, Tom, Donna, and I settle down under an umbrella on the patio to have our first conversation.

Tom, tell me a little about your young life. How old were you when you first discovered your interest in painting?

"I grew up in Ontario, Canada. I was born in Hamilton in 1947 and lived there until I was four then we moved to the outskirts of Toronto where I was surrounded by beautiful farmland. I rode horses and lived a pretty idyllic existence. My Dad was an engineer, a smart guy as well as a great artist. He never really developed it but he could have been a good painter. He was a good father but I suffered growing up because of my mother's problems. I think I started drawing when I was five. It was my dad who took me out for my first plein air painting. I began getting prizes for my drawing in school but I liked to write too. I always thought I would be a writer. I don't know whether you're interested in all this stuff.

I am. Did you go to art school?

"I went to the Ontario College of Art in 1966. My work got high marks but that wasn't good enough because by that time, everything had gone cerebral, hard edge, that kind of thing. I was interested in Impressionism and traditional painting but they weren't doing that anymore. I discovered that I was irrelevant at art school. Even though I loved painting and was technically skilled, I had been at it for ten years by then, they were into 'installations'. At the end of that first year I just wanted to escape. I felt absolutely destroyed. The reason I don't like being interviewed is that the memories are painful. 'Validity' was a big term back then and I found out I was invalid. So I took off. I just wanted to get away. A girl I knew in art school had told me about San Miguel de Allende and it was in that summer that I discovered Mexico and, in the process I discovered a lot about myself. I didn't discover validity. That took about twenty years. I'm still left with a lot of bitterness over what happened at art school and in the years afterward. I didn't paint seriously again for a long time."

"That first summer in Mexico in 1967 left a huge impression on me. The people and the colours were so different and I did little sketches but I didn't show them to anyone. I was embarrassed by them. I went all over the country until finally, when I was absolutely broke, I went back to Canada. I lived at home for a while, then I went to Vancouver and to San Francisco but I was never able to find anything that seemed real to me. Things kind of clunked along for a few years until I met Donna. I don't think it would be overstating it to say Donna saved my life."

How did you two meet?

"Donna and I met in 1970 in Ontario through Circle Arts, an artists' cooperative gallery. I'd been used to meeting girls at art college who were pretty artificial and she was the most honest person I had ever run into. When we met it was like we had known each other all our lives. Donna was one of the few people who encouraged me to paint. Nobody else really seemed to care. One of the first things we did was come back here to San Miguel then we went out to the coast. We got to know each other and tried to re-establish who we were. This is all very difficult for me to explain. I tried to reconnect with what I had been before I lost my confidence. After six months in Mexico we went to

Vancouver, and eventually we made our way back out to Ontario. I stayed with the Circle Arts Gallery in Tobermory. Tobermory is a beautiful place in the summer. It was a fishing village and it became a tourist destination because of the ferry to Manitoulin Island in Lake Huron. I still didn't paint much at that time because I didn't have a lot of faith in what I was doing."

Donna interjects to say that during that time they traveled to Greece and while they were there Tom began to show her some of the basics of painting. "I couldn't understand why Tom was so modest about his painting. I thought he was an amazing painter and I thought I was terrible, even though Tom kept encouraging me."

"Donna's work showed a connection, a real spark. I made her practice because I thought she would discover something about herself that would impress her."

Donna smiles. "I was surprised at how I improved with Tom's help. But it was frustrating because when you are seeing something beautiful you want to get in touch with that but your skills aren't good enough to render what you want. I know what people struggle with when they are just getting started and I remember that when I'm teaching."

Tom continues. "In Ontario we started canoeing and camping in the northern part of the province. We'd go into the bush when there was still snow on the ground and spend all summer going up and down rivers, painting on lakes in the footsteps of the Group of Seven. We kept having to work at odd jobs in the winter to make money. I spent some time spraying cars. They had heard I was good with paint."

"I didn't take painting seriously again until 1986 when I finally decided I didn't care what anybody thought. I was going to become a professional painter, paint full time and see if I could make a living at it. We took a trip out to the east coast and fell in love with it. The landscape and the old fishing villages appealed to us. We were on the coast close to Peggy's Cove. Once I seriously decided to become a painter, within six months I got a gallery and became their best selling painter. By that point I realized that a lot of the people that had impressed me when I was younger, even though they talked about insight, were not doing what they said they were going to do. I realize now that they want the public to believe their art work is saying something, but it's not. Once I turned that corner, I became interested in painting again."

Was that what helped you regain your belief in your own ability?

"It wasn't art so much that did it for me, it was politics. Ever since the sixties I believed in going back to the land, in overthrowing a system that was corrupt. I watched, I read. I became aware of the influence of certain powerful families and their interest in oil. I must have spent twenty thousand hours thinking and reading about politics. I listened to short wave. People are not used to operating with intellectual depth. I carry around half a ton of knowledge that I picked up over those years and I don't even talk about it anymore because very few people are interested and they think you're a radical, but I regained some self-respect. I'm interested in astronomy as well. It connects you. I hope this isn't too... I feel like I'm just centering on myself."

Donna comes to the rescue. "Being an artist is a pretty solitary kind of occupation. The openings and the gallery events can seem superficial and we don't get involved much with it. We have a few good friends here but they tend to think along the same lines as we do."

Tom agrees. "We largely ignore the art scene here. It is partly my fault. I don't really have the interpersonal skills that allow me to find common ground. Other people go around in a kind of personae. I go around wishing I was invisible most of the time.

It's a quirky trait of mine. I hate walking through town with my painting equipment and being seen as 'an artist'."

When did you make the move to San Miguel?

"We came in 2005 from Hornby Island in British Columbia where we lived for fifteen years. We both wanted a change from the west coast and our trip here in 1987 by motorcycle convinced us that this is where we ultimately wanted to be. San Miguel has changed a lot since then but it still has that spirit. We go into the campo and they are still planting corn, beans, and squash, the triumverate, the traditional foods in the same field. They plough with a horse, seed by hand, and we are lucky to get to paint that. Five minutes past the train station and you are in the past. The tie in with nature is one reason why we have always loved painting. The city itself has grown of course. When we were here in '87 there were hardly any cars and it was very quiet. There has been a lot of development on the surrounding hills but the historic centre of the city is pretty much the same. We are out nearly every day painting either here in town or in the country. I seem to find more to inspire me all the time."

Have you cut your ties with Canada?

Donna has family back in British Columbia and she goes to see them now and again. We don't have children so we don't have that connection. The people here are very kind and we are enjoying getting to have a greater picture of the lives of the Mexicans. They are very interested when we are painting here in town and they encourage us with smiles and congratulations. In the countryside, I think they wonder what we are doing. Generally, Mexicans prefer religious subjects and people to landscapes. I'm not sure why. Maybe they are so much a part of the land they can't separate themselves from it, objectify it. They are very puzzled by our interest in the landscape as a subject for painting."

Tom and Donna do what is known as plein air painting, a term I learned comes from the French meaning "full of air or open air". It means they paint outside. Plein air painting began with the Impressionists in France and was carried on by artists living in California in the first part of the 20th century. Donna explains. "When you look at the work of the early Californian plein air painters, you realize each painting is very precious. You can tell what it was like when they painted that picture. They are a great inspiration to modern plein air painters."

Donna regularly instructs groups of aspiring artists who live in or are visiting San Miguel. When I ask if I can accompany her students on a plein air outing I am welcomed without hesitation. Tom is going to be joining the class on location and I am to meet them high above the city on Sunday morning at 9:00 a.m.

* * *

I ask the cab driver if I can get to the top of the stairs of Salida de Queretero some other way besides climbing the couple of hundred stairs. He says sí, he can get me there. We drive up a sharply rising road and then along a dirt roadway that is more of a footpath until the driver stops and says aqui. I look skeptically at the open field on my right and then turning to my left I catch a glimpse of Tom disappearing down a long flight of stairs, moving easily with his backpack and easel over his shoulder. This must be the place.

It is a beautiful bright morning in San Miguel and Tom and Donna are out with a dozen or so adult students to do some painting on location. Officially it is Donna's class but Tom has come along as he routinely does, to provide another example of a skilled professional at work. They have chosen this spot because the houses that border the long set of stairs offer many visual treats for a painter and the distant view over San Miguel's signature church, the parroquia, to the mist covered hills, provides a perfect backdrop. As I approach, Tom is deciding where to set up his easel so he can get a good view of one of the houses that lines the stairway. Donna is encouraging her students to find a vista they want to paint and soon they have scattered themselves up and down the nearby stairs, each having chosen a preferred aspect. Most are using oils although I see one man has chosen watercolours and another woman is using acrylics. Donna tells me she prefers oils to acrylics. She herself has opted to paint the scene facing down the stairs toward the distant hills and is applying a thin wash before loosely blocking out the main elements in the picture with a darker colour. She sets the horizon high up on the page. She tells me she came out about a week ago and did a thumbnail sketch. As Donna paints she explains to the students clustered around her, "The perspective lines are all going up to the horizon. We use our thumbnail sketch and a reference photograph to register the shadows because within twenty minutes all the shadows will have changed. When you get back to the studio to finish up you can refer to your photo to remind you of what you saw. We're going to ignore that trellis in front of the parroquia. I'm just putting in some dark, it doesn't matter what colour, I'm using blue to remind me it's shadow." Donna uses a broad brush to sketch in the houses, stairs, and distant hills. "We'll put in a little more bougainvillea, improve on nature."

I leave Donna to seek out Tom who is further up the staircase and has chosen to paint the purple doorway of a house flanked by crimson bougainvillea on the left and a rust coloured wall on the right. He is holding a pencil sketch, looking at it and then at the scene before him. I ask him what he is doing.

"I'm doing a quick thumbnail sketch to establish what the problems are. I just refer to this. It won't be exactly like this in the painting but it is a reference to start with." He holds a piece of heavy cardboard about eight inches by four inches. It has a rectangle cut out of it on one side and there is a piece of paper attached on which Tom has drawn a pencil sketch of the scene before us.

What do you like about this scene?

"It's very abstract. There is some nice stuff. The stair railing goes up and then turns left. I like the glare on the wall. There's some nice sympathy between the crimson of the bougainvillea and the colour of the wall. It's going to be kind of poetic. The purple door of course is very intriguing."

It is a wonderful clear day and up where we are standing the air smells fresh. It is quiet except for the sound of the birds who call to one another from the trees behind us. I am warmed by the increasing intensity of the sun and I take off my shawl to feel the slight breeze on my arms. Tom tells me that in the spring and summer he and Donna like to paint in the early morning to avoid the heat of the afternoon. "In December and January we come out in the afternoon. It is kind of nice because half the year we are out in the morning and half the year in the afternoon so we get some variety."

How does painting outside differ from painting inside?

"Painting outside is harder but it is more inspiring. You're right there surrounded by everything. I like painting on location so much better than studio painting. When I find myself back in the studio it is hard to get motivated. Plein air is really challenging. In the studio there is always something to divert you. The phone rings or you have to get a coffee but on location you find yourself pretty much just going at it hard for about three hours. If you are painting from a photo in the studio you can analyze colour more easily using photoshop and that sort of thing but out here you have to be able to analyze what the colours are without any of those crutches. It's direct. You go from inspiration to analysis to putting it down."

"Sometimes you are dealing with bugs, sometimes with people. We were in the jardín yesterday and I painted the whole time with about ten people behind me. They changed over the course of a few hours but there were a lot of people taking pictures of the painting and of me, and you know how much I like having my picture taken. It's a distraction."

"It's tough but the inspiration is much greater on location and even if you don't finish the painting, when you take it back to the studio you remember. The next day your colours are still there, on your pallet, and it takes you right back. Even after the second or third day you remember the sights and sounds, you remember people that went by. The other way seems artificial. The more I do this, the more I want to do it exclusively. It's exciting because you have to make so many decisions, technical things, getting the colour right, getting the perspective right, leaving things out. You have to make hundreds and hundreds of decisions over the course of a few hours. Sometimes they're wrong but I think if eighty percent of the time you're right, you are doing pretty good."

Tom goes to the top of the section of stairs to set up his tripod and says he hopes he doesn't fall backward. A student who is already set up beside us welcomes Tom and tells me that he learned so much the day before from watching Tom paint. I ask him what he learned and he replies, "Tom uses very dramatic contrasts in colour, the dark and the light, bold strokes, really rich colours. He has a lot of confidence in what he is doing. It's just more complex than what I am capable of."

The easel securely in place, Tom takes out his box of paints already on the pallet, and assesses the scene in front of him with an expert eye. He tells me he doesn't seem to be as well organized as usual. I think he is a little nervous about my presence.

"I seem to be a bit dithery this morning. I didn't sleep all that well", he says. "There was a lot of noise for some reason. There were fireworks until late last night." The years in San Miguel have taught me that the noise was probably due to the fact that this is late February and it is the lent season which heralds a lengthy period of celebrations, parades, and special occasions, from Primavera when the jardín is crowded with paper flowers, intricate paper puppets on sticks, and confetti-filled eggs to smash over little girls' heads, to the fervid dancing of the Chichimecs decked out in elaborately feathered costumes dancing to drums that shake the heart inside your chest if you get too close. The activity culminates forty days later in the silent solemn march of hundreds of San Miguelians dressed in black, stepping slowly to the beat of a single bass drum through the city streets, following the larger than life, bloodied statue of Christ on the cross. For a newcomer it can be disquieting to be a part of the hush that falls over a normally boisterous population. For those of us who are not Mexican or Catholic, the very graphic wounded Christ figure seems exaggeratedly gruesome. I recoiled from the image until I read a very sensitive article in the San Miguel newspaper *Atencion* explaining that Christ covered in blood, in agony, is a stark reminder of the compassion we should all share for our fellow sufferers in this world. Then it made a bit more sense to me.

Any and every event is punctuated by an explosion of fireworks, some showy and funded by the city, others simply a few brief bangs in a neighbouring colonia. The effect is the same, sleepers suddenly wakened, dogs barking. Our young Australian visitors assumed it was gunfire and that all the reports they had heard about Mexico were true. When we stopped laughing, we assured them they were not about to be gunned down like dirty dogs in the dusty streets of San Miguel.

A couple of women come down the stairs on their way into el centro. As they pass, one asks, "So are you guys painting the city?" She doesn't wait for an answer. It's a long way down.

If that door was green could you make it purple?

"There are no rules in painting. If you want to move things around, you can but you have to admit this purple door is pretty pleasing just as it is. Generally you try to simplify. If an element works to enhance the painting you include it. If it doesn't, you leave it out. It is like a science. You have to figure what perspective is going to help and what isn't. The reality of a painter is to evoke a feeling, to get in touch with the poetry. It is a big deal to me to do that."

Donna comes to check on how a couple of the nearby students are doing. She asks to look at their thumbnail sketches and discusses their blocking in of the basic elements of the painting. To one of the students she points out the interesting shadow of the door handle on the door. "You might want to do a little sketch of that shadow before it changes." She mentions to Tom that one of the neighbours has offered his bathroom to the class members. Working outdoors presents it's own unique problems.

Tom is using a large brush and a thinned black paint to define the buildings and the stairs in the scene. The students around us are using lighter paints, more like the colours we see in front of us. Tom says, "I find that I use the big brush for at least half the painting. The choice of black or grey in the early stages means that I can go over things like that bush with a lighter green and it will come out looking more as you see it there."

There is silence while Tom works. He apologizes. "It's kind of boring isn't it? It takes a while to develop." I reassure him that watching him work is quite the opposite of boring. A student near us says, "I saw Tom develop a painting yesterday. It was like watching a miracle."

As Tom outlines a corner of the building in front of us, he uses his left hand to support his brush hand. "When I was sixteen the other kids would remark on how steady my hand was but this is my sixty-six year old hand. I have to do something. Steady hands would be nice but I don't want my lines to be too straight either. Perfectly straight lines can look too stiff."

Donna has joined us and I tell her how lovely it seems to paint outside. She agrees. "You are taking part in the world passing by, all the sounds, the smells. When you look at your painting again later it brings back the memories of the day you painted it. A long time ago when I was just beginning to paint, I met a man who showed me some of his plein air paintings. As he went through them one by one, he told me a whole story describing exactly where each one was painted. I didn't think it was possible to remember all that detail but now I realize being fully aware for several hours as you paint will mean the painting can reawaken all those sensations whenever you look at it."

Tom says they have given the students some information to read about the basics of colour. A student comments that the material is difficult to understand at first but is proving to be useful. Tom summarizes for me. "Value is light and dark, saturation is intensity of hue, hue is the basic colour of the spectrum but hue can vary in intensity and value. Those three things working together are very complicated but that's part of the fun. The light on the objects effects how you interpret what you see. You don't see glare. Your mind sees the basic colour of the wall. Most people don't notice the shadows, the light and the dark. You have to learn to really look. You can be entertained all by yourself seeing those different tones and when you are painting every day you can get pleasure out of analyzing the visual landscape wherever you are."

Could you tell me a little bit about the process you go through when you are painting?

"My work is very personal. I'm not sure where to begin in order to talk about it. We usually work on location, even the large paintings are started outdoors but I finish them in the studio. I am meticulous and I work and work at paintings. I have killed the odd painting by working it to death."

Donna speaks to Tom, "I think you are very concerned about the nuances, the subtlety of colour that brings out the atmosphere and I think it is the atmosphere, the colour and the mood that attracts you to the scene because to actually capture that you have to get into the little changes that make the atmosphere clear."

Tom elaborates. "Composition is a big part of it too. There is visual poetry there if you can find the right combination of colour and structure. It's a different language, a visual language. It's certainly not Spanish or English. It takes a lifetime to be able to get in touch with that, to feel that you are in control enough that you can start to write those poems. It doesn't come easily at first. I try."

Donna goes on, "Some people might think you are just copying but it isn't that at all. That feeling you get in touch with. You have to simplify, sum it up, distill the essence of a scene. There is a lot more depth to it and it does take a long time to get to that point. Along the way you are discovering how to render those things, learning the tools, the use of colour, the brush work, gaining experience as you go."

Tom agrees. "That is why it is important for a young person who is interested in painting to begin early, not let ten or twenty years slip by. A kid that shows some promise should be encouraged and given the guidance of a mentor, a master. I sometimes think I would like to teach some young people who show that kind of promise but I don't know, I haven't had any practice. Donna's the teacher."

Your work is very distinctive Tom. Do you think it is your technical skills that make your paintings so remarkable?

I think something else has to be present before you develop the skills. When I was a little kid I saw the world differently. I didn't realize it at the time but I used to drink it all in and it was that visual poetry I was talking about that I was relating to. Everything was beautiful to me, absolutely beautiful. When I first came to San Miguel when I was twenty, there was enough of that left in my character, quite a bit of it actually, that the place had a lasting and profound effect on me. You have got to see those things in nature, or whatever, and see the effect it is having on you. The skill comes later. That's where the fight is and that is what I wanted out of school. I knew I didn't have that kind of skill. I had rendering skills but I didn't know how to get at that stuff that was in me that would appeal to the soul of an onlooker. You can get that kind of skill, it just takes you your whole life."

As you are both artists, do you and Donna ever disagree or find yourself in competition over your painting?

Tom's response is immediate. "We've been asked that question before. People ask don't you criticize each other. Don't you have fights but we don't. Donna and I still talk and talk and after all these years, we are still discovering things about each other. We both know how hard it is to achieve what you want in painting. And we certainly don't worry about validity anymore. We like to be in touch with all aspects of the world. We like to be in touch with reality. We don't like artificiality. Painting is very satisfying for me now. I just wish it had happened twenty years earlier. I still wonder what it would have been like to have gone to art school and found some mentors there who were really good painters and who could see it was really worthwhile, that it connects you with the planet and keeps you connected."

I take a moment to look around at the paintings of the students near me. Each one is remarkably different from the next. I comment on the fact to Donna and she confirms what I have observed. In addition to the different perspectives and styles, the students have chosen different mediums.

I notice some of the students are using acrylics and some are using oils. What is the difference?

"Acrylics are basically plastic. They dry very quickly and they dry flat. I used to use them in the seventies but I like the feel of oils so much better." A student adds that here in San Miguel, oils are perfect for capturing the vibrant colours. Donna tells me that she and Tom prefer to work in oils almost exclusively although she did watercolours for a long time. "Working in watercolours takes a lot of experience. You have to think ahead and go from light to dark. With oils it is the opposite. You go from dark to light. I worked in watercolours for twenty-five years and you can see the effect of that in my oils which are a kind of hybrid. Watercolours have a delicacy I like. You can be more precise with your colour with oils because you are using white paint to get the specific colour you want to achieve whereas in watercolours you are using the white of the paper which does limit you. Other aspects like the accidental effects you can achieve with watercolours make it interesting."

"Everyone has their own approach. I don't like to change an individual's style. I will point out errors in colour or perspective but I think it is important not to discourage painters. When my students are struggling with the paint or the composition, I tell them the challenge is interesting. I remember I took a course recently from a teacher who was not very gentle in his criticisms but I prefer to find things to compliment about students' work. I enjoy teaching because I can see many different versions of a scene. Many visions."

Tom says that after you have done this for a while, you can read the personality of the artist in his painting. I ask him where he is in the painting before us.

"I like to put a lot of drama in my paintings. I take things pretty seriously. And it's kind of musical. There is a relationship between painting and music. You compose a picture just as you compose a piece of music. That whole thing of value and intensity that we talked about, the saturation of colour is like orchestration. The horns are bright and lively and you notice them. Some of the other instruments are dark. A painting is like that."

I ask Donna to describe the process she goes through when she decides to paint a particular scene. She is eloquent in her response. "You feel it first and then you have to analyze what makes you feel that way. That is the essence of painting. It is the tricky part of painting. Whether you can achieve it or not is another thing. The ratio of light and shade, the delicacy, the intermingling of colours, the composition, it is all these things. The painter has to be able to step back from the emotion that first grabs him, and analyze it. If it is a successful picture, the emotion will be caught there and the viewer will feel it. A beginner painter is more concerned with the mechanics. When you get beyond the mechanics of painting you can look at a scene and think, 'I like this. I like this a lot,' and then try to figure out what you are reacting to. It is usually about the light, the degree of warmth and colour. One teacher I had said the passion is the light."

A woman comes up the stairs doing her morning workout and is delighted to see Donna. "We want to come to your studio and get one of your paintings." She agrees to call later to make an appointment. I am interested to know whether Tom has experienced a change in their ability to make a living here in San Miguel.

"Yes, we sure have. When we first came here six years ago we sold a lot of paintings. We were doing pretty well and we are still doing ok but people are buying small paintings. Mind you we sell big ones once in a while so we are doing well enough. Money never meant that much to us anyway, Donna and I."

When you select a scene, do you ever consider whether or not the picture is going to sell?

"I have to say honestly, yes we do but if I am excited about something, I will go ahead and paint it anyway. I guess I should care more about the economics of it but I don't."

Tom is thinking he might take a bit of a break but is aware of the light changing and wants to get a couple of things in. He has put a pale yellow line horizontally to one side of the door and it seems to me that it is in exactly the right place and is exactly the right colour. He says he likes it too.

Are you happy with what you've done so far Tom?

"Yes, it has been pretty exciting. It has the drama I was hoping for. It is like music again because you lead into a piece and then it builds and it builds and there is a kind of a surprise or a focus and it is what I tried to do here. It was a good choice."

I am reminded of a poem by E.E. Cummings about maggie and millie and mollie and may, four young girls who have dramatically different experiences at the same beach. I think about the varied lives we lead and the understanding we gain if we are fortunate to encounter the right teachers along the way. Sometimes it is our parents who teach us, sometimes our peers, sometimes we learn the most difficult and important lessons from our children. At times it is our own foolishness that we eventually decide to abandon in favour of an easier path. A surprising conclusion by scientist Stephen Pinker tells us that more often than we think, it is simply chance that determines how our lives will unfold. However much we differ, nobody gets very far or learns very much without a struggle, and if we are lucky, we find the life that fulfills us, the one that was meant to be. As Mr. Cummings concludes, "For whatever we lose, like a you or a me, it is always ourselves we find in the sea."

I can hear Donna not far away, speaking to one of her students about his colour choices. I turn to look at Tom beside me painting in the San Miguel sun. "You are a lucky man", I tell him.

He holds his brush still for a moment, considering what I have said, then he smiles. "Yes", he answers. "Yes I am." He is completely absorbed in the splendid green leaves of the crimson bougainvillea as I begin my descent to the city below.

Christina Sol

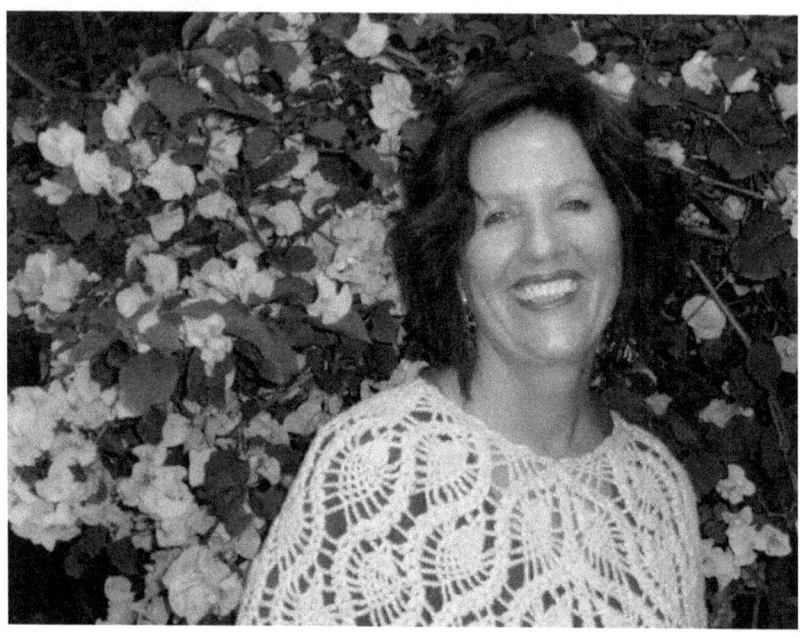

It is well known in San Miguel that within the non-Mexican community, women outnumber men at least three to one and among the men, a significant proportion is gay. Some friends who lately came to dinner told me a joke that underlines the inherent difficulty in meeting an eligible male. A woman sits down on a bench in the jardín beside a nice looking older man. She asks him if he is new to San Miguel. He says yes, he has just arrived in town. "Where were you before?" the woman inquires. "In jail," he replies. "Really!" says the woman. Why were you in jail?" The man explains, "I murdered my wife." "Oh my!" answers the woman, "Does that mean you're unattached?"

Women of a certain age are plentiful in San Miguel and if you are a female looking for a mate, best to look elsewhere. The fact is, women that do come to this part of Mexico are frequently in recovery and have no specific interest in a relationship with a man. Often they have endured addictions, heartbreak, financial hardship, betrayal, or depression and they are looking to reclaim their better selves. Some are searching for long absent joy, others require refuge and a community of support. Most discover that San Miguel allows women of limited means to be independent while they establish an understanding that it is alright, even healthy, to put themselves first. My encounters with many of the single women here have been revealing. A very few have a desperation about them that is disquieting, but the majority of women I meet are involved in some creative endeavor, they do charity work in one of the hundreds of organizations in town, have a loving social network, and are enjoying a life that is free from the demands of caring for a house or family. While few of the women who express themselves through the visual arts could be called great artists on any world stage, I have the deepest respect for their accomplishments and for their pursuit of fulfillment. My first encounter with Christina Sol was on the weekly house and garden tour sponsored by the biblioteca. I was part of a large group who had come to see a whimsical home owned by two eccentric artists a few miles from San Miguel. Being a friend of the owners, Christina had offered to help out with crowd control and when I first saw her, was wearing a gold tiara. After a brief exchange, we agreed to meet to discuss her life and her art. I had never seen her work, but the woman intrigued me and I wanted to hear more about how and why she had come to Mexico.

Christina's own home is perched on a steep hill overlooking the city and is an expression of her beliefs and her creative energy. Symbolic images are reproduced in the wrought iron railings and in the decorative moldings. In every room, light floods the space from several directions and the walls are filled with her colourful paintings. Our conversation began with her description of the circumstances that prompted her to leave California at the age of twenty and to make Mexico her home more than thirty-five years ago.

"I grew up in St. Helena in the heart of the Napa Valley. I was waitressing in a restaurant there when I met Jim, a carpenter who came to work in the Valley in the summers and in the winters lived in Teposlan just outside Mexico City. When he asked me to make the trip with him to Mexico I said yes, so off we go but it takes us two and a half months to get there because you never knew with Jim what would happen. We'd meet people and wind up staying and there were lots of parties. Anyway we got to Teposlan and then finally a week later we went to Mexico City. I wanted to see the Anthropology Museum so Jim said to meet him back at a restaurant in the Zona Rosa and when I got to the restaurant Jim was at a table with twenty people I had never met. I sat beside a man who turned out to be a photographer working for an attractive man named Jose who was seated across the table. Jose published a magazine, a Mexican version of Playboy, which at that time had a circulation of 100,000 and employed the best artists and writers in the business. By five in the morning we were at Jose's apartment on Reforma and all of us decided to go to Acapulco. Jose and I spent an amazing few days in Acapulco and then we went back to Mexico City where I said good-bye and I didn't expect to see him again until he invited me to lunch and from that day on we were together."

Christina tells me her first year in Mexico was rocky. "I mean it is one thing to come here for a vacation but it's another to live here with a Mexican man within a different culture. For a time, he had a lot of intercambios with the magazine so we went all over Cancun and Europe, but then problems began to arise with the magazine. In Mexico in those years, there was repression, no freedom at all, and the magazine hired a famous writer to do an article and in it he accused a powerful politician of talking too much and very soon after, the magazine was closed down. For a year, we lived in Teposlan on almost no money. I made necklaces out of beads I had gotten in Morocco and Jose would sell them and we'd get a hundred dollars and travel around and have a great time. Finally when all we had left was about two pesos, Jose went to work for his father at his printing factory. The printing business was profitable but its success made the family a target and Jose's father got kidnapped. After 23 days, we did get Jose's father back but he had been seriously effected by the experience and he began to make bad decisions. His printing empire started to crumble and eventually Jose's father's health failed and he died. In the meantime, Jose had started a raunchy Mexican comic book that was doing well, and to help with the failing printing business he took out a loan for $300,000. This is a sad story and it happened to a lot of people. It was in 1994 and by the end of the month with devaluation, his $300,000. loan had become a $900,000. loan. That was the beginning of the end for his business and his own health. We lost everything. It has taken me a long time to understand what happened. The man I married seemed to have disappeared. I hit rock bottom and I don't know how I found the strength but I left and came here to San Miguel."

"I came to San Miguel a broken woman, to rebuild myself. I had nothing when I came here- no support, no money, nothing, except for one good friend. Jose and I had come to San Miguel over the years to visit my friend and every time we came we walked in what is now the Jardín Botanico. It is a beautiful, peaceful place." The Jardín Botanico or Native Plant Garden is one of San Miguel's treasures. It is an expansive area on the edge of the city that is dedicated to the preservation of plants from the arid and semi-arid zones of Mexico. The garden is run by a local non-profit organization that provides educational programs, conducts tours, and does research related to the sustainability of the local eco system. Once a year there is a major musical event at the garden for the purpose of fund raising. Last year an orchestra played in the canyon while the audience perched on rocks above them and the sun slowly descended in the clear western sky. This past year a gifted pianist who was in San Miguel for the Baroque Music Festival agreed to give a concert and again it was a remarkable evening. Residents of San Miguel regard the garden, El Charco, as it is known, as a place of unique spirituality and value it much as a national park is cherished as a gift to all who use it.

"When I left my husband I could only think to return to San Miguel." Christina pauses to retrieve a picture of her two children, a boy and a girl now in their twenties. She is enormously proud of them, "They are beautiful and talented and strong. In Mexico a mother never leaves her children and I was condemned for it but I had to save myself and it turned out to be the best thing I could have done. Unexpectedly, my mother died and left me a small inheritance and it made it possible for me to find the land and build this house. When my ex-husband had a stroke I was able to provide the children with a place to come. It was wonderful to have them here but they want their independence now and I have to let them fly."

Christina describes the release of her children as a natural but painful progression, one that every parent understands. Today, she projects a self-confidence and a faith in the future which is very different from the darkness which enveloped her years ago. She talks about how that transformation took place.

"It has been nine years since I came to San Miguel and I have managed to rebuild myself by walking in the Jardín Botanico every day, by giving up alcohol which had become my means of coping with all that was happening to me during the last few years of my marriage, and by doing my art." Christina is certainly not alone in her prior dependence on alcohol. There are many active AA groups in the city and these are important sources of strength for individuals who have fought to free themselves from their addiction to alcohol or drugs. Perhaps if one seeks them out, one would discover the multitude of services available to addicts and their families in any city in North America but I have been struck by the numbers of people in San Miguel who are in recovery and my impression is that the group assistance extends into people's social lives and often leads to close, enduring friendships.

Christina continues. "When I came to Mexico, I could have gone to art school and Jose would have supported me in this but I was too terrified. I am a very creative person but I had to do a lot of different things before I found the work I am doing now. I was a make-up artist, I did some black and white photography, then I went into clothes and started designing rebosos, the Mexican shawls. I had painted off and on over the years but at the age of forty, the urge to paint couldn't be repressed. It has taken many years for me to reach the stage in my painting that I am in now. Before I came to San Miguel when I was so lost, my painting was rigid. There was no creativity, but when I came here I started painting the jardín, the plants and the birds, over and over again for two years. In 2001, I met a dream teacher who is a spiritual guide and has helped me interpret my dreams. He and I have worked together for several years. He began to explain what significance certain colours have in dreams and as I gained understanding, I began to paint the images that came to me in my dreams. In 2002 I met a shaman from Peru who was doing workshops in San Miguel and he introduced me to a plant called iowaska, the awakener, the great mother who comes to teach us not to abuse ourselves, not to abuse others and not to abuse the earth. She shows you where the obstacles are inside yourself. She shows you all your faults without judgment and it's up to you to do the work based on what you learn. For people with addictions, she is a purifier and gets the toxins out of your body and tells you what to eat and you get the equivalent of years of therapy in a very short time. But you can't hide or be afraid of what you will discover. This is not a drug. It is not about numbing out. She is opening your consciousness. From that has come my true body of work."

Although iowaska (or ayahuasca) is a hallucinogen that has been used by shamen in the Amazon regions for hundreds of years, to the average person Christina's experiences with the drug are unfamiliar and even suspect. They invite the conventional observer to discount her insights, but there is no question that her quest is sincere. Her efforts to understand herself and the world are entirely genuine. In our culture it is the norm to equate the taking of drugs with rebellion, illness, or addiction, a failure to function as a productive member of society. In other cultures much more ancient than ours, specific drugs are cultivated as a means to an altered perception of reality, a practice which is integrated into the community's set of beliefs and behaviours thereby creating unique and varied understandings of existence. Because diversity is the very linchpin of a thriving planet, that which keeps the wheel on the axel, I am prepared to keep an open mind. Christina Sol hasn't devoted a lifetime to painting nor could her work be called avant-garde, yet when one looks at her paintings it is difficult not to be moved by her honesty. Her brave representations of all aspects of her personal experience are a testament to the equilibrium that for the present, imbues her life. Christina describes her paintings reverently, as a form of communication which travels through her, rather than being strictly of her own invention. She relates each image to what she now understands to be true through the interpretation of her dreams and her experiences with iowaska.

As our conversation draws to a close, Christina describes for me the profound influence San Miguel has had on her recovery. "San Miguel is a healing place. Even if you don't know that you have come here to get healed, you do. Without even trying, you trip into it. The beauty heals me all the time. I feel safe here. I feel I can be myself. My painting began as something that came from the outside but for a long time it has been from the inside. I had a journey in which a tree spoke to me and the tree said I would receive energy from above and that my feet were planted and would receive energy from the ground. 'Put your branches out so people can come under them and be refreshed.' The source comes and nourishes me so I can be the tree and nourish others. When I came here, I never imagined I could build a house and by being here I discovered I could do all these things and all the abilities I didn't know I had, came out. I know I've chosen an unusual path, but for me, it's a rich path. It is important to bring the images from that other side back here and paint them because they resonate with people. When I started painting the dreams, people said, these paintings mean something, rather than these paintings are pretty. They meant something to me and now as I keep growing there is more purpose in what I am doing. I've come to realize we paint what we are."

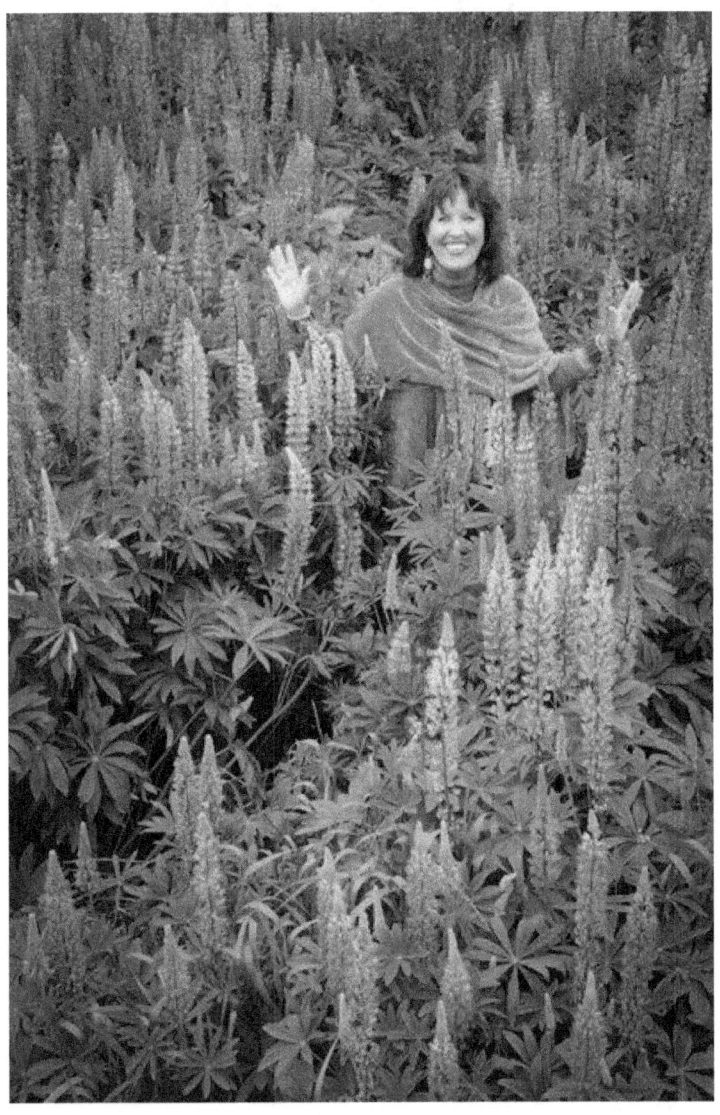

Santiago Corral Gutierrez

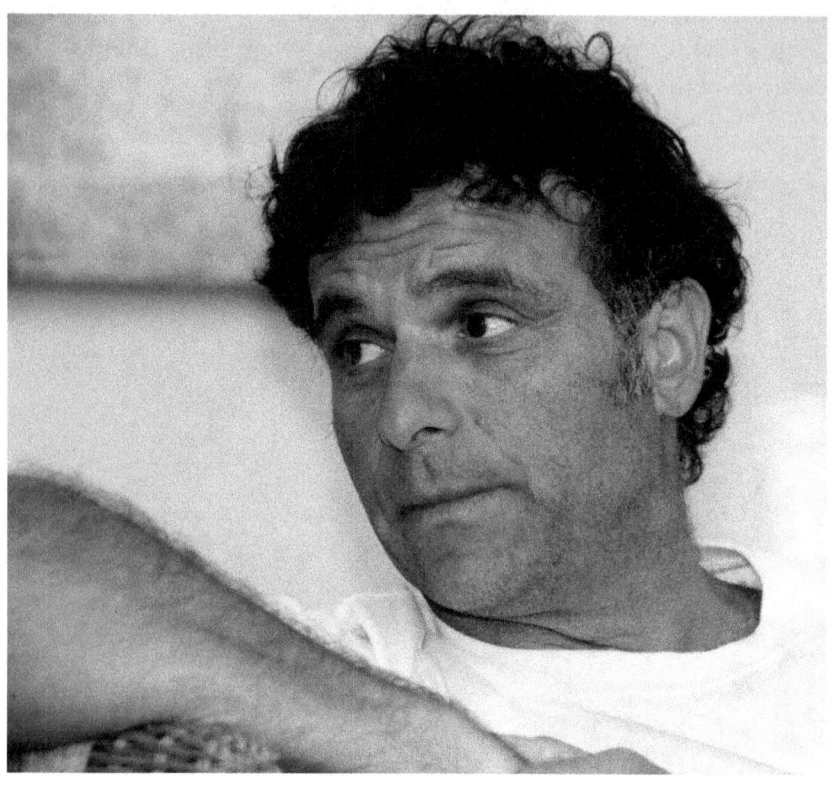

Voici mon secret. Il est très simple: on ne voit bien qu'avec le cœur. L'essentiel est invisible pour les yeux.

Here is my secret. It is very simple. It is only with the heart that one can see rightly; What is essential is invisible to the eye.

(Le Petit Prince by Antoine de Saint-Exupery, 1943)

Santiago Corral is a solid, muscular man with thick brown curly hair that is graying slightly, just slightly. Today he is wearing a t-shirt and jeans and seen alighting from his truck, could be a labourer on a construction site, probably the foreman, a physical person with a job that requires focus and good management skills. He moves efficiently through space as though he were taking the shortest route to a destination, but when he sits down to speak with me on the ample couch in his gallery at Fabrica Aurora, he relaxes his body, flinging his arms back and open wide. His face is handsome, eyes bright and discerning, mouth set but ready to smile, a man who inspires confidence yet has little patience for fools. I discover he is sensitive, very smart, and someone who has learned from his considerable life experience.

Are there other artists in your family?

"Several. My family consists of artists and aviators, kind of like Antoine de Saint-Exupery, we are two different types of spirits. When he was a young guy, my grandfather went to Esmeralda Academy in Mexico City, one of the country's most important art schools, then he became a business person and never did art after that. He created a big coffee brand in Mexico and ran that business for many years. My mother has painted all her life. She lives in Los Angeles and makes a living painting trompe l'oeil and murals. Some of her brothers and sisters enjoyed painting and drawing as a hobby and a couple of my cousins are also painters. My brother makes a living as a painter and my sister draws for pleasure. As a child living in Spain I learned a lot from my mother and from the museums we went to when we lived in Madrid. We always visited museums and we always had art in our house, Valasquez, Goya, all the classic painters."

Was there a moment when you realized you wanted to be an artist?

"When you are surrounded by artists there is never a realizing point, you just know. Your drawing, your painting, you are always close to it. You imitate. If your parents do art also, it is natural. I did decide to devote myself full time to painting when I was twenty-six. Before that I was a pilot and I taught flying. It gave me the travelling I wanted. I always worked but I always carried some pastels with me and I continued to draw. Eventually I realized it was time to stop moving around so much and start dedicating myself to painting fully, and to make a living. It never came to my mind to do it as a hobby. It was never that."

"Although I knew I wanted to be a professional painter, I didn't go to art school for formal training. When you look at other artists as I did, you absorb information. Of course there are many things I probably missed by not going to school, like how to use different mediums along with some technique. Still there is a research side to art and I have done a lot of that on my own. Talking to other artists can help and it is also what you see, what has been done. Until recently I stuck to regular oil and canvas but now I am moving into different mediums. From what I have heard and read, good art schools are trying to encourage students to create their own language. That's what it is all about. People ask me if I teach and I tell them if I was going to teach you something I would teach you how to paint like me and it is totally not the way to go. It is really from your own point of view. I can't teach you, but we can talk about art and I can tell you what I know from what I have seen. You have to find a certain balance and geometry of composition and at the end, nothing is certain. It is all relative to your own eyes."

"But, I also believe there is a beauty for everyone's eye. That is why masterpieces go through so many generations and transcend and touch everyone's heart because it's beauty for everyone. Some say that for me it is beautiful, for you it is not, but when we talk about good art, real masterfully done art, composition wise, colour wise, there is something there that captures perfection. You might not want it in your house, it might not be your style but it has some quality that makes it beautiful and gives it a broad appeal. I believe in that. When we talk about good art, there is something there that attracts you. That is why I think in the art world collectors usually agree when something has that beauty, that quality that nobody will deny. It is when a work of art becomes a masterpiece and reaches a universal standard."

Do you try to achieve that when you paint?

"Yes, of course. I have a few paintings, not many, that have reached that point. The paintings I am most proud of have all the qualities I was searching for with respect to colour and composition. I don't consider myself a hyper-realistic painter even though people see my work as hyper-realism, my definition of hyper-realism is imitating a picture, with a very flat surface. I try to leave some brush strokes. I don't want to hide the artist's hand so I leave some texture even though it is not obvious when you see the painting but it is there. There are some paintings where I would say I have surprised myself, or impressed myself. And that is what I am looking for, always. When you are impressed with a painting it is because you exceeded your own expectations. I'm not sure how you achieve that. You have to be working, you have to be connected, in that mindset but it is not just about working. You know I spend a lot of hours in my head. Many hours go by just trying to figure out what I want to do and that is a kind of a maturing process, taking not just days or months, but years. Sometimes you may not know exactly what you want but you have certain clues as to what you want and sometimes it leads you to where you want to go. At the end you know you have found the right path and then everything becomes clear."

"I decided to start doing human figures a few years ago, something I always avoided because painting the skin, the body, is probably the most difficult thing to achieve. I'm not talking about just technically. The skin on the body is very important but there is also the atmosphere, the feel. The Spanish have the expression, to have *duende*. The magic. You could go out to see a concert for example and the musicians might be virtuosos but there is no soul. There is so much perfection that you lose the charm. Flamenco dancing is a perfect example. Flamenco dancers do have a lot of technique, steps they have to follow but at the end flamenco is about that spirit. There are a lot of hyper-realist painters that are impressive but their work can be cold and empty. I get compliments, 'Oh your painting is so real.' If they are referring to the technique, to how I did it, that is not a compliment for me. The compliment is if it creates an emotion. It might not be perfectly done technically but if it has an impact on the viewer, it is a success."

After our conversation I consulted Wikipedia and discovered that a duende in Latin American and Spanish mythology is a goblin-like creature. According to Christopher Maurer who edited *In Search of Duende* (1998), "duende is a demonic earth spirit who helps the artist see the limitations of intelligence, who brings the artist face-to-face with death, and who helps him create and communicate memorable, spine-chilling art. Quoting from a lecture given in 1933 by Federico Garcia Lorca, *Play and Theory of the Duende*, Maurer explains that duende is an alternative to style, to mere virtuosity, to the classical, artistic norms dictated by the muse, or to God-given grace and charm (what Spaniards call *angel*). To a higher degree than the muse or the angel, the duende seizes not only the performer but also the audience, creating conditions where art can be understood spontaneously with little, if any, conscious effort."

I am put in mind of a concert I attended at the Royal Theatre in Victoria some years ago during which a very elderly guest conductor was on the podium. Decades before, he had been the orchestra's resident conductor but his appointment had long passed and the current orchestra members were of a different generation. The first half of the concert was difficult. The musicians did not look at the conductor who held the baton down low where it was hard to see and the music seemed to flounder unattended. After intermission, without much enthusiasm, the audience members returned to their seats. I expected more of the same, but whether because of words said during the intermission back stage, whether it was the piece of music itself, or whether it was the presence of an earth spirit, the musicians played the symphony as though they were possessed. They never took their eyes off the conductor and I found myself too, sitting forward on my seat, spellbound and captive to the music. When the final note was stilled, I and others present, including many of the orchestra members, cried spontaneous tears. A friend who was a violinist in the orchestra told me later that such an experience is rare but when it happens, it is never forgotten. That is duende.

Your paintings seem to convey a sense of something about to happen.

"It is the vertigo of life. The next moment is so uncertain." Santiago smiles. "It's terrible. It is almost a fear. A lot of people tell me there is a sadness in my paintings even if the subject is happy. In my series of open suitcases, there is that fear hiding. Some people see loneliness, but at the end I think there is a fear of the next moment alive. The next moment alive means death. You are there but you might not be. It is behind the scene, not very obvious. I don't intend to do it but it just comes subconsciously. With conceptual art it is very obvious what you are trying to say. It is very direct just like communications are today, but I think there has to be the subconscious part of the artist in the work, the artist's soul, the deepest part. There is a part that comes through the intellectual but the other part, the mysterious part should be there too and you might not control that, is what I'm trying to say. If you are being honest, it will come out."

Do you feel there is sadness in you or a fear of life?

"There is fear for sure. I'm not a sad person. But especially in the suitcases there is a nostalgic feel to the paintings. Maybe all the travelling, because we moved around quite a bit, not always on good terms, immigrating for other reasons, family problems. At the end that series was really about those losses, what they call in the psychological field, your drama, the people that you lose, that series caught that. The food series is about the moment, the ephemeral. It is not about food. I love food but it is about form, aesthetics, also about the porcelain, the ceramics, the table, the fun part. I like materials, the texture of things. Basically it is about light. My painting has always been about light because when you grow up with the classical masters, that's what you see. The chiaroscuro is very obvious. It has always been about light anyways but these guys were very focused on that. You will see a ray of light hitting a hand or a face. That really struck me and you will see that in my figure paintings."

Near us hangs Santiago's painting of an empty cardboard box. The box has been opened and is torn a little on one corner. A bright light is coming through a mullioned window that we cannot see and is shining on the surface of the box giving the impression that someone is present just outside the frame of the painting and we wonder who opened the box and what was in it. I comment to Santiago that the light is an important subject in the painting and he agrees. "Also where it is hitting. Light creates the form."

Some people say that San Miguel has a light that is favourable to painting. On the west coast where I am from, the winters are gray. When I'm in San Miguel I wake up happy every morning.

Santiago laughs. "That's why they come here."

What brought you to San Miguel?

"When we lived in Mexico City it was a popular place to come for a holiday or for a weekend. It was always very appealing. I didn't want to live in Mexico City so I was living in Valle del Bravo where we have another gallery but there is nothing to do during the week. It's a very quiet town although it gets very crowded on the weekends. I wanted some social life and I decided to come to San Miguel, not because there are artists, none of those reasons. You can go out on a Monday morning and have a coffee, have different options. I felt it was more of a normal economy. It was nice to find there were a lot of galleries and artists of course but I love the town. I love the architecture. I have been able to walk and feel very comfortable. No matter what time you walk in town, it is pleasant. You feel the same way when you are in Paris, even if it's gray there is something in the air that is very magical and I think San Miguel has that. And the light, yes it is special. As far as the influence on painting, I don't know. I think artists can create in any environment and really, any environment has a lot of things to inspire. My art dealer from New York warned me. Be careful living in San Miguel. All those colours may not be good for your painting. He had a point. He helped me understand that gray is very important because it is a neutral colour. It is not just about throwing bright colours at a canvas."

You have a dealer in New York. You have lived in Paris and Spain and the United States. You have spent time in the Middle East and in Europe. What have your travels done for you?

"It opens up your mind. You learn to adapt. I first moved to France because I wanted to learn French but not as a tourist. I wanted to be part of the society. I went to work for a hang glider company in France, one of the best in the world. I happened to meet the owner in Mexico City and I asked him for a job and he hired me. When I was there working many long days, I was also doing my painting, that ego part of one, showing that you have another talent. Don't think I am just a pilot. I know about other things." Santiago chuckles remembering his younger self. "I was doing murals in Mexico City in children's rooms, and car shops, and stores. In the end I did it to survive. I have always had to work since I was eleven years old. I had to do it for a living.

Even though I had a job and I would get paid for flying and teaching, it wasn't always enough so I also relied on painting. I sold my first painting when I was thirteen, a typical still life with wine and grapes. When I was in France I offered to paint a mural in my boss' house, in the master bathroom. It took me seven months because I could only paint at night, bit by bit. I painted the French landscape, the Alps on one side, a little village, the whole ceiling was clouds, it was beautiful. In seven months when you work little by little and you don't rush it, you can make something really nice. The owner, my friend always came to watch me paint. After I finished it, he and his wife closed the bathroom. That was their bathroom but they never used it again. I said 'Just varnish it. There are ways to protect it.' But they said no, no, and they kept going to the bathroom downstairs. A few years later they sold the house." There is more laughter, this time softened by the shared knowledge that trying to preserve the past is often impractical.

Tell me about living in Israel.

"My girlfriend moved there from Toronto with her twin sister. They had a clothing business in Toronto called Cat's Cradle, very popular in the eighties, knit wear, casual clothing, great designs. She and her sister were two beautiful twins, both of them funny and gracious. We met in Acapulco and then she came to live with me in Valle del Bravo. After our relationship ended she went to live with her sister who had moved to Israel and then a year later I took advantage of our friendship and went to live with them in Jerusalem for eight months. They were living in an apartment but I made myself a little studio out of one of the bedrooms and I painted all the time I was there. I was painting surrealism at that time. When you are young you have all these existentialist ideas. You mentioned the light in San Miguel. The air in Jerusalem is the same, very powerful. It is semi-desert, high in the mountains. It has the same feel and the same blue sky, very sharp. They use a lot of stones in the buildings and at sunset, everything turns golden. It is a beautiful city. You get the historical influence which is so vivid and alive, all the traditions."

"I was in Jerusalem all through the winter. I used to walk to the old city, sometimes it would be snowing and it was very beautiful. I am not religious, nor am I Jewish although my father says we have some Jewish heritage from northern Spain. It could be. I was raised in the Catholic church but I'm not interested in religions. In Israel, life can be difficult. People have to be hard because they live under pressure, very stressed. The money seems not to flow very much. When I was there, there was a lot of cheque writing and giving credit. Even in supermarkets you could sign a post-dated cheque. And yet it seems like Israel gets a lot of help from the outside. They have large parks and beautiful buildings. Everything is expensive. The quality of the food is great. I like the diversity of cultures in Jerusalem. Everyone enters the military. I watched the young men and women going out at night dressed in green and carrying machine guns. It seemed natural even though we are against war. There are many great things about Jerusalem but I wouldn't live there. People live on their last thread."

In Israel, the men and the women share many of the same roles. Has your travel produced any conflict within you about gender differences, particularly living here in Mexico where machismo is said to be alive and well.

"In my travels I have found machismo everywhere. I don't tend to generalize anymore, but more than male chauvinism it is ignorance that bothers me the most. Machismo is a bi-product of terrible ignorance, a lack of education of any kind. Not everyone has the opportunity to travel but they can still be educated. The Cubans don't travel because they can't, but they read. Here in Mexico, ignorance is really a result of the miserable education we have. Not so much in my social status because I grew up with a wealthy family even though my mother was thrown out of the dynasty for marrying a man who was not approved of by the family. We ended up having to work because my father was brought up in the old way, very strict. He was an immigrant from Spain. My mother was born in Mexico but all her family is from Spain. My grandfather was brought here by his father who was very hard. They came here in a boat with no money and immigrated to the New World, to America the continent, looking for fortune. That was the reason he was never an artist. He was pushing to make money because that is what they came here for and that is what they did. He was brought up in a tough way and he was tough with his children. My grandmother, like other women, was like the Virgin Mary in an altar. Women are the most important thing. That is the contradiction in Mexico, the idea of the Virgin but as the woman, you don't speak, you don't say. It's everywhere like this. I think it is all ignorance. If it was an educated country, machismo would be gone. It's as simple as that. I think we need to break a lot of these traditions, these totally wrong misunderstandings. I believe many of these traditions are not healthy. The ways of thinking are very *arraigado* as we say in Spanish, deeply rooted. There are ways of changing that through education but it needs to be taught to children. In spite of the problems, I feel optimistic because I believe it is changing. I will encourage my daughter to travel. She is already learning French from her grandmother who speaks five languages. I see girls dressing up and breaking away from the male oppression and violence that is also part of the ignorance. Maybe I'm being unrealistic in thinking that education would fix everything, but it could certainly help. Despite the lack of opportunities, there have always been famous writers and artists that come from very small villages in the country. Some people are born with a drive and an ambition. In Mexico we say even if people have an education some choose not to have it. Take any child. Any child wants to learn. They might decide they don't want to go any further when they are adults but with an education they will have more instruments, they will have more tools. They might choose not to do anything else, but they will have a choice."

"I was a teacher and I think you are right that circumstances will change for the better in Mexico as educational opportunities improve."

"Well, because information is so accessible. Unfortunately the education I'm talking about is the one that occurs slowly and gives you the idea to expand your life. At the end, all that we see is information. We are bombarded by it. That's why my next painting is a two metre high i-pod using multiple images. I am working on it now. I will do a painting and then I will take a photograph and mount it on plexiglass using the same theme, using the i-phone as an icon of our time. It is not the artifact itself but the idea behind it that represents our time. I want to present a clear concept using images that have the same theme. I want to develop something I have never developed. Up to now my paintings have shown more of my unconscious side and not as much of my intellectual side. I want to start doing paintings that have a more direct message. For example, I did a portrait of my daughter on a camouflage fabric. It's about children and violence. *Intentionality* is what I am talking about. It is something that I want to explore and develop. It's an exercise but I think it will help my career if you want to call it that, my path. I want to communicate better, not just the beauty, which is what I have been concentrating on all this time, the beauty of an object, the beauty of the light, the composition, but the message."

Santiago tells me of Francisco Toledo. Born in 1940, Toledo is a Oaxacan artist well known in Mexico as a passionate defender of his Zapotec culture and its mystical roots. He studied for a time in France and became adept at using a variety of mediums including ceramics, oil paint, ink, and fabric. He is still a prolific artist himself but today he devotes much of his time and creative energy to the education and encouragement of younger artists. "I read something about Toledo in one of his biographies, something that caused a 'click', very important, something I was doing without knowing it. I was accomplishing it without realizing. He said the message is always the secondary thing.

First is the beauty of the painting, after that is what you want to say. Both can live together. One doesn't negate the other. Some people have a very strong message, a strong intellectual idea that they want to convey and they emphasize it over the pictorial aspect. I'm against that. For me first it is the beauty of the painting, the colour, the composition, the light, and the feeling that it gives you and then the realization that there is something very strong there. They both go hand in hand but the two must remain very balanced. One shouldn't dominate over the other. In any case, if one is going to dominate, it should always be the pictorial. If you were going to measure my paintings, the pictorial has always been very strong. Still lifes are always more focused on the beauty, painting for the sake of painting, the beauty of things. When I get into the figure painting I want to make it clear why the person is expressing what he is expressing. Really develop it. It will help me and inspire me if I can make a statement or say something in a more direct way without losing the other part, that part which is really for everybody, seeing the beauty before everything else, without having to think."

Are you saying you intend to make your paintings more political?

"I suppose you could call it political, not in the way Tomayo or Rivera were political but political if you use that word loosely like the painting of my daughter with the camouflage. I did another painting of my girlfriend with a mask over her mouth from when we had the swine flu scare here. The widespread fear was government induced but also self-induced. We were fearful for a few days but then you realize you are being sucked in. In Spanish we say you almost stepped on the stick, *pisando el palito*. Someone put it there for you to step on and when you step on it, you are in the trap. I want to make more paintings where there is beauty but where the message is clear."

"I have plans for my next series but sometimes it is difficult because I don't work as much as I want to. I have very limited days and hours. My daughter is here and I commit a lot of time to her and I have my airplane. I have to deal with that duality. It is always a war inside of me. I am not one of those painters who can work for twelve, fifteen hours a day. I have a need to paint but more than a need to paint, I want to make a painting that is going to impress me from the first moment and if it doesn't, it really drags me down. Any artist will relate to this. Every artist is trying to make this impressive painting. That is really what is going to make you work more, to get more involved. Since I was a kid I always had dreams of grandness but I am also very objective and there are so many great artists today, so I am not so interested in becoming 'the artist', not at all. I want to make a painting that really impresses me, and not just one. It is as if you were mining and you finally find a *vita*, a seam, and you just go for it and really excel and what I mean by excel is you can be a well known artist with access to great museums. Probably that is the biggest reward, being able to be in a great space where you can make a great painting, something big and it is going to hang there and look great and many people will see it. It is like having a power but before any of that, if you can impress yourself with great work you are probably going to impress other people. I have had shows in many museums in Mexico, for example in Chiuaua I had a show in the Sebastian Museum, a very famous museum in Mexico, very contemporary, very modern, in an old building, but very modern inside. The walls were beautiful. It was very well set up. It really felt wonderful. The night of the show, the municipal president of the city came with his wife and three or four hundred people and many more people came in the following weeks. That night was so special. People loved the paintings and they were very, very happy. They left smiling. It's a province after all so they don't get many great shows. I'm not saying mine was great but it was very nice and I enjoy that so much and I can imagine having that in a bigger spectrum, the Guggenheim or another large gallery in New York. A premier in one of those great spaces would be a real achievement. I think if I concentrate on my work, on the quality of the work, it will make the crossover. As long as I am exhibiting, eventually my paintings will make their way into other places outside Mexico."

"I want to say that I don't consider myself a Mexican painter. I grew up in many countries, many places. I don't want to be recognized as a Mexican painter, or any nationality. It is that universal thing. When I was younger, I had several realizations that were very important and that was one of them. I didn't want to paint people with hats and Mexican themes, not at all. I also thought my colours weren't very well developed, not very mature so I decided I was going to work one painting with all reds, one painting with blues, one painting with yellows and I discovered many tones in each family of colours. I did that for a year and a half, almost two years."

It makes me think of Picasso's blue period.

"Picasso was probably just playing with colours but I didn't go to school so I had to do my homework. I had been painting about three years when I decided, I'm a painter now and I want to take the next step up. So I started with simple objects and I learned a lot about colours and when I met my dealer in New York I went to museums, got some great advice from him, and learned many important things. It helped me organize my head, to stick to something, develop a subject, finish it and move to another. I needed that badly. I needed that discipline of being organized and knowing what I was going to paint next instead of wandering around, oscillating between ideas. I still need that structure which I didn't have as a child. As a boy, I was spontaneous, free, left out there to do whatever I wanted. I focus now. This conceptual work is going to be a whole series. If it goes for years, it might develop into something else or it might just be that, and I will go back to painting in the more traditional way, but I will follow it until it is done."

Can we go back to something you said when we began this conversation? You said there are two kinds of spirits in your

family, the pilots and the painters. What's the difference between them and how can you be both?

"That's what I'm trying to figure out. I have been in the flying world all my life and it seems there is no relationship between it and the art world. I think you use different sides of the brain. Flying has more to do with science. You have to be methodical and disciplined, which you do in painting but it is a different kind of discipline. In painting you have to set your mind to work a certain number of hours. In flying the rules are very strict and it is always by the book. Stay on the safe side. It is all about safety. You are dealing with your life so you have to read all the technical books and commit the information to memory. Flying has no relationship to painting other than when you are flying you have a different view, a bird's eye view. If you notice in my paintings most of them are from a bird's eye view, even if I am painting a coffee table or a suitcase, the view is from a forty-five degree angle above, never vertically because when you fly you usually don't look vertically down. You are looking forward and down and you are looking where you are heading. That's probably the most interesting thing about flying and being an artist. You can really bring that perspective into your art and it makes something different. It is a different point of view.

Do you do that consciously?

"Not any more because I have been flying for a long time and now it's natural. I do very few paintings from a horizontal viewpoint as the classical painters did. Most of my work is from above and I have explored that. In some of my work it is unconscious and in other works I purposely use that view. In classical paintings the horizon is more or less in the middle. In my paintings it tends to be further up or further down. In my landscapes the horizon may be in the middle of the canvas but if you look at my landscapes, you can see I try to obscure the horizon. I don't like that line, maybe it is from flying too much. If you have a line you set yourself in a certain fixed position. My landscapes often have trees or other objects obscuring the horizon. When I think of painting I think of something more spherical, no beginning and no end."

"Flying lets me be free, out there in nature, feeling the air and being part of everything around me. Painting is more of an inner activity, something that forces me inside my head. And of course, flying is exciting. I like the rush of adrenalin I get when I am flying. I have done a lot of hang gliding which can be dangerous because you have no motor and you must know the wind conditions. It is very physical but my father was a football player and my brothers and I have always been very athletic. I think the challenge of flying is my way of facing my fears. I feel a need to push myself and by doing this I am able to tame something that at first frightened me. It's true some people set the bar too high and so they never try but I continue to try and when I succeed, I want to attempt something even more difficult. I suppose painting is like that too because I enjoy the challenge of making something that surprises me. Sometimes if I am working on a painting that is going well, I can't sleep because of the excitement so in that way also the two activities are similar but the conflict is always there, to paint or to fly."

A few years ago I flew to France to see a young German friend Tim, who I got to know when he studied at Pearson College of the Pacific, one of the United World Colleges. We had arranged to meet in Paris so we could travel together to his parent's home near Dresden. Knowing Tim's fondness for cars, I had broken the bank and rented a large BMW for the trip. Tim is trained as a pilot and he concentrates when he drives a car just as he does when he is flying a plane. After a couple of days' vacation in Germany, Tim flew back to work in London and I was left to return the BMW to Paris alone. At this point I hadn't driven the rather intimidating vehicle at all so before he left, Tim and I went out to a local parking lot to practice. After witnessing my ineptitude from the passenger seat, I could tell Tim had decided I would never make it to Paris alive. He told me I drove like a Canadian, absent minded, not fully committed to the task at hand. Despite my national handicap, I did manage to get to Paris in one piece but I never forgot the collected proficiency with which Tim flew along the German highways and I thought of him again during my conversation with Santiago. Although we have never been in an airplane together, I have no doubt that Santiago Corral devotes the same zealous attention to his flying as he does to his art. He knows where he wants to go and what he wants to accomplish, and certainly no one could fail to appreciate his current achievements, the consummate technical skill that is so visible in all his paintings. But what sets Corral's work apart is what reaches out to the imagination, a quality that emerges from beneath the surface like a floating object, buoyant but often hard to identify, something that is recognized most instinctively by the heart. Perhaps the artist and the pilot share more than they know. Antoine de Saint-Exupery, himself an aviator, understood that the eyes are likely to see a hat, whereas the heart in its wisdom, knows the hat to be a boa constrictor digesting an elephant. It simply depends on one's perspective.

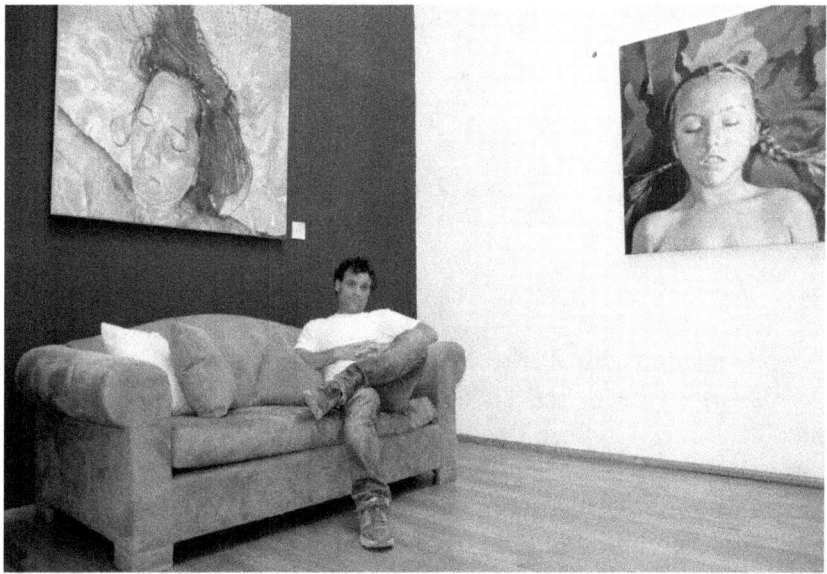

Pedro Friedeberg

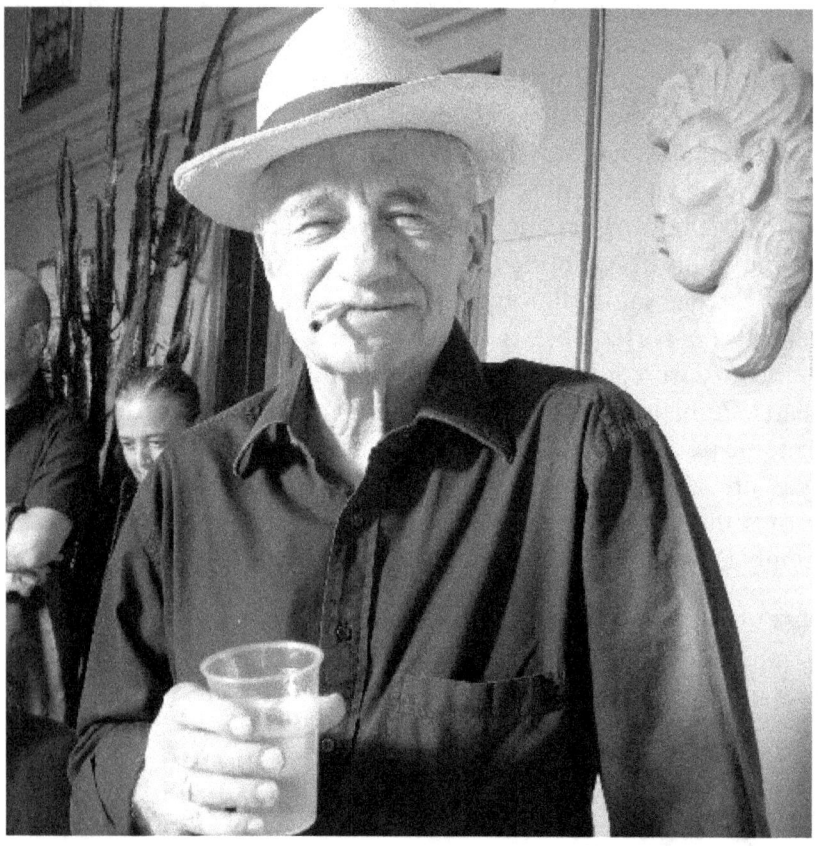

A conversation with Pedro Friedeberg is not a frenetic volley of words tossed back like shots of whiskey on a night out in the local cantina. It unfolds thoughtfully, seductively, like a fine wine that has overtones of honey and a long finish. While others have told me that Pedro can be intimidating, I find he is obliging and good humoured although I do get the distinct impression that he is amused by my attentions. I am aware too that I am working hard to secure his good opinion.

We meet in Pedro's former home in San Miguel where he and his wife Carmen lived for seventeen years. The two are divorced and Pedro lives in Mexico City so I am delighted to find him visiting his ex-wife for a few days. They remain friends and recently traveled together to Europe with their adult children. The room we sit in is part of Casa Diana, the successful art gallery that Carmen owns and operates, where we are surrounded by art and the sounds of people coming and going in other parts of the house. Periodically the intrusive roar of a passing vehicle forces us to pause until once again I can hear Pedro's somewhat husky, measured voice. He tells me that twenty-five years ago San Miguel had ten taxis and a handful of private cars. One could park easily on the street in front of one's house. Now San Miguel like so many other cities, suffers from what Pedro calls, "overcarification."

Just his name is evidence of the fact that Pedro Friedeberg is a man of the world. He was born in Florence, Italy in 1936, his Jewish parents having left Germany shortly before the Second World War. At the age of three, he and his newly divorced mother boarded one of the last ships in Hamburg heading for Veracruz. Pedro describes it as carrying eight times as many people as it should. "My mother would have preferred England or the United States but the quota was full so we took what we got. Mother had distant relatives in Mexico City, among them a cousin named Friedeberg whom she eventually married. He paid for my education, sent me to Europe when I was a young man. He was a very good father."

As a child, Pedro was attracted to the elaborate and the absurd. His favourite book was *Alice In Wonderland*. "My mother who was very German would say 'Why do you read that nonsense? Why don't you read Dostoevsky or Tolstoy?' But I found them to be sordid. When I was about ten, my parents would give me money to go see the movies in Mexico City. 'You must go,' they insisted, 'You have nothing to do all afternoon. You must go see *The Bicycle Thief* or *Shoeshine*' but I preferred Hollywood movies with lots of girls coming down stairs in feathers. At home again they would ask, 'How did you like the movie?' and I had to invent. 'It was very interesting, very sad.' But they never caught me because I was a very good liar and besides, they never asked me too many questions. Even then I didn't care for realism or things to do with poverty. I wanted to live in a different world where magic is possible."

I am later reminded that twenty-five years after De Sica made *The Bicycle Thief* and *Shoeshine*, he directed *The Garden of the Finzi-Continis,* a film which hauntingly encapsulates the desire to escape a chaotic and painful existence and instead, to reside forever in a place of order and beauty. In the movie the garden is ultimately destroyed by fascism, but it is my impression that Pedro Friedeberg preserves his own sanctuary through his art.

"From a young age I used to draw, especially houses and churches and that's why later I studied architecture just at the wrong period, in the late 1950s and early 60's. Everything then had to be in the style of Mies Van Der Rohe and the Bauhaus. Everything had to be square, which I hated so I wasn't very successful." When I ask if he knew Luis Barragan, Pedro says Barragan wasn't too well accepted because his work had a lot of blind walls. "His teacher was Mathias Goeritz and I worked with Mathias. We did some projects together. We painted a little mural for his offices. I was just an assistant when he collaborated with Luis Barragan to do The Torres de Satelite, the five towers in Naucalpan de Juarez. I assisted, sort of helping and learning. While I was there Goeritz designed the windows in the cathedral and in the church of San Lorenzo in Mexico City that are in the German expressionist style. Mathias was a very creative and funny person so it was a delight to work with him. He didn't take anything seriously. At the same time he was very generous. He was a very special person." I ask Pedro if perhaps some of the humour in his work could have come from Goeritz. "I think that is why we got along so well. We understood the same things. We had the same outlook on life."

Friedeberg gets up to retrieve a book that was published in 1972 and contains a picture of him taken in the late sixties. Here is a compact, handsome young man standing in his house "before it was full of clutter" and wearing a zebra patterned jacket. Pedro tells me he had a tiger suit as well as the zebra jacket because it was important to attract attention, to set one's self apart. "In the 1960's Mexico was a much smaller city and you were still able to get to know everybody and you could get near the collectors. You could invite them to your studios, show them your work and they were delighted to come to artists' studios. I wanted to be original. I liked original things. When I went to New York in 1960, everyone was doing abstract paintings so I began to despise abstract paintings and preferred to do figurative or geometric paintings. I have always liked playing with shapes. I like ornamentation. Victorian art, baroque art, these appealed to me but they were not fashionable at all. I liked painting and sculpture that were not popular, not known, like art nouveau. This is fifty years ago or more. The Pre-Raphaelite painters were not popular and I liked them. I always liked things that were not fashionable. This was pre happenings or installation. But that kind of art has gone too far. It has become boring. When all the second rate artists copy something, it becomes déjà vu."

Do you think anything new is possible in art today?

"No. I don't think anything new is possible in art but it is always possible to find a new combination. For example, you see women wearing pants from the sixties, shoes from the forties, and hair from the two thousand and twenties. Everything is eclectic these days although I still hate minimalism, cubes made of glass. My house in Mexico City is very cluttered. I have many things that I like. I even have things that I hate. People think that because I have so many things I want more things. Last week someone gave me a bird made in China that starts singing and wiggles its head but it is done with no taste."

In the room where we sit is a large table with a glass top being held up by enormous hands. I ask Pedro what gave him the idea for the hands which he has used in many forms and are a kind of trademark.

"When I went to Rome I saw the museum on the Capitoline Hill, fragments of the statue of Jupiter. There's a large foot and a hand too. I loved those. Years ago Mathias Goeritz had a wood carver that worked for him and when Mathias went to Europe for a few months he said please give the carver a job to do because he needs money and I will be gone. That's when I had the idea for the hands."

We exchange remarks about Italy that stir Pedro's memories of a trip taken long ago. "I love the atmosphere in Rome. You feel you are in an Italian city as opposed to Florence which is now so crowded with tourists. Once when I was in Rome I got caught in a downpour. I got lost in the narrow streets and I had to walk two or three miles and there were no taxis. The palaces have overhangs but it rains twice as hard under them. I was two hours late for my appointment. Even so, I loved the experience. I first went to Europe in 1962 so I must have been twenty-five or twenty-six. I was supposed to go for a year but I ran out of money and came back after nine months. I did all the things you're supposed to do, flew to Paris, went up the Eiffel Tower. I was with a girl friend and we rented a car. There were no freeways. You had to go through every village on narrow roads. It was wonderful. It took three days to get to Provence. Nowadays you just whiz by. I think the food was much better then."

"When I went home to Mexico I was working full time as an artist. I was having shows, trying to sell things. Sometimes I had no money. Sometimes I had what I thought was a lot of money. I was happy doing what I wanted to do. Mathias knew some people from Germany so he introduced me and they invited me to have a show in a very fine gallery in Munich the year after, in 1963. I had met the French Ambassador in Lisbon while I was in Paris and he said he could get me a show in a prestigious gallery in Lisbon so I said, Oh sure, why not? When you are young you will do anything. The next year I couldn't pay for the freight so I packed all the paintings I had, including all the ones from the year I spent in New York, and made the trip on a creaky ship built in 1930 from the time of Mussolini. I got off in Lisbon with my thirty or forty paintings and hung them in the gallery. I didn't speak Portuguese but if you speak Spanish it isn't hard. For a month, I lived in a three star hotel with three meals a day for seven dollars. It was true what those books said about living in Europe on five dollars a day. For seven dollars you could live like a king."

"From Lisbon I took a trip on a bus to Spain. There were no big roads then. It was the holy week in Seville and all the hotels were full. I asked the taxi driver, 'Where can I stay. The city looks like it is popping.' He said not to worry, I could stay at his house. The Spanish used to be very proud. He would take no pay. We got to his house at about two in the morning and he told his six daughters to sleep in another room and I slept in the daughters' bed. I had all those old fashioned experiences that I don't think one can have anymore. I spent a few nice days in Seville and then I said I wanted to go visit some friends in Malaga so the taxi driver said for the price of gas he would drive me but he had never driven on country roads before and we almost fell into many ravines. I spent another month there because the show in Lisbon was going to take two months. It was wonderful in the south of Spain. The coast wasn't ruined like it is now. Then all the paintings had to be flown to Munich for that show so I took a train to Munich and I had my show there. The people spoiled me a lot. They were very kind to me. We never talked about Jewish or not Jewish. I stayed in a house owned by a woman whose husband had been killed in the war. I noticed his picture on the wall of my room. He had been a Nazi but I didn't say anything. What could I say? During the month in Munich I sold a lot of paintings. They loved my work."

"In Germany I had another revelation which were the castles of King Ludwig II. Now there are six hundred buses full of tourists in front of each, but you could almost drive up to the castles in those days. You could even take souvenirs if no one was watching, little pieces of castle. The art dealer in Munich was very kind. He drove me around to visit Nymphenburg, Neuschwanstein, Linderhoff where Wagner's operas are staged, and Herrenchiemsee which is a copy of Versailles but a metre longer. That was quite a fantastic experience. When I was forty-five, I went to Sicily. It too was a revelation. I discovered the baroque buildings which had all been rebuilt after the 1695 earthquake."

"You're Jewish."

"Mostly."

"Is it important to you that you are Jewish?"

"No, although now I have a mezuzah in my house for the first time because I have a new art dealer who is also a rabbi in Mexico City and he insists. He's a wonderful person but I love to go to good restaurants and he can only go to two restaurants in the whole of Mexico City because of the kosher diet. I enjoy his company but I don't enjoy the food. He lives in one of these high-rises in the suburbs of the city where they have a pool and a gym. I notice half the people are quite fat in spite of the exercise. I don't do any exercise. In those places there are no libraries, no bookstores. To me it seems such a sad life, although I suppose they are happy. I would rather live in a village, a dusty village with maybe a little air conditioning."

Behind Pedro on the floor is a canvas that at the moment is blank except for a spiral of tiny detailed drawings moving out from the centre. He brings it over to where we sit. "My work is very inside, very private. Why is there an alligator in this picture? Because I love animals. A picture has to have some relation to life, to anatomy or botany. I never liked abstract pictures. It is not enough. I guess you could say I was influenced by magic realism but I'm not realistic enough. Many years ago when I had shows here, I was told my work is very German. I like very regimented things, very orderly things." He draws my attention to another of his paintings on the opposite wall. "This painting is the second of that kind. It has cats and more colour. Sometimes when I like a painting of mine I try to repeat it, not exactly, but a variation. DeChirico used to do many versions of the same thing. He did eighteen paintings of a woman made up of geometrical shapes in an architectural setting. Matisse, Monet…Picasso did hundreds of variations on the same subject, a guitar and a bottle of wine. The first version of this picture was black and white but black and white pictures never sell. People want colour. Generally people buy painting for colour."

"Do the figures in your paintings have some symbolism?"

"Everything has symbolism if you want to find it. The crowns are here because I love aristocracy, kings and queens although I realize they are as corrupt as non-aristocrats. Sometimes I use an image just because I like it. See these little horses. I've always been fascinated by sea horses. I always liked stories that took me away from nagging parents, boring school, difficult play mates. Life seemed to be humdrum but when I read *Sleeping Beauty*, it was fanciful. Maybe that explains why I fell in love with the castles of Ludwig II."

"A few years ago I met a Columbian writer Fernando Arellano who has written a number of excellent books. He wrote a terrible book about the Catholic Church, he's Catholic of course, and it describes the corruption of the church. On the other hand religion has been responsible for ninety percent of the art in the past twenty centuries. I sort of got hooked on Catholicism. I always loved the altars and the statues and the cathedrals. My parents were atheists but I loved the cathedrals, maybe it was my Italian background. You know the church that is next to Bellas Artes here in San Miguel? I took my son there when he was three years old and he looked at the statues way up high and he asked what are they doing up there? I think he thought they were alive."

Now as I write, I am distracted by loud explosions that sound like small cannons firing but which I know from experience are fireworks set off to mark another festive occasion. This being the first week of October, the commotion is part of the annual celebration honouring Saint Michael the archangel, patron saint of St. Miguel. I judge this event to be particularly merry because it has brought a parade down my narrow street consisting mainly of four and five year olds dressed in native costumes of tan paper or cloth, each child with a painted face and a colourful headband. Here and there among them are taller figures in extravagant feather headdresses and at the rear a band plays music which is not the militaristic march of parades I am used to in Canada, but the quick drums and horns of a joyful dance. Proud parents walk along the sidelines taking pictures and offering encouragement.

"Are there any clues in your work that you have spent your life in Mexico?"

"I suppose the *animas del purgatorio*, then those butterfly chairs. I got the idea from a house in Mexico City. A Mexican architect went to Belgium when art nouveau was still new and in 1902 he did his house in Mexico in art nouveau. Each room had a different theme. One bedroom was done in art nouveau Red Riding Hood. There was a Snow White room. The house has been torn down since but I loved to go there. It wasn't open to the public. You had to knock and ask if you could come in and sometimes they would let you in and sometimes not. That's where I got the idea for the chairs but I made butterflies instead of flowers."

"I love ornament so maybe I was influenced by the churches like in Oaxaca or the church of Santa Maria Tonantzintla in Puebla which is covered with angels carrying fruit and flowers. It is a fantastic place. Cholula in Puebla is supposed to have 365 churches, one for each day of the year but I have only counted about 40. It is an Indian version of baroque or rococo and is very primitive. That is the charm of it. The Spanish and native cultures married very well. There are two churches in Queretaro, Santa Clara and Santa Rosa which have fabulous churricueresque painted in a crazy Baroque style which is almost psychedelic, covered in gold leaf. When I was younger, I was fascinated by the Spanish architect, Gaudi. Not many people knew Gaudi at that time but I always loved his designs."

"As for the Mexican landscape, I don't take much from nature. Maybe if you come here at twenty-five, you say wow have you seen this colour, but when you come at the age of three, you take it for granted. My mother bought flowers from the flower vendor every day and our house was filled with them. I don't have an interest in landscapes. If something can be photographed, why would you want to paint it? One hundred years ago the impressionists were experimenting with light and Seurat was discovering that colour is a series of little dots but that is from the 19th century. It isn't valid anymore. I know people still enjoy painting landscapes. There is nothing wrong with it but I wouldn't go out in the country to paint mountains or deer reflected in a pool. I am most fascinated with arabesques and patterns. I loved the Moorish art in Spain. That is what I use most, patterns. I try to invent new patterns."

I study the detailed painting that is still close to us on the floor. **"Is it comforting to do this work?"**

Pedro's eyes widen in acknowledgement. "Yes, very comforting. I start with something and it grows like a plant. I started this a week ago and I don't know what is coming next."

Finally, as we are both beginning to tire, I ask Pedro Friedeberg to tell me if his life has been a happy one.

"I don't think anybody has a totally happy life. There are ups and downs. Regrets? Yes, very many. Sometimes you do the wrong thing. Sometimes you wonder why didn't you get to know this person better. I see that every day there are two paths. You are taking one or the other. Sometimes you should have taken the other one. They say one shouldn't regret anything, but why not? Some people think that God is up there saying that tomorrow you will have cornflakes for breakfast not eggs but I can't say if our lives are predetermined. To me, it is a puzzle."

Pedro asks about my career and I explain that I was a teacher of children with learning difficulties. I tell him it gave my life meaning. He considers for a moment. "I feel my life has been sort of meaning*less*, just making art. But that's what I enjoyed doing. My parents wanted me to be an architect building glass cubes and maybe I should have been more aggressive, painted bigger things, worked harder. But that's what is nice about being an artist. You can be lazy and not feel guilty. You can wake up and paint or go to Acapulco instead. Your whole life is a vacation. I think I have had just three jobs lasting only two months, in my life. The first one was in the sixties working for a magazine. I was useful to the woman editor because I knew a lot about Mexico, the churches, Mexican customs. Another job I had for three months was selling records. The shop was owned by the husband of the painter Remedios Varo who was a friend of my parents. So it has not been a very disciplined life. I don't feel I have had to do things that I don't enjoy doing. Even so, now I find you have to do horrible things and it gets worse and worse. There is all this paper, the water and the electricity and the car. You have to go to government offices and take eight copies which you lose on the way. Half the people I know have computers that are out of order or they have a virus or they can't get into the something. I don't even have a computer or a television, or a cell phone."

"Have you been entirely undisciplined?"

"I have been disciplined in that I paint every day, not because of the Protestant work ethic but because I enjoy it and I have nothing else to do in the morning. I sit down and do little squares or squiggles or doodles. I read a great deal. I have about 10,000 books in my house in Mexico. They start choking you. I have made a vow that I won't buy any more books until I have read all the good books a second time. So that is what I am doing now. I enjoy people coming to interview, like this. Lot's of people say wow, wow. I don't think they think my work is such great art but it is full of detail. Recently someone came to my house about fifty times and wrote my memoirs. It was interesting because I was forced to remember. It is very flattering to one's personality. In October there is a major exhibition of my life's work at the Bellas Artes in Mexico City and they want pieces from the 1960's and 70's but I don't have them. Just to get rid of things I sold them for very little. I should have kept a record but I was too lazy to go to all the bureaucratic work. I just painted something and if someone came and said I love it, I would say take it, take it so I could travel, keep my vacations going. I have lived in my house in Mexico City for nine years but about four years ago the beams were full of termites, and the stairwell collapsed. If I had been there, I would have been killed. Then last year when I was in Europe, the entire ceiling in the library collapsed. The whole roof crumbled. You could see the sky. Fortunately there was little damage to the books. It took six or seven months to rebuild. Such a stupid expense because in Mexico we are not insured against acts of God."

"In Canada, I think we would be insured against that kind of event."

"Naturally. You don't have these old wooden beams or Mexican termites."

As I say my good-byes to Pedro Friedeberg, I am conscious of the fact that I have been bewitched by this charming man. Even the Mexican termites have become exotic characters in a fairy-tale world of Pedro's invention. And like all the artists that I have met, the art is an extension of its creator, a product in this case, of a complex and rich imagination.

This past week I attended the opening of Pedro's show at the spectacular Palace of the Bellas Artes in Mexico City. It was a glamorous affair with cameras and speeches and a crush of beautiful people. Pedro's work was plentiful and much admired. Alone with my cocktail, I happened to notice a large poster describing Friedeberg as an architect of "impeccable confusion" and though the juxtaposition of these contradictory ideas had some appeal, I couldn't agree with them both as descriptors of Pedro or his accomplishments. Impeccable, yes, but confusion…I don't think so. Pedro Friedeberg possesses a clarity of intention which informs his life in all its aspects and which is certainly evident in his art. He is a romantic, a man who has long preferred refinement to the crude struggle which frequently defines human experience. Whether by providence or by his own design, Friedeberg has articulated a yearning for transcendence that most of us share but lack the ability to express. Such a vocation is surely not meaningless.

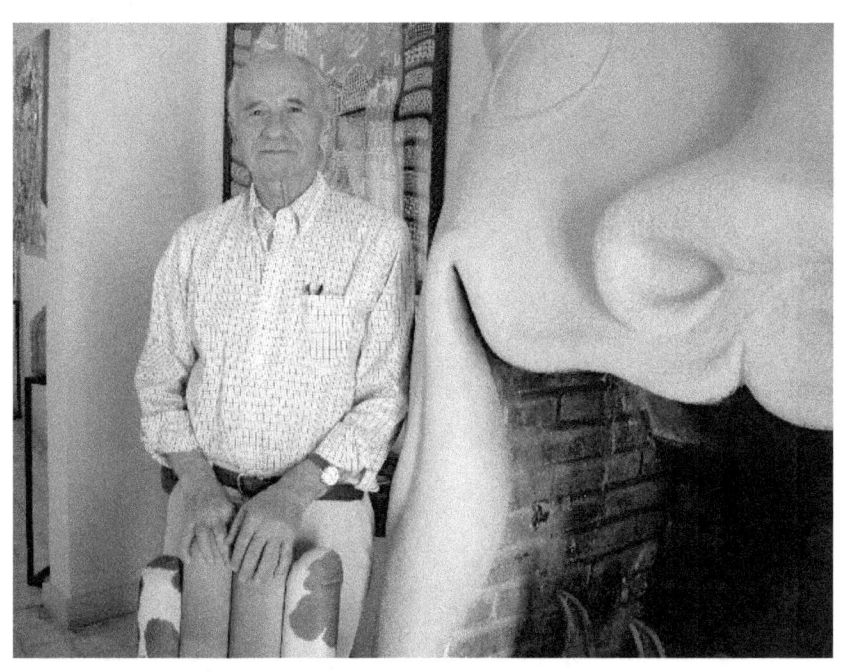

Stephen Eaker and Bea Aaronson

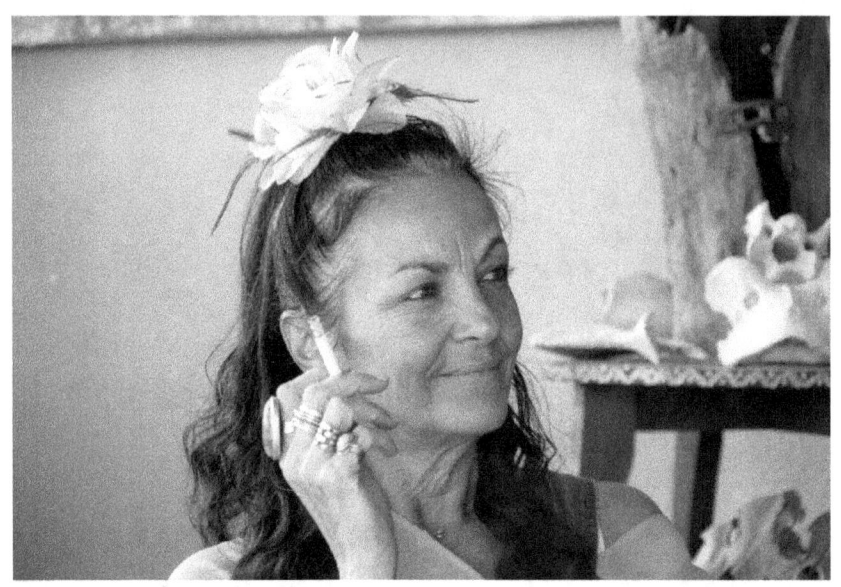

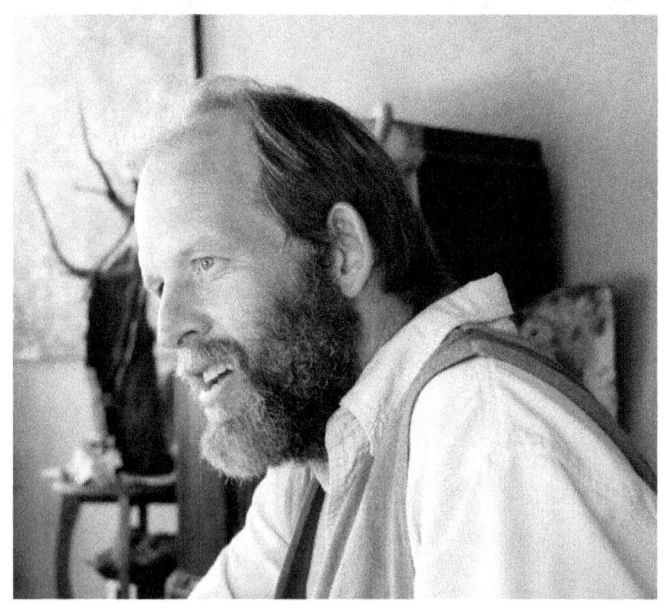

When Bea Aaronson lived in South Africa she joined the protest against apartheid. In the eighties when Nicolae Ceausescu controlled Romania, she attempted to publicize the brutality of his regime in a mural she hoped would emulate Picasso's *Guernica*. More recently she exhibited a series of works intended to draw attention to the right of every person to have access to clean water. Although she would deny it has been her raison d'etre, Bea has long been an artist with what she calls a "political edge". Stephen Eaker, Bea's partner, had his own political epiphany when he came to Mexico and discovered his ideas about the country were in fact prejudices he had formed as a result of the stereotypes he encountered in his birthplace, the United States. The two now live in San Miguel de Allende where they paint and are active members of the local community.

It was on Leonard Brooks' recommendation that I contacted Stephen and Bea who enthusiastically invited me to their home and studio across the street from an automobile repair service. Some might be deterred by the noise of industry so nearby but Stephen and Bea are thrilled to be in a place where people are "doing real work with their hands". We sat on their terrace overlooking the desert hills of San Miguel and the morning was spent in animated conversation about art, politics, and life in Mexico. Bea is a beautiful woman as only French women can be, classically educated, worldly, and impassioned. Stephen is charming in the tradition of a southern gentleman, intelligent, and candidly critical of his former bias' about Latin America. Despite their different beginnings, or perhaps because of them, Stephen and Bea share a love and respect for one another that is immediately apparent and as I soon learned, both are artists in the truest sense.

Bea makes a point of saying that she was born in France on the same day and in the same hour as Rainer Maria Rilke, the Austrian poet, whom she greatly admires. She lived in Paris until she was twenty-one, when she married and moved to South Africa with her husband who had taken a job in a Red Cross hospital. While in Capetown, Bea did an Honours Bachelor's degree in art history. She became politically active, protesting apartheid whenever and wherever possible. She was not dissuaded by a day spent in jail but when she became pregnant, Bea and her husband decided for the safety of all, they would take advantage of a job offer for him in Charlestown, South Carolina. In the U.S., Bea obtained an M.A. in French Literature and a Ph.D. in philosophy. Although she never formally studied painting, she says she started drawing at the age of seven when her family moved and she found that the trauma of the move could be alleviated by "her true friend", artistic expression. She tells me that she can endure anything, go through every hurdle of life without the pain, if she can, as she describes it, get into her world. "Because I didn't go to school for art, I found that there were no rules, there is no right or wrong. The only rule is authenticity. Do not pretend, just do."

Stephen adds. "Making art is the only thing that I know where you can take any rule and not only break it but wipe your ass with it, throw it out the window, and you won't go to jail for it. And, you might even succeed in breaking down barriers or making something beautiful that inspires or helps other people."

Stephen tells me he first became interested in art when he was three years old watching the weatherman draw sweeping H's and L's across the television screen. "My twin brother Stewart and I used sticks to draw similar lines in the dirt. When my mom got tired of us getting our clothes covered in dirt, she cut up the brown paper bags that were common in those days, and my brother and I drew on them with pencils. I could spend hours experimenting with shapes and lines. It became an escape if I was bored or unhappy. In the ninth grade I discovered Picasso. I think cubism appealed to me because it has most to do with line, and form, with architecture and playing with these elements. It was only natural that I would be drawn to Picasso because as a kid, I loved to take things apart to see what else they could be. I wanted to understand, to possess cubism. I didn't study art at university because I didn't want someone else telling me how to paint. I wanted to keep my art free. Instead, I studied biology and worked for fifteen years as a scientist, first in the pharmaceutical industry and then as a marine biologist, but I always felt I wasn't doing what I was really meant to do. Deep in my heart I felt I was going against my own grain. Living in Charleston I met some other artists and got a taste of the life I wanted to live. Then I met Bea at an art opening and we have been inseparable ever since. We were waiting for an opportunity to put our real identities forward when we discovered San Miguel de Allende through a friend, and everything came together. For the first time I am doing what I want to do and I am where I want to be, not just in location but in spirit."

The two came to Mexico in part because they found the atmosphere in Charleston creatively stifling. Bea says that after one exhibition, she received anonymous letters accusing her of being on drugs, which wasn't true, and even of being an unfit mother because the writers felt her work was not appropriate for display in a public place. "No gallery would give us the time of day because we didn't do palm trees and egrets." Initially the two considered relocating to France, but like others before them, they found San Miguel affordable and stimulating. As Stephen says, "Here in San Miguel people are more aware, more developed, and more curious about different artistic expressions."

Bea leans forward. "I am especially drawn to the Nawal which is when the animal spirit inhabits the human body. I feel it resonating inside of me. The geography and history of Mexico, its hybridization of pre-Hispanic and Hispanic culture is surrealism in its first state where you have creatures, half animal and half man, wings and teeth and sculls, swarming with colour and energy. It's an explosion of everything possible."

Stephan remarks that when Salvador Dali and Andre Breton came to Mexico in the thirties, Breton, the founder of French Surrealism, declared the surrealism in Mexico to be for real. He concluded, "They are faking it in France." Dali complemented the Mexicans on their vision and their dynamics by calling them crazy. "When you see the Indians here in their costumes, covered in paint and feathers," says Bea, "in comparison, French surrealism in the 20's in Paris seems sedated."

Do you think it is necessary for a serious artist to obtain a formal education in the arts?

Stephen responds first. "Every human being has, as a child, danced to the music, attempted or performed or participated in some act of creativity. Between the age of zero and seven most children did finger painting, played with paper, experimented with colour, and then a lot of them stopped, the drive to create was suppressed. Their innocence was subjected to criticisms, conditions, no, no, your line must go here, don't use that colour there. The magic gets destroyed. It's sad. When people tell me they can't draw a straight line, I say good. What use is a straight line in a painting anyway. So many art schools don't nurture creativity. Many of the greatest artists abandoned a formal art education."

Bea suggests that art is a form of language and as such, it requires a vocabulary. "Going to fine arts school can teach you the vocabulary and the syntax but that doesn't make art. Art is an alchemy. How are you going to change, to transform? You can learn the vocabulary and syntax by being aware, by observing, and then by copying, making the brush strokes, but eventually you realize it isn't you. You must create your own language and for that, the real school is life. A work of art surpasses technique. You need the scales to play Chopin but when you hear Chopin being played by an artist, even if the piece contains the odd missed note, it takes you to another place. Not all art schools are bad certainly, but a teacher's first responsibility is to nurture his or her students' enthusiasm. A real teacher will guide you to finding your own voice."

"I have no formal training," Stephen says, "but I have the desire to paint. Art schools all around the world are loaded with talent, but talent isn't enough. You can teach someone how to hold a brush but you can't teach the fire, the ambition. Leonard Brooks has that. When I met Leonard here in San Miguel, I felt I had met a true master. In Charleston, there were good painters who wouldn't give you the time of day but Leonard loves to talk shop. When I am with him, I feel like a young Paul Gauguin hanging out with his mentor, Camille Pissarro. Leonard is a maestro in every sense of the world. He challenges you to show him what you've got. If we take some of our work over to Leonard, he looks at it with joy. He'll study it, he'll exclaim over the reds or the blues, or he might take out his charcoal and suggest a line, but he never imposes. He says this is an idea you might want to consider. He invites you in. That is the sign of a great artistic being. Good teachers recognize that becoming an artist is a rough road. If they see a fire in someone, they want to encourage it but they don't need to make it their own inferno."

Does a successful artist have to be personally ambitious?

Stephen remembers that Picasso did not set out to become successful. "He likened himself to a man who goes walking in the woods and finds a pile of gold. He wasn't looking for a pile of gold. He was simply walking in the woods."

Bea feels some clarification is necessary. "I want to make a distinction between the producer of images, the businessman for whom art is a commodity, and the true artist who is a creator. Of course we need the basic materials to live but art is not a commodity. It is something holy, it puts you in touch with something beyond. We are bridges between the profane and the sacred. We are rooted to the ground like trees but we have branches that reach upward. We are endowed with a sensitivity that makes it possible to register the seismos, the earthquakes inside of us but also outside of us. Marcel Proust was not a painter but he was a lover of art. He said basically everything is illusion. We are hovering between disappointment and disillusionment. The work of art is the only redemptive factor whereby you have linked yourself to something beyond you and where past, present, and future are coalescing in one little ball of ecstasy."

The relationship between artist and viewer is a topic I have explored with other artists and I am interested to hear what Stephen and Bea's thoughts are on the subject.

Bea's response emanates from the visceral first, the place from which she draws her own inspiration. "The relationship between the artist and the viewer is complex. When you are in a trance, making, creating, there is nothing else but you, what's inside and the substrate, whatever it is. You talk with it, you wrestle with it, you make love to it. That's a phase. Once it is finished, it doesn't belong to you anymore. It belongs to whoever is going to look at it and maybe see something you didn't see in it. That's the beauty of it, the need to share, to have a dialogue."

"Art is the illusion of illusions, yet it is the path to truth. In the past century, the shock of the new was the definition of 'good art' and like all fashions, it didn't last. Jose Luis Borges said originality in art is the curse of the 20th century. So what lasts? What lasts is the instant, the intuitive confidence and vitality that pushes us to do the seated woman or the shaman mask or whatever. If this instant throughout time is relived, it is alive. A work of art can transform someone's life. You need the gaze of the other. Without the gaze of the beholder painting is not alive."

"It requires the same amount of energy to look at art as it does to make it. When you encounter a work of art, don't analyze, let yourself be raped, from the Latin rapere 'to be seized' by the colours, the shapes, whatever is in front of your eyes. Don't think. Then go back to it and think. Start to look at the perspective, the colours and you will see they form a symphony and you are totally enveloped and this makes you better because it forces you to go deep inside yourself and to also remain on the periphery. If you can pass by a work of art, it is just surface decoration. If you feel an urge to go back to it and entertain a dialogue with it, then it has become art. It has touched something inside of you that you must respond to."

Stephen continues. "To walk past and to deny a great piece of art should be virtually impossible. And why does some art touch us? Because the artist has successfully fused his being to it. Van Gogh's paintings are like that. Whether Van Gogh painted a pair of shoes or a chair or a bed, his paintings are all self portraits. You can't look at his paintings and not see it. How the hell did they not sell? It is unbelievable that he sold only one painting in his lifetime."

Stephen maintains that artists are observers and recorders of their time. "The public can be critical of an artist if he emulates an earlier master, yet in other professions, like medicine for example, it is considered necessary to learn from the masters. Art is a continuum. Artists speak to further generations through their work. To understand it you must consider the chain. You can't understand the links without the chain."

Bea agrees but she reminds us that trying to explain something like a work of art can sometimes get in the way of experiencing it. She points out that sometimes the more you explain something, the less you understand it. Stephen admits she is right. "People will accept calculus and statistics and mathematics more easily than a painting. You can put the most brilliant person in front of a painting and watch him get confused. Most want to understand rather than experience. The great Spaniard, Picasso said, 'What's all this talk about understanding painting? Do people try to understand the songs of birds?'"

For a few moments we talk about the profound experiences we have each had in the presence of great art. Stephen remembers seeing his first Picasso in Paris in 2003. He calls it a "true Zen moment". At the same time, he has mixed feelings about showing his own work. "When I paint, I never wonder how this painting is going to look over somebody's couch. But when I invite the public to look at my work, I want to know what they think. It is a paradox. Andrew Wyath said when an artist has an exhibition he might as well walk into a room full of strangers completely naked because he is putting himself out there to be criticized and picked apart. I have to think, if they get it fine, if not, fine, it is still going to be done."

Is it possible that art has lost its significance in the twenty-first century?

Stephen answers. "Certainly it is less usual today to encounter artists discussing art with the passion that was common a century or two centuries ago. In Montparnasse people argued fervently about such things as a line or colour. They would get so vehement that fights could ensue. In 1905 Picasso happened to be carrying a Browning pistol he had been given as a gift. When someone began to bad-mouth Cezanne, he took out the pistol and said, 'One more word about Cezanne, and I'll fire.' Artists even challenged each other to duels. In fact when Diego Rivera was in Paris, he was a second to Polish artist Moise Kisling who got into a sword fight over a difference of artistic opinion."

Bea quotes Martin Luther King who said, "Until you find something worth dying for, you are not living." In her own words she says, "If an artist can put his life on the line for art, then you don't have any existential problems with life because it is right there and you are fighting for it."

Stephen tells us that when Van Gogh died there was a letter in his pocket in which he said he was risking his life for his art. "In his letters to Theo, he says death is not the greatest concern. One of the ironies of art history is that when artists were at points in their lives where there were financial limitations, no money, deprivation and hardship, and they were a breath away from the end, a part of them said to hell with it, why should I hold back if I'm this close to the edge, and when they let go, they created something that launched them. When they had nothing, they had it all."

"Creating is a humbling experience," admits Bea. "We approximate, that's all we can do. Artists are makers of images. The word *image*, in Greek, means an idea. Each image is a part of your identity. We are traversed in one day by different identities that make up who we are. That's why my images are so diverse because each work paves the way to a harmony of identities. I have recurring obsessions. The eye, the hands, throughout my work you can see an eye or something grasping. And bones. I love bones. If I have a problem, I press my hands to the skull beneath my skin and I remind myself to let ego go. I am just a bag of bones."

"The thing that is magic about making art, is that if you don't have the money to buy paints, you find leaves, cardboard, you can make colours with vegetable skins. There is no end to creating. If you can't buy, you find, and you find treasures all around you. When I don't have money for a month, ok I go into the street. What can I find? I remember when I was about eight years old, my parents had put a beautiful rug under the dining room table. One day my mom served beets and spinach and I didn't like them so I put some portions under the rug. A couple of weeks later my mom found them and insisted I clean it up. I didn't throw the dried mass away. I went into my bedroom and I started to make something with the remains. Now I am in my fifties I still take leftovers, banana skins, beet skins, and make sculptures with them. With the simplest materials, I can give new life."

"There is another dimension in making art. It is perseverance. An artist must persevere every day. *Perse* means to pierce, and *ver* is to see, but it also means truth. So when you persevere you pierce something to see a little bit of truth. We need to get away from the Platonic notion that the goal is perfection and that if something isn't perfect, it isn't worthy. Plato discarded the poet from his city. In the poet there is no perfection. He maintained there is only one perfect table, and what you make is a lesser copy. That is fascism. Imperfection is a blessing because it means that every day you can get better, so you give meaning to your life every day. Perfection is death."

Stephen recalls that Van Gogh once said if one of his figures was ever perfect he would be terrified.

Bea explains, "The Impressionists challenged the public with work that didn't have a polished finish, it was in a constant state of movement. People were taken aback. They didn't recognize what they were seeing. The invention of photography freed art from being representative. It allowed the impressionists to go right to the source of this hovering movement. No more orthogonals. You couldn't decipher the lines that built the perspective. What helped the impressionists to be accepted was the philosophy of Henri Bergson who was called the philosopher of the painters. He based his philosophy on impression and élan, inspired impulse. If you can get to this first impulse, you are there. But it means you have to shake the tree. It is dangerous because you have to be mentally strong to get to this first impulse. Once you have passed the fear, there is no danger. It is the fear that creates the danger so if someone says you are not an artist or you are not fit to be a mother, who cares, because you know that you have tapped that source and no one can take that away from you."

The process Stephen goes through when he paints is a mystery to him. "I may have an idea of what I want to paint but what the final image is going to be, I have no idea. I take from the artists that have come before me. I think an artist that doesn't learn from others is a fool. Picasso was influenced by Toulouse Lautrec for example, but his genius was taking what he wanted from other artists and extracting it for his own use and purpose.

Art of the present can't exist without the art of the past. If something moves me, I don't worry about its origin. Bea and I are prolific and our work changes so much that in six months you might come back and not recognize it. Every artist has a father. I have about fifty. All the artists that have come before me lead me in different directions. I know I'm going to paint tomorrow but I don't know what. That keeps it fun because if painting becomes a job, I shouldn't be painting on a canvas. I should be painting your window trim."

"A long life," says Stephen, "allows a creative person to throw off any yolks of restraint and experience a second childhood. When an artist comes up with a masterwork, he uses it as a springboard to reach another level. With Picasso and Matisse, every ten years roughly, their art changed. It was a stripping down to the essentials to show the maximum human emotion by the most economical means possible. As artists grow older they are often trying to express the essence without being bogged down. Charles Baudelaire said genius is the ability to return to childhood at will."

Bea lights a cigarette. "What is it when we talk about this state of childhood? What actually do we mean by that? I think it is the ability to surprise yourself, to marvel at things, to have an unalloyed enthusiasm! And if you can do that when you are forty, fifty... But no, people are jaded. They have been put in boxes and drawers with a little label. A child can marvel at anything. This ability allows you to cross boundaries, to where there are no boundaries. *Enthusiasm*, (words are magic), it comes from the Greek, en-theos asthma, it means literally the breath of God."

"Liberation," Bea concludes. "Picasso said it takes a very long time to become young."

We are quiet for a moment, then Stephen stands and walks over to the terrace's edge to gaze at the neighbouring houses and beyond them, the surrounding countryside. "It is not only the ungodly beauty of this place, but it is the spirit. It is an ancient nation that has not forgotten its identity. I love the people, the importance of the family, the traditions that are kept alive. Until a few years ago, like most Americans, my attitudes toward Mexico were slanted by what I was told. In the U.S., Mexicans are described as criminals, as lazy, and yet I have never seen people with such a harmony for one another, that work so hard. When a Mexican goes to the states, he is treated like a piece of shit. When an American gringo comes to Mexico, for the most part he is greeted with sincerity, compassion, and open arms. When I came here I was eating humble pie. I was ashamed and embarrassed that not only had I believed the lies about Mexico, but that it was my own country that had lied to me. Living here has given me a different perspective. I am so glad I have had a chance to experience this place."

Bea and I join Stephen as he looks out to the sage coloured hills filling the horizon beneath the blue sky. Bea shares her own deep appreciation for San Miguel and its inhabitants. "I love the physicality of life here. People hug and dance in the street. Women are women with hips and bosoms. The colours aren't shy. I feel part of something larger than myself. Some argue that it doesn't matter where we are, that each work of art from authentic artists around the world is part of the nomadic truth. We don't own property. We don't own nature. The nomadic truth says you carry civilization within you. I was born in Paris, I have lived in Israel, London, Africa, America and I didn't feel at home in any of those places. I came here and I felt at home."

Stephen is the last to speak. "For me, there seems to be more of a soul here. Look at this beautiful place. It looks like Vincent himself painted it. I feel a connection to the past lives of artists that is very important to my work. Here I can live and I can paint and I have an incredible appetite to do so. San Miguel has awakened something in me that I never knew was there. People may not have much but they have more of what is important.

Here the human spirit seems more alive, more authentic, and closer to the divine."

Amen.

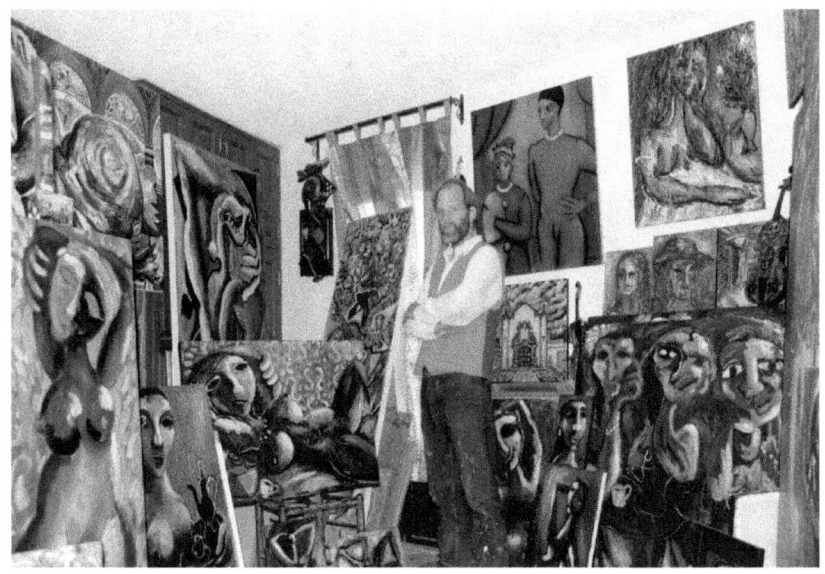

Edgar Soberon

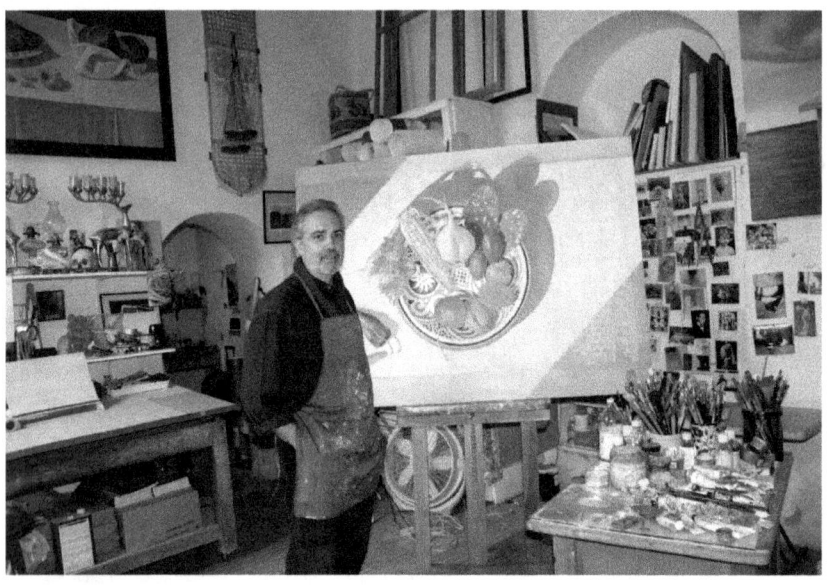

In an essay he wrote in 1917 called "Art as Technique", the Russian formalist Viktor Shklovsky discussed what he called 'defamiliarization'. He wrote, *"the automatisation of perception must be zealously guarded against, otherwise life is reckoned as nothing. Habitualisation devours work, clothes, furniture, one's wife and the fear of war....Art exists that one may recover the sensation of life; it exists to make one feel things, to make the stone stoney.... to impart of the sensation of things as they are perceived and not as they are known....to make objects 'unfamiliar', to make forms difficult, to increase the length and difficulty of perception because the process of perception is an aesthetic end in itself and must be prolonged."*[1].

By chance, I came across Viktor Shklovsky's name and the term "defamiliarization" while I was working on my article about Edgar Soberon. I had interviewed Edgar in 2008 and had only begun to put my notes into some kind of cohesive form nearly four years later. Shklovsky's ideas immediately struck a chord in my attempts to understand Soberon's work and his approach to art. When I met Edgar again in the early months of 2012, I asked him if he knew of Shklovsky's essay *Art as Technique* and he responded enthusiastically. "Victor Shklovsky is one of my influences. I read his wonderful essay in art school. Since then, his ideas have lingered in my mind. If you see his influence in my work then I feel I have succeeded in some way."

At this moment, Edgar is working on a huge painting, which sits on an easel in the centre of the large room that serves as his studio. The subject of the painting is a selection of common vegetables on a round plate against an intricately patterned background of muted pastel colours. In the centre of the plate is an outline of a square surrounding a handful of seeds. I experience a sensation of falling as I look at the seeds and I feel as though I am perceiving the painting, not with my eyes but with a different unnamed sense. I ask Edgar if he has intentionally tried to draw the viewer into the painting as if into another world. "I am painting this shadow here in the corner. Now I am having to go into it to take the light back out. The pattern behind the plate began as a very colourful idea but I ended up taking all the colour out of the background. It was too much. I want all the colour to be in the centre so that there is focus. When you start to work like this you can lose yourself and you have to remind yourself to be more objective. I put seeds in the centre of the painting and it was only afterwards that I realized I was copying the design in the centre of that ceramic platter up there." Edgar points to a large, very old plate hung high on the stone wall near us. "The symbolism of the sun and the seeds and of course, life, these are an ancient tradition in pottery. All of these images connect and it is kind of nice to plan some of these things in advance but it is also pleasing to discover their hidden symbolism as you're working. This opens another door for selecting, editing and emphasizing certain elements. Beauty is found in the process. It's not just the idea. The ideas that the image can evoke are important but one should also be creating something beautiful which evokes an emotion. When I taught in New York, I used to send my students to the Forbes Magazine gallery next door where often there were original documents or drawings on display. I still recall one particular document, it was Lincoln's Gettysburg Address. It wasn't only Lincoln's words that were beautiful but their execution, the way the ink was applied on the paper. Something wonderful happens when those two things meet. There is a connection between that which is made or manifest visually or physically, and the idea behind it. There is a unity or a wholeness about it all when they come together that makes one kind of happy."

"In his essay, Shklovsky talks about literature. In the most erotic literature, parts of the body are given other names. In order for them to become erotic you can't have a direct cognitive approach. A metaphoric approach allows a thing to become whimsical and beautiful. The breasts are pidgeons or doves for example. In this painting of vegetables on a plate, the forms are voluptuous. They have personality, texture. I try to do that with my still lifes. They are a metaphor for something that in many ways can be personified and they can be related to as we relate to the body, to our anatomy. I use nature, fruit, flowers and forms, in a way that brings to mind the human body, but I strictly keep the human form out. Strangely enough, by denying the human form, it always seems to be present in the work. I was trained using the figure and I still think it is the best way to train the eye and to to learn to see form. In most museums we are confronted with depictions mostly of faces, and heads, portraits of important people or not so important people. Or there are nude bodies engaged in heroic or mythical events. My paintings are in some way a response or perhaps even a rejection of these obvious historical hierarchies which define portrait and figure painting as lofty and landscape and still life as lowly genres. My still life paintings are a way of representing the world through a very limited set of principles and ideas that are based more on drawing, design, and the formal elements of painting. I would like people to look beyond the surface of my paintings. The viewer might say things look so real but in fact they are not. I am interested in that duality or ambiguity. As Shklovsky said, art should cause us to see the familiar as though we had never seen it before, as though it was strange. Many years ago I read a book called *A Tree Grows in Brooklyn*. In it the main character, a young girl, talks about the "first time and the last time" of anything. I never forgot that. I believe we should try to live our lives as though we were doing things for the first time, or the last time. I try to incorporate that into my paintings. It connects back to Shklovsky, to see something again, as experienced. Experience itself should become meaningful and the only way to bring meaning to experience is to be present, to be present with all of your being. That's what painting should trigger. That's what poetry should trigger. Of course, you can't do all of these things intentionally. Art does not come to us that way. You can't say I'm going to be an abstract painter or I'm going to be objective, now I'm going to express sorrow, now I'm going to express joy. This is not possible but what you can do is to have some ideas and principles that guide you and which open the way for something to happen. Perhaps then joy and sorrow will be expressed and the viewer will receive the work in the same spontaneous way, if he is open. Works that are didactic and hit you like an axe have an immediate impact but the effect quickly dissipates. They are trying to drive home an agenda and art shouldn't do that. My idea of great art is Vermeer's paintings. There is a woman in a room reading a letter. Apparently not much is happening. It is a moment in time but when you get into that little painting, it becomes a world. You begin to dream with her about the letter. The light coming in the window, everything becomes part of a narrative that is personal to the viewer. Never mind what Vermeer was thinking. That's not important. Through the process of making something, he has you engaged in your own personal relationship with this woman from the 17th century. One can spend hours looking at one of Vermeer's paintings as if reality had somehow been transcended or made more mysterious, seeing it as if for the first time."

Edgar and I were meeting again after a long interlude but as he spoke, my memories of our first conversation returned and with them my admiration for this expressive, intelligent man who still paints in the same studio at the top of a steep hill at the end of Calle San Francisco. Here he is surrounded by three hundred year old stone walls replete with history, art and history being two of Edgar's favourite subjects. I remembered that when we met for the first time, before I could turn on my tape recorder, we were deep in conversation about the differences between artists in San Miguel today and those who came here in the past.

"Artists who came to San Miguel fifty or sixty years ago had already accepted that they were not going to be rich or famous. In some ways these artists were monastic. They knew the financial rewards would be small. They came to San Miguel to live a life that allowed them to paint without being consumed by the system. The art world has changed over the years and the proliferation of art institutions and degree programs has certainly affected all of the Arts. The Arts became a career. But even before the advent of the art careers track, the seeds had already been planted with the likes of art personalities such as Pollock and Warhol in the United States, and I think to some degree before them, maybe with Picasso. Artists became a kind of celebrity, 'les enfants terribles' who were world famous. In today's art world, the media, television, the Internet definitely play a big part in the creation of an art star or an icon. Manufacturing a persona who is supposed to embody an entire generation is a distortion. It creates monsters whose role is to lead us into yet another bright, utopian future in art. The cult of personality is what I am talking about."

"The truth is, art evolves gradually. It takes time to cultivate, like the word 'culture', like a plant, art needs the proper light and circumstances. Nowadays a young person leaves art school and immediately wants a show, expecting a part in this world of fame, glamour. It is not so much how talented that person is but how they play the game, how they market themselves. The dealers are behind it, and now the museums as well. Museums, dealers, and curators act as a triad. They run the show like the fashion world, what's in, what's out for the season? Years ago, artists often worked with one dealer who bought work from them outright. Dealers came to your studio, looked at your work and if they liked what they saw, they promoted the work; they made a commitment because they believed in what they saw and in the artist making it. They printed catalogues, had shows, placed the work in reputable collections, and so on. Now galleries take artists' work on consignment. They display it, they might give you a show, they may or may not make a catalogue and distribute it to those on their mailing list, but regardless of their stature in the art world, whether they are large or small, galleries will take 50% off the top on every sale and they won't budge. It is insulting that a gallery who doesn't represent the artist, publish catalogues, or promote his or her work with collectors and museums, can take five hundred dollars from every thousand dollars it charges for a painting. The art suffers and the artist who is trying to express something solid, is pushed more and more to the margin."

"Artists nowadays have strategies. They come up with a theme; it could be political, religious, whatever. They package it, they put together twelve or fifteen works, put a price tag on them, and then try to get the dealers to jump on it. Younger artists do it but older artists are sometimes guilty as well, if they don't see the public responding to the slow development of their skill, the honing of the eye, the refinement of what they are trying to say. So you see, not only have artists changed but also the system itself has changed. That is what has happened to the art world. It is reflected everywhere you go. In New York, what I am describing is a very sophisticated machine. I know because I lived in New York for twenty-eight years. I taught drawing and printmaking at Parsons for ten years."

Parsons New School of Design, as it has been known since 2005, is an art school in New York city which was founded in 1898 and despite having gone through some structural changes over the decades, has always prided itself on being a leader in the field of design, particularly in the industrial arts. I ask Edgar to trace his journey from Cuba, where he was born, to New York and now to San Miguel.

What influenced you to become an artist?

"Two things. One, I was born in Cuba in 1962 when Cuba was in transition. The revolution had started in 1959 so I was born in the midst of all that. Many Cubans left in the sixties but we stayed on. Because they didn't want to go into exile, my parents decided to stay and experiment with Castro's dystopia for eleven years. Finally, in 1971 we left for Spain. From an early age I had an ability in art. I had always been able to paint and draw. It was something that was part of my life. Not a family trait as far as I know, it was more of a genetic mutation. My circumstances growing up encouraged something that was natural in me. You can have a gift but if the environment doesn't encourage its development, it will come to nothing. I think leaving Cuba was a shocking event for me. Painting and drawing helped me make sense of the world, helped me make a whole out of the pieces that resulted in our case, from being cast out. We were leaving and not coming back. People who are exiled are left with fragments of who they are, not only personally but the entire family is also affected. Art is a kind of refuge for the mind. It gave me something solid to hold onto. We went to Spain for three years and on to New York. I am thinking back as we talk. I was thinking about this a month ago. How did I get here? It is funny you ask me these questions now. The second thing was visiting the Prado Museum in Madrid as a boy. I remember walking into those rooms filled with great paintings and being absolutely thrilled. It was the first time I had ever been in a museum and it was there where I first saw still life paintings. That memory has remained with me ever since.

Edgar indicates a collage that hangs on the wall behind us. "I used to do collages like this one about fifteen years ago before I began to paint still lifes. The collages were influenced by Schwitters and Picasso, and were a way of putting together the pieces. I called them my Cuban cubism. I was trying to interpret ideas and images I had when I was in art school. Later I moved to still lifes, which are my way of creating serenity, a stasis, symmetry and a balance. That's what I look for in my work. There is a thread there, back to the circumstances of my growing up."

"One also has to give credit to the teachers that guided me. It was a high school teacher who recommended I attend Parsons. He also went out of his way and made all the phone calls necessary to get me an interview. I went there on a scholarship in 1983 and graduated in 1987. In 1992 I was called back to teach and I spent ten years on the staff. Looking back now, I can't help but see the events in my life have something of a unity. What did Socrates say? The unexamined life is not worth living. Self-reflection is important because it forces you to think about what you are doing and why. In all the things I have done, it seems like there was a plan. There was an unintended intention. What is guiding us is usually what is inside. If you are listening to who you are and you are doing what you want to do, the right things happen. I feel lucky to be doing what I was doing as a child. Most children are natural artists but it is hard to keep the child alive. I am making collage and painting and drawing and it looks more serious but it is still a kind of play."

"My work is not like the constantly changing experience that seems to dominate the art world today. It seems that now the only thing you can count on is change. Artists are constantly changing because that is what the market wants. A lot of what you see is not so accessible. As an experience, the viewer is not really sure what he is looking at. It has nothing to do with the old dichotomy of abstraction versus representation. There is no immediacy in a lot of what you see today. It seems it has been all very well orchestrated and packaged. A good painting is something that is very immediate. It is intelligible or not, regardless of its style, technique or school. It either works for you or not but it reaches you on a one to one level. Art today seems to be mediated by something else and in order to get to it, you need to know what the artist is trying to convey. There is always something in between you and the art. There is a disconnect here and the viewer often feels stupid because the art isn't accessible. As a painter, if you don't speak the current language, if you don't use the fashionable pattern, you are not wanted." Edgar looks at the painting he is currently working on, a still life of fruit on a table. "A picture like this is based on value, tradition, drawing, skill. If you paint a picture like this, they don't want to see you and simply deride the work as academic. They want something that stirs the pot. They are looking for novelty. This is passé. It has already happened. But as I often told my students, why be a victim to one's own time? Why not paint something that would have communicated three hundred years ago and will still communicate three hundred years from now, as it communicates today? All great art is timeless. One learns this lesson in the great museums. I had students who could draw so beautifully but that skill was not valued. In a few years they had either dropped out of art school or had joined the Duchampian ranks. It requires courage for young people to follow through on their own terms or find a teacher who will encourage them to cultivate their individual talent. This is especially true for a nineteen year old who is told in art school, limit yourself to this prescribed language. Limit yourself to what is happening now. That person has to somehow search out a teacher or support system that will help them stay on the right path."

"By all of this, do I mean that we have to return to the models of the past in a desperate attempt to erase the mistakes of 20th century modernism and art education? The answer is obviously no; we can't go back to the nineteenth century models or any other period for that matter. We must work from were we are and accept all of the great contributions of modernism. The art school system has to go back to its foundations. Kandinsky, Picasso, Mondrian, the most revolutionary artists of the 20th century were great because they understood and were trained in the fundamentals of art and design. We have to go back to those fundamentals, teach the humanities, history. We need teachers who can draw and paint and can teach those skills. This is what we tried to do at Parsons in the 90's. A student needs to be provided with the knowledge, guidance and appropriate tools. Given this training anything he makes will be modern or contemporary because he is living in the world as experienced today."

You obviously have a lot of knowledge about art and you have thought a lot about what it currently takes to become a successful artist.

"In 1996 I was awarded the Teaching Excellence Award at Parsons. That's an award that is given by the students to one teacher in the entire university. To receive it was a great honor. I was working with students who were go-getters. They wanted to be artists and designers. I was in my thirties and at first my students thought I was too young to be teaching but once they connected to me, they saw me more like a friend than a parent. I was able to get them to do things that surprised them. The students had a synergy with what I was trying to teach them. That same year I met my wife Paulina.

Tell me about how you met.

Paulina was born and grew up in San Miguel. Her father was an American, Jim Hawkins, and her mother Carmen Masip was an exile from the Spanish Civil War. Carmen devoted much of her life to the cultural center in San Miguel called the Bellas Artes. When we met, Paulina was in New York to visit her friend, Victoria Roberts. Paulina and Victoria were childhood friends in San Miguel. I knew Victoria from an etching studio in New York where we met and became friends. She's a cartoonist for the New Yorker, one of a small number of women on staff there. Victoria had talked about San Miguel many times but to me it was kind of a myth, like Shangri-La. I never thought I would ever go there but that year Victoria introduced me to Paulina and I came to visit for the first time in December."

"I loved San Miguel immediately because of the light and its colonial architecture. Entering these homes I felt transported back to my childhood days in Cuba. I thought this was a place where I could paint the pictures I wanted to paint. The subjects, the colour, it was all right here. I thought this would be a wonderful place. I was teaching at Parsons but I kept coming back to San Miguel during breaks. Even though I had a great apartment in Chelsea and a great job, it was 9/11 that ultimately made me decide to leave New York. It was a turning point for me, what I now recognize as part of my life's plan. I also turned forty that year. It was time to move on. The writing was on the wall as they say. The first thing I had seen entering the New York harbour in 1973 was a crane on the top of one of the towers. They were finishing the towers when I arrived and they went down when I left. I remember the day it happened. That morning I got a call from my mother saying that one of the towers had been hit by a plane and it was going to fall. I said no, it can't fall and I reprimanded her for watching television so early in the morning. After I calmed her down and said good-bye I turned on the TV myself and realized she was right, this was serious. By the time I got out into the street the first tower had collapsed. I tried to get downtown on my bike but they had closed all the streets. Just ambulances were going down and people were walking up. It was a sad day."

"The day after the towers were hit, classes weren't

cancelled. The students came to the studio and there was absolute silence. I didn't know what to say. I had hired a model and I think I told the class the best thing we could do was draw. I said, 'We are here. Let's just draw the figure.' I think I said something about World War II never thinking this was an event the students probably couldn't relate to. I didn't know what was coming out of my mouth but I was trying to give them some hope. I reminded them that destruction takes place in an instant but making something worthwhile takes time. To do something constructive is a sign of hope. There was no way you could wrap your mind around the reality of what had happened. Reality is a kind of construct that floats around us. People are looking for something they can point to and identify with, something that is tangible in a meaningful way. I don't mean it literally but people are looking for that experience. In the right hands, art can provide tangible meaning about reality. It doesn't necessarily lead to realism. Abstraction can be a tangible reality that's ephemeral while it holds itself in time and place."

Your paintings seem to depict a reality in which things have come to a standstill yet at the same time, the reality that is presented is moving toward becoming something else.

Edgar responds, "That feeling is a kind of zeitgeist of the times we are in. San Miguel is an island. Here we are in a protected bubble. When you live in a big city you start to feel there is something strange about the age we are living in. Reality itself becomes more and more elusive. The center doesn't hold as they say, or in effect there is no center at all. Time vanishes. That's what I felt when I left New York in 2002. I still miss New York but I'm also glad to be out of the race. I felt the city was winning. I could see myself doing the same thing until I was old, time having run out and my energy sapped. I felt my work was suffering. In many ways, being here is like a salvation."

Do you ever feel out of touch here?

"In some ways, I do. I still miss my job, working with young people. My parents and my brothers are in New York so I go back often. But at the same time, I am very happy here with my studio and my painting. I have some autonomy. I couldn't replace this in New York where to have a studio and a place to live is so expensive it is prohibitive. I feel privileged to be here while at the same time, I feel disconnected. In a big urban centre like New York everything is available. It is kind of a soup. You swim through it and you find the experience you are looking for. It gives you all of the points of view. What is a painting? What is music? What is the novel? What is the stock market? It depends where your head is at but what you realize later is that you have seen the very best and the worst of everything, it's a life lesson. In a place like New York you can find the best people in your field, all that which makes you thrive. I had the benefit of being surrounded by people who really knew about art; teachers, colleagues, students, the galleries, the access to culture, I had it all and it formed me. The Frick for example, has three Vermeers (the Met has five), two el Grecos, a Bellini, a Goya, two Rembrandts, two Turners, Piero della Francesca, Gainsboroughs, several Chardins and they are all masterpieces! I can tell you the whole museum room by room. I have it in my head. It scares me that I don't have access to it now but I have it in me. I have been to see it over and over. There are thirty-three Vermeers in the world and eight of them are in New York. It terrifies me that I don't have that at my finger tips anymore but I go often and I breathe deeply and I tell myself, it's ok, it's ok. It is still here."

"I am fortunate I can travel. Although I will never go back to Cuba to live, one day when Cuba is democratic, the country will open up and I will definitely go back and visit. I am Cuban by birth but I have been shaped by so many things. Now that I have lived here all these years, I am in some way Mexican as well."

Do you think of yourself as Mexican?

Edgar laughs. "No, not yet. I'm still working on that. Mexican culture is rather complex, one can spend a whole lifetime learning these things. Going back to the beginning of our conversation, the people who came in the fifties and early sixties came to San Miguel with a different outlook. Many were artists, writers perhaps wanting to escape the rigidity of American culture but they also had a genuine interest in the Mexican culture. They mingled and they fused with the culture. That generation were adventurers, in the Kerouac sense of the word. Many of them married Mexicans and today have Mexican grandchildren who are bi-cultural. The people that come to San Miguel now are looking for something else, a more affordable way of life, a place to retire. Maybe some are escaping from a different set of circumstances. In many ways people who arrive now have fewer hardships because all of the infrastructure is in place. You don't even have to speak Spanish. You get a realtor, you buy a house and settle down. It's safe and the large community of foreigners makes it easy to navigate and remain in closed social circles. These comforts in effect make it more difficult for foreigners to integrate into the Mexican culture."

I turn to look at two paintings that sit on easels near us. Both are of a religious nature and both are almost but not quite complete. Edgar explains. "According to the old woman who owns this building and is the caretaker of the church right next to us, the Calvario, the building was full of humidity. The whole chapel has had to be renovated. In San Miguel the Easter procession ends here at what is the last station of the cross. Not too long ago, the old woman who had obviously seen I am a painter took me in the church. She told me that on either side of the altar there had been an exvoto, painted on copper. They were old ones, framed and beautiful."

The practice of making exvotos can be traced back to the 1500's in Mexico. Most often they are personal expressions of gratitude for a recovery after an illness or accident. In Mexico today, they are painted on tin or wood, or embroidered on cloth and are valued as folk art. Edgar continues. "I don't exactly know what happened but these two exvotos were taken, so she wanted something to replace them. She showed me two small postcards, one of the death of Jesus and one of the annunciation and she asked me if I could enlarge them photographically. I knew they wouldn't look good so I told her I would think about it. I decided to ask my two students who are both Catholic, if they would copy these two pictures and they agreed. This one is a copy of The Annunciation by Fra Angelico in the San Marco convent in Florence and the other is the death of Christ. Both are in oil and as soon as the chapel is ready I will put them in these frames and they will decorate the church. The caretaker is ninety and she is the last in her family. She doesn't have any children. She is the third generation of her family who has looked after the church, which dates back to 1730. On the back of those paintings I put a legend stating that these paintings were commissioned for the church and should not be removed. My students signed their names and one put the names of all her deceased family members. These pictures are a labour of love and devotion."

Today, Edgar and I gaze out the open door of the Calvario church and along the street to the beautiful and ancient buildings that line Calle San Francisco down to the Jardin and to the hills beyond. We have come into the church to see the completed ex votos that Edgar's students had been working on when we first talked four years ago. The paintings are beautifully displayed in the Baroque frames that had been carefully guarded by the old woman who lived long enough to see the paintings hung on the walls of the small chapel. She died at the age of ninety-three, a couple of weeks after the pictures were hung. Edgar confides that he felt a sense of having fulfilled some greater purpose in overseeing the making and hanging of the paintings in the church and to ensure that they would not disappear, he made a formal gift of the paintings to the priest at the Parroquia. "Anyone with bad intentions would hesitate before stealing from the Catholic church, an act which would be a serious matter." From where we stand in the narrow chapel, Edgar points to the holes that have been drilled in the walls to help alleviate the moisture problem that plagues the little church. Constant maintenance is required and although this is an important monument, he feels it is not sufficiently valued as such. "Because this church is in such a significant location at the top of this hill where the road turns, it would have been an important stop on the route to Mexico City. Travelling from the silver mines to the city was a dangerous journey in the 1700's and 1800's. This was a chapel where travelers stopped to pray for a safe journey."

I remind Edgar that last time we met he had lightly referred to himself as a Mexican. I ask him if he feels more Mexican with the passage of these past few years. "I have always felt like an exile. My parents left Cuba, never dreaming that Castro would remain in power so long. It was equally difficult in Spain under Franco and so we moved to New York. Even though I lived in the United States for twenty-eight years, I have never felt I belonged anywhere really. I don't feel an allegiance to any particular country. I'm Cuban by birth and I'm also American, perhaps even a bit Mexican and at the same time none of these. As I grow older, I don't feel it is so important to attach oneself to any particular place. At the age of fifty, I am beginning to feel complete in my own being."

"I can't say that it is true but maybe when we are very old, looking back one can see more clearly the direction of our lives. Already we have been in San Miguel for more than ten years and a lot has happened in that time. San Miguel has changed. Our lives have changed. In 2008, Jim Hawkins, my wife's father, passed away."

Has Jim's death affected you?

"It has affected our lives completely. When Jim was alive, we had lunch with him every day. He might have been eighty-two but he had a youthful outlook. He thought like a young person. He was open minded, very interested in many things, so well read he could talk about any subject. People like that really leave a hole. Jim's wife Carmen helped found the Chamber Music Festival and directed the Bellas Artes for more than thirty years. They also opened in 1959 The Academia Hispano Americana, the oldest Spanish language school in town. They and many of the others that came here long ago like Felipe Cossio de Pomar, Leonard Brooks, Stirling Dickinson just to name a few, helped make this town the unique place it is today. They attracted painters, musicians, writers, creating the culture and reputation we often take for granted in San Miguel."

Like most of us who have entered or surpassed middle age, Soberon is aware of time passing. He has been an exile in a world that continues to alter itself, a world that is almost unrecognizable as the home we once knew. For many of its residents San Miguel exists as a place that has managed to elude the passage of time in the same way that Edgar Soberon's still lifes, aptly named, still life. The beautiful images he paints are exquisite moments frozen on the canvas and we the viewers are captive to the stasis, to the tranquility visible there. But even as we look, we feel the pull of conditions about to change. As much as we might wish to remain in that pure, sensual space, we are summoned by routine, and time moves on. Thankfully, it is possible to return to the sublimely unfamiliar whenever we choose and that is Edgar Soberon's and San Miguel's gift.

1. Russian Formalist Criticism: Four Essays. Eds. Lee T. Lemon and Marion J. Reiss. Lincoln: U. of Nebraska P, 1965. 3-24.

Mary Breneman

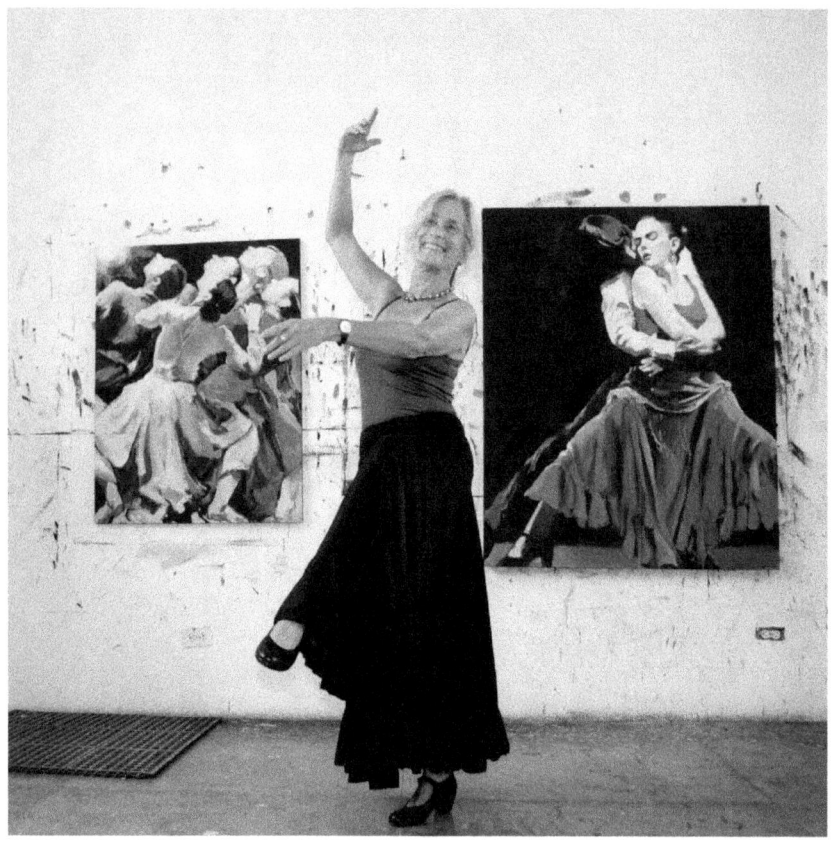

If you Google TED TALKS and search out the most popular presentation in the past five years, you will find that over ten million people have watched a man named Ken Robinson speaking about how the education system worldwide, fails to honour or develop creativity, particularly in the arts. To illustrate what can result from nurturing more than one of the multiple human intelligences, he tells the story of a woman, Gillian

Lynne, who many years ago at the age of eight, was taken to the doctor because she couldn't sit still. She fidgeted and made trouble for her teachers and in today's context, Gillian probably would have been diagnosed with ADHD (attention deficit hyperactive disorder) and she would have been put on medication. Gillian was lucky. The doctor asked her to wait in his office while he and Gillian's mother left the room. Before they left, the doctor turned on the radio, then outside through the slightly opened door he and Gillian's mother watched as Gillian, left by herself, moved around the room to the music. The doctor turned to Gillian's mother and spoke, 'Your daughter isn't sick. She's a dancer.' Gillian Lynne was given dance training and went on to choreograph *Cats, The Phantom of the Opera,* and many other original productions. Something reminded me of this anecdote during my conversation with Mary Breneman perhaps because Mary too is a dancer and although she paints for a living, she dances when she paints.

Mary Breneman is one of San Miguel's best known and best loved artists. She usually chooses bold colours, large canvases, and subjects that vary, from goats who are smiling at some private amusement, to horses that gallop in air, to landscapes enlivened with green cacti and sunshine. My first meeting with Mary was at her new gallery in the Fabrica Aurora where she had just launched a large show of older and more recent works. The expansive rectangular space with the high ceiling reminded me of a riding ring, giving her paintings room to move. We had never met but when I saw the animated woman wearing jeans and a colourful blouse pushing back her straight shoulder length hair as she spoke to a client, I was sure she had to be the person who had painted the energetic images around us. When I approached her to introduce myself she greeted me with a lively smile. I was with a young friend from Mexico, one of our United World College graduates who was spending the week with us in San Miguel so while Mary finished her conversation, Jose Armando and I played a game of choosing a painting we would each like to take home. I chose a landscape with an expansive cerulean blue sky and he chose a landscape full of lime green because he said it would make him happy whenever he looked at it. Later Mary and I sat down to talk but before I could question her about her life as an artist, she asked me what had inspired me to undertake this writing project and I found myself telling her about my pilgrimage to India.

In 2006 I took a small backpack and went off to India alone. It was not an easy trip to make because forty years ago a good friend had gone to India and had returned seeing ghosts. He shot himself a few months later so in my mind, India was a place to be feared, a place that could drive you mad. Emerging from the Bangalore airport terminal building on a hot night I was met by a sea of dark faces. Lit only by the spotlight behind me, they pressed forward against the wire fence dividing us, too many people too close together. My first reaction was to insist I be allowed back on the plane, but instead I chose to surrender to the dirt and the smells and the noise and the visual chaos and ultimately to the spirit that sustains India's people through the hardships that manifest themselves in a country of over a billion people living on just over a million square miles. It was three months later after many miles of bus, train, and plane travel, that I was staying in Trivandrum on the southwest coast in a small bed and breakfast where fisherman still swim out to place their nets in the ocean each evening and haul them in empty each morning, the fish having been taken by international trawlers just visible on the horizon. There were three other guests, a nice English couple and another woman who spent a lot of time sketching in the garden. One afternoon I asked to see what she was drawing and as we chatted we exchanged details about our intentions once we left the B&B. She was moving on to an ashram further south and I was going to Mexico, to San Miguel de Allende. She looked at me. "San Miguel is my home," she said. The woman's name was Laumuq, and it was she who encouraged me to contact her friend Carmen Gutierrez, owner of the Casa Diana Gallery in San Miguel who she promised, could put me in touch with some of the city's artists. I decided that if a woman from San Miguel was in India telling me to do something, the message was coming from somewhere important and I should listen. Upon hearing the story of how I came to write this book and how one artist seemed to lead me to the next, Mary told me she wasn't surprised. "That is so San Miguel", she confirmed. "It sounds like it is flowing gracefully, which is the way a project should be."

This morning Mary Breneman has come to my house on Reloj for our meeting and when she arrives she recognizes a painting hanging in my front hall that she did in the Caribbean. I tell her I have always liked the painting. It has given me pleasure every day since I bought it and the fact that now I know where and under what circumstances it was done, my enjoyment of the painting is deeper still. And I like that I know the woman who painted this bright yellow and orange tropical scene, that she is someone who has endeavored to get it right, a brave person, a woman who has withstood loss and has determined that she will be strengthened by life, not beaten by it.

Will you tell me how you came to San Miguel?

"I've got a unique story but maybe not so unique for here. Twelve years ago I was living on the north shore of Boston where I had been a decorative painter and a muralist for quite a number of years. My children were grown and I knew that I wanted to have some sort of adventure. I was in my early fifties and I wanted to move to a place where I could paint full time. I had taken various painting courses but primarily my work was in the commercial field although my desire all my life was to be a painter. Another thing that consumed a huge part of my life was dance. So anyway, I took a trip to Italy with a bunch of painters and I became good friends with a man in his seventies who had been coming to San Miguel for thirty years. Each year he would rent a studio in the Instituto for a month. I was toying with the idea of returning to the Caribbean where I thought there would be tourism and an economy I could probably afford which would allow me to open a gallery but there didn't seem to be enough culture there for me and I felt like it might be a little isolating. So one day back in the States I was at my friend's house for coffee and he had just come back from San Miguel and he was showing me some photos and he said, 'You know Mary, I think that's where you need to go.' and I swear to God that moment I made the decision. I had never been to San Miguel but I went home, I sold my house, I sold everything I owned, not speaking any Spanish, I arrived here with two suitcases. That really is the truth of it, and everybody said Mary you're crazy, don't sell your house, but my feeling was I could always go somewhere else if I didn't like it but the whole experience has been very positive. It has been totally the right decision."

"Ok, I had to make some adjustments like when I came through Houston and there were all these guys wearing cowboy boots and coming from New England I thought, oh, oh, what the hell have I done. When I got to San Miguel I was a little frightened. I didn't speak the language. I didn't even know how to buy a bar of soap. But you know how welcoming this city is. I just seemed to meet people right away. Everything opened up for me. I rented for a couple of months and then I met a man in a sketch class who had just bought a huge artist's studio where you could live with a beautiful garden and he asked me if I would house sit for him and I did that for almost six years. It was really great."

Did San Miguel have an influence on your painting?

"I paint the world around me, I paint what stimulates me and there is just an enormous amount of stimulation in Mexico. Sometimes I'll turn a corner and just feel like weeping, at a face, or light, or a child, or a festival. It is unending. There is so much vibrancy and life. But my beginnings here in San Miguel were difficult and I'll tell you why. In my first apartment I was trying to paint in a small studio and I hadn't been a full time painter and I didn't know how to approach it. I did struggle and part of the problem here for me was the social aspect of the city. It seemed like I was meeting more and more people. Everybody was going to *comida*, there were events at night and after six or nine months I was feeling a little depleted and I realized it was affecting my work. I made the decision that I was going to work during the day, this was my job, something I wanted to do, and that I would save my socializing for evenings and maybe not so much of it so that I could get more in touch with myself and what I really came here to do. Then I rented a studio at Margaret DaWitt's and that was fabulous. I painted from the model, there were other artists around, and I would work all day and I'm such an admirer of Margaret and her husband Nacho's work. They are formidable. Eventually they decided to close down to focus on their work and I was again very lucky because I found a huge studio on Tenerias where I went every day. I was painting five, six, seven hours a day. I did plein air painting with a group here for five or six years. We'd go out on location and I'd come back and finish the paintings in the studio and then I got into the charreada, the Mexican rodeo."

Many aspects of Mexican rodeo can be compared with North American rodeo although the events do vary somewhat and as with any rodeo, critics argue that the animals are subjected to abuse and therefore rodeo has no merit. My own childhood in rural Alberta acquainted me with the world of man against beast. As kids, it was every farm boy's normal practice to try to lasso the dogs or ride the pigs. Naturally the latter objected actively with high-pitched squeals until the offending young rider had been successfully thrown into the dirt, a ceremony that never took very long. Girlfriends' older brothers who had graduated from pigs to broncs were my heroes, their modest valour the stuff of my dreams. There is a rodeo ring on the outskirts of San Miguel and there is a bullring right in the historic centre, its entrance nearly invisible on Recreo unless an event is taking place, but I have grown too conventional to appreciate the contests; nevertheless, the rodeo and the bullfights remain enormously popular in Mexico.

Mary continues. "I had met a woman who was a yoga teacher here and she was dating a matador and she asked me if I wanted to do a show based on the corrida (bullfight) and I said sure, why not. I remember when I was a child I watched a movie about matadors and I fell so flippin' in love with these matadors and I thought one day I'm going to get to see a matador and finally here I got a chance to paint the matadors and the bull fight and the rejoniadors (matadors on horse back) and I have to say a lot of people think I'm gross but I enjoy all the pomp and beauty and the music. Of course you can't paint in the bullring so I took a lot of photos and started painting from photos there and then I went to the Mexican rodeo and I love the escaramuzas, the women on horseback with the beautiful dresses. One thing that I love to get into my work, I mentioned before that I am a dancer, and I am very inspired by energy and movement so it is one reason why the corrida interested me and the charreada and I try to get that in my landscapes, that layering, that movement, the way the landscape here swirls around. It is not a static landscape at all. And now I'm into dancers, now I'm painting dancers."

The bullfights are a big part of the Spanish traditions in Mexico even though a lot of people are revolted by it.

"Well, they kill the bull."

How do you reconcile that with the beauty of the pageant?

"I don't like to see them kill the bull, especially if it is not a good matador and I'm not crazy about the picadors but I don't question it is part of this culture and I enjoy the ceremony. And they are great athletes. My favourite part and the part I only go to now is the rejoniadors. They are like dressage riders and we have a guy who has a ranch just outside town here, Pablo Hermosa, who is the second best in the world. They dance around on the horse while the horse and the bull are two inches away from each other and it is gorgeous. I went to the lucha libres, the wrestlers, the other night and I don't question it. I'm an American, this is what they do and I have a curiosity about it. Many Mexicans love ceremony and they love machismo. I saw it at the lucha libre, I see it with my gardener, and yet the women run the society. They are the bosses in the house. You know something, I don't think I will ever understand this culture but I do know there is no confrontation here. Everything is done in a gentle respectful way. You can say what you need to say but politeness is essential. To suggest that someone is at fault takes away their honour so there is a lot of going through the back door."

I know what you mean about the need to follow the rules of courtesy here and elsewhere. In France you can't walk up to someone on the street to ask for the time, for example. You have to first introduce yourself, greet the other person and after you have gone through that ritual, you can proceed with your question.

"It's really nice. In New York it's more likely to be, 'Gimme the time. Did you hear what I said?'" Mary speaks in an exaggerated Bronx accent that makes us both laugh.

My husband and I were walking along the other day when two horses ridden by beautiful young men came trotting down the street. Behind them sat equally beautiful women with their ruffled skirts spread over the rumps of the horses. It seems we are constantly being delighted by the unexpected in San Miguel. Do you find that?

"All the time. There is a sense of vitality and magic. I am not one of those who say they can't live in the U.S. anymore. I love the States, it's my country and I love going up there but the States feels kind of homogenous after living here. The economic situation and the state of the world have affected things. There is a lot of fear in the States. I don't feel that here. I feel like Mexicans live in the moment. Here's a story. I have a friend who has been married to a Mexican man for about thirty-five years. She's a very intelligent woman from the States and he was from the campo so they had very diverse backgrounds and she told me that after they had been married for about six months they had a huge fight and she said to him, 'I cannot be with someone who doesn't think.' and he appealed to her saying, 'Well, I've never done it before.' Mary laughs heartily and slaps her knee. 'Let me learn how to think.' and I thought oh my god, that's what the Mexicans are, so experiential. They just are. I think they just experience things. That's not to say that many aren't very poor and have a tough time but I don't think they go around worrying like we do. They are more focused on living and celebrating life. They celebrate all the time. Also the sense of family is so rich. There is a lot of support. I know you do hear of older people whose families are gone and they are abandoned but for the most part the Mexican family is really impressive."

Do you have a family?

I have two sons. The oldest is a singer songwriter named Luke Temple who has a band called Here We Go Magic. He went to art school and could have been successful as a painter but he wanted to pursue his music career. My younger son is a chef in a great restaurant in New York City. I have a real right brain family. There are no accountants. There are no bankers. There just aren't. A few years ago a relative called me to tell me she had done some research into our genealogy and she found that my father's mother was an Emmett and among the Emmetts there were three or four women who were society portrait painters who travelled with John Singer Sargent. What I saw in the family tree was that we are descended from a lot of artists and lawyers.

It sounds like you come by your artist genes honestly. What about dance? Did you start dance training when you were young?

I used to win dance contests when I was in high school. I came from a family of five kids and I was the oldest and I remember every night I had to do the dishes and I had a ribbon tied to the cabinet and I would be in there with the radio on, dancing. My mom would come in an hour or two later and I was dancing. Eventually I got the dishes done but I loved dance. I had a Russian ballet teacher when I was a girl but she was mean and so I quit that but after I had my first son, I was twenty-eight, I started belly dance just to get in shape and I ended up performing a little bit with a small group, then when I was about thirty-three I was invited to participate in a show called Art in Harmony and it was going to be about dance and art and theatre and music and I was going to represent the dancers, as an artist. So I went to sketch the dancers and they were doing ballet and I flipped out. I started doing ballet and then I started taking modern class and I was taking ten, twelve dance classes a week. I was completely and totally obsessed with it. I ended up in a semi-professional company. I was really passionate about it. And then I got divorced when I was thirty-eight and so I had to cut back. Up until that time I was a freelance illustrator and began to get into decorative painting but then I really needed to focus and I couldn't pursue my dance in the way I wanted to. Since coming to Mexico I have studied all kinds of dance. First I took ballet, then I took tango for a while until I got a frozen shoulder, and now I'm obsessed, totally obsessed with flamenco. I go to three classes a week and I just found out she's having a fourth and I'm there. It's a huge passion in my life. My teacher is a really great dancer from Mexico City who is very formal and I'm learning good fundamentals with her. I'm having fun."

How old are you now?

I'm sixty-six.

You look and act much younger and you have certainly chosen activities that are going to keep you that way. Is it your character to respond wholeheartedly to things that interest you?

"I'm passionate and I get very obsessed with things and I have been accused of bouncing around a lot. It used to really upset me because I used to think my work had to look a certain way, but it is not who I am. I decided I needed to paint from my insides. I might be passionate about horses for a while and then all of a sudden I will see a landscape and I will say, oh my god I have to paint that landscape and I will be off into landscapes and then it will be cactus and I'll take a trip to Chiapas and the children will be so beautiful I have to paint them. I accept this part of myself now and I don't worry about it. There's something for everybody, it's not all horses and it's not all landscapes. I have to be true to myself as a painter. I have to follow what excites me. Right now it is dancers. I am totally turned on by a German choreographer named Pina Bausch. To my mind she is the best choreographer of the century. A documentary has just come out about her that I'm going to see when I'm in Dallas next week. It's a combination of modern dance and theatre, very forward. It can be slow and repetitive but it is so effective and her dancers are exquisite. Stay with her awhile and you will see what I mean. Somebody told me about her about six months ago and since then I've been watching her choreography on Youtube, plus I've been thinking of painting flamenco dancers but I want to do it without looking trite so since I'm dancing so much, all of a sudden it hit me, I want to paint dancers. That's how I've been carried away into that."

In spite of your changing subjects your paintings are still very identifiable as belonging to you.

"Yes, people say they can tell my work. I was an illustrator years ago and I do love to draw. Sometimes I will just do drawing for a while and maybe my love of drawing is what is recognizable. I also like to have movement in my brush stroke. I want the painting to somehow dance around the canvas. I have heard people say they know my brush strokes. I just did some small works recently for a collaborative show and they were relaxing for me in the sense that I put something in front of me and there was some decision making about the colours but working small doesn't have the same energy. I feel like I am freer working large. When I have a large canvas in front of me I can get my body into it and I just feel more able to express myself. People keep telling me I should do some more small paintings but I really don't want to."

How did it happen that you moved to an acreage on the outskirts of the city?

"I had to move when the man I was house sitting for decided to sell and I thought building a house would be a good way to invest my money. I wanted land because I had always been a gardener in the States. I grew vegetables and I had fruit trees and I love flowers and I was lucky to find a little piece of land just over the train tracks so it is an easy commute to town and I could even walk but it would take too much time. I built my own house. I had an idea what I wanted so I hired a man here to design and build it. It is small but it is totally light filled and I really love it."

Do you ever feel you are out of touch in San Miguel, or as you get older that health care is a concern?

"We are behind, most definitely. It dawned on me about five years ago when I went to the States without a cell phone that I had a problem. I said to myself, 'Where the hell are the pay phones? Mary, you gotta get on board.' Some people like the fact that we are out of the main stream but I don't want to be left behind. I don't want to be an old fart. I am in a lot of ways but I try not to be. As far as health care goes, I don't worry about it. I had my gall bladder out a while ago and it cost me $275 and I got great care. Besides, the U.S. health system isn't perfect either. I feel problems exist everywhere you go these days. There is a whole world transition happening. It's a spiritual crisis. I don't have answers but I think there is a bigger picture. Look at the climate change. Money and power runs it all. Anyway, I just have to trust in the wisdom of the universe. You can get too caught up in it and too angry and too frustrated and I feel it is has to be more about changing our consciousness and taking personal responsibility."

Whatever the reasons, it seems people are staying away from Mexico in droves.

"They're fools. They're fools. I grant you there are places I wouldn't want to live in Mexico. When I first came to this country I saw men standing around with machine guns and I thought what the hell is that, but you get used to it. They're not going to shoot those machine guns. Yes, the drug cartel has made some places unlivable but I live in the countryside by myself and I feel totally safe. I'm attentive when I am walking alone at night but I'm not afraid. The difference is there is less employment now and many of the problems have to do with that. Mexico has tremendous potential. There are a lot of natural resources but unfortunately there is a huge disparity between the rich and the poor and that encourages nepotism and corruption. When I first came there was a lot of greed on the part of developers. They were buying properties for very little, fixing them up, and then selling them for big profits. That has changed in recent years. The Texans used to come down in the summer time and they don't now. They were good customers but I have to say I have been very, very lucky as far as my own work goes. I consistently sell my paintings."

Are you here in San Miguel to stay?

"I'm not going anywhere unless something catapults me. I think I'm here for the duration. In my first years I used to feel sometimes that I needed to get out but I don't feel that anymore. I really love it here. I can't imagine living anywhere else. I miss the big trees at times but that's not worth moving back. There is a large gringo community and I like that. I think basically by nature people are clannish and we feel most comfortable with people who understand our culture and our ways of behaving.

It's one of the reasons I like San Miguel and I love that there are endless opportunities to see and meet people with enormous talents. It's not your average Joe that gets drawn here. It is people with a sense of adventure, people who can see outside the box. We're seekers, we're open to life."

Mary invited me to attend her Flamenco dance class one morning so I took a cab out to Los Fraites, a suburb on the south side of the city where, in a large yellow house on the corner I found Patricia Linares' dance studio. The woman who let me in was tiny, under five feet tall, probably in her forties and had a deferential bearing. She could have been a member of a religious community receiving a visitor into the cloister. I wondered if she was the maid. I followed her into a front hall and then into a large room like a miniature gymnasium with a concrete floor over half of which a wood surface had been laid. The boveda ceiling was almost thirty feet high and a large skylight cast a square of light on the floor. I was offered a chair facing the dance floor and a wall entirely covered with full-length mirrors. Seated, I waited for the class to begin. Within a few minutes five women emerged from a door to my right where I assumed there was a change room. They ranged in age from twenty to seventy and all were wearing long black skirts and black fitted tops such as gymnasts would wear. Their black shoes had medium heels about an inch wide and an ankle strap to secure them. I noticed that in addition, some had used wide elastic bands that went entirely around their feet under the instep to keep their shoes in place. A slender woman wearing a long yellow t-shirt and loosely fitting black pants entered and took her place facing the other women. She looked perfectly ordinary as she spoke quietly to the group, then she raised her arms above her head in a graceful arc, her hands found their comfortable familiar place, shoulders erect, head still, every muscle composed and ready, she was transformed. A guitar began to play forceful strumming chords that demanded attention, then a voice joined the guitar, a strong clear call released with such assurance and passion that I found myself searching for the source. Turning, I realized the music was coming from the humble woman who had opened the door to me but like some miracle, she had grown in stature, elevated by her skill. Later I learned her name is Silvia Cruz, a talented musician. I watched, mesmerized for an hour as the women practiced footwork that necessitates the placing of the toe and then a hard descent of the heel making a loud, firm knock on the wood floor. The palms of the hands are clapped together to emit quick syncopated rhythms called palos while the intricate footwork and body movements require imagination, energy, and daring. As someone has said, flamenco dancers reach for the heavens with their arms but their lower body belongs to the ground. At one point all the women danced together to a lullaby called a nana. I presumed the moves had been rehearsed but later I was told the students were following the teacher's lead and that much of flamenco is improvisational. After the lesson I found myself struggling to express my feelings of gratitude to Senora Linares and even today as I write, I can't entirely account for the depth of my reaction. I think it was the sudden unexpected beauty of the women that caught me by surprise. Superficially unremarkable people were made luminous, and it was dance that effected the change. The arts move us all so much closer to grace than power or money, and judging from the joy in her paintings I think it is safe to say Mary Breneman understood that a long time ago.

www.ingramcontent.com/pod-product-compliance
Lightning Source LLC
Chambersburg PA
CBHW051635170526
45167CB00001B/194